SHARON HAYS

The Cultural Contradictions
of Motherhood

Yale University Press
New Haven and London

Published with assistance from the foundation established in memory of Philip Hamilton McMillan of the Class of 1894, Yale College.

Library of Congress Cataloging-in-Publication Data
Hays, Sharon, 1956–
    The cultural contradictions of motherhood / Sharon Hays.
        p. cm.
    Includes bibliographical references and index.
    ISBN 0-300-06682-1 (cloth: alk. paper)
        0-300-07652-5 (pbk.: alk. paper)
    1. Motherhood. 2. Mothers–United States. I. Title.
    HQ759.H37 1996
    306.874'3 — dc20   96-10262
                            CIP

A catalogue record for this book is available from the British Library.
The paper in this book meets the guidelines for permanence and durability of the Committee on Production Guidelines for Book Longevity of the Council on Library Resources.

10 9 8 7 6 5 4 3 2

To my mother, Doris Hays Sudkamp

Contents

Preface

This is a book about mothering. In the course of writing it, I have spoken about the subject before various audiences. Most people, I have learned, have strong emotional responses to this topic. They tend to be either highly appreciative or deeply offended by what I say. I sometimes believe that my public presentations would meet with equal levels of success and failure if I simply stood before the audience and chanted the word *mothering* over and over. It seems that the word itself, without any embellishments on my part, is a highly provocative one. After all, we all know something about mothering: we've been mothered, we are mothers, we know mothers, or at least we think we know what it *means* to be a mother or to be mothered. It is partly because of this widespread familiarity that the topic tends to elicit such powerful, and often conflicted, responses.

But there are two further reasons that my analysis of mothering generates diverse reactions. First, part of what I analyze in this book is the issue of mothers who leave the home to work for pay. Although most Americans have accepted the fact that women with young children will participate in the labor force, many are still unsure whether they approve of this state of affairs. My acceptance of women's paid employment may lead some to worry that I am implicitly attacking mothers who stay at home. On the other hand, my discussion of mothers who stay at home and the selfishness they attribute to paid working mothers may lead others to believe that I am suggesting all mothers should be at home with their children. More important, in this book I analyze mothering as a historically constructed *ideology*. Although most Americans recognize that certain aspects of mothering follow from socially developed ideas, many also believe that other aspects are sacred, inviolable, or at least commonsensical and that they follow from the natural propensities of mothers or the absolute needs of children. My treatment of child rearing as an ideology may thus lead some to complain that I coldheartedly neglect the truth and value of current methods of raising children. My treatment of the mothers who use these methods may lead others to think that I unfairly portray mothers as too emotional, too gullible, or too sentimental. Following my analysis through to its conclusion, still others will claim that I am insufficiently critical of mothering and that it is I who am too emotional, too gullible, or too sentimental. All these contradictory responses are indications of the cultural power of the concept of mothering in our society.

My intent here is not to attack mothers or the work they do. Rather, my intent is to systematically unpack and analyze the cultural model of mothering. But part of my job in this unpacking process is to take the familiar and attempt to make it strange. The primary device I use to accomplish this is to approach mothering as if I were a disinterested outsider. I take that position not because I imagine that one could or should develop an objective or scientific view of mothering but because I think that this dispassionate stance is the most efficacious one for encouraging my readers to step back from their beliefs about mothering and to begin to explore its meaning anew, without any preconceptions about what mothers naturally do, what children naturally need, or what is best for mothers, fathers, children, and society.

It is my argument that the contemporary cultural model of socially appropriate mothering takes the form of an ideology of *intensive mothering*. The ideology of intensive mothering is a gendered model that advises mothers to expend a tremendous amount of time, energy, and money in raising their children. In a society where over half of all mothers with young children are now working outside of the home, one might well wonder why our culture pressures women to dedicate so much of themselves to child rearing. And in a society where the logic of self-interested gain seems to guide behavior in so many spheres of life, one might further wonder why a logic of unselfish nurturing guides the behavior of mothers. These two puzzling phenomena make up what I call the cultural contradictions of contemporary motherhoood.

To understand the bases for these contradictions and to demonstrate the development and prevalence of the ideology of intensive mothering, I drew on three types of data. First, I analyzed the history of ideas about child rearing, attempting to uncover the development and logic of notions of appropriate mothering and to understand the connections between those ideas and the social contexts in which they emerged. Second, I conducted a textual analysis of the best-selling contemporary child-rearing manuals to uncover their underlying themes. Finally, and most important, I talked to mothers. I conducted depth interviews with thirty-eight mothers of two- to four-year-old children. I talked to them about their everyday child-rearing practices, their styles of discipline, their sources of information on child rearing, the advice they liked and did not like, the qualities they wanted to see in their children, their male partners' child-rearing ideas and practices, their feelings about day care, their own upbringing, their positions as stay-at-home or paid working moms, and their visions of how child rearing would be organized in the perfect world.

These interviews were conducted in 1991 in San Diego, California, the sixth largest city in the United States. I used a modified snowball-sampling technique, asking the mothers I interviewed for referrals to other women. In order to avoid becoming enmeshed in groups of like-minded mothers, I limited the number of women that I interviewed from any given initial source to three. I spent two to four hours speaking to each mother. All interviews were tape-recorded, transcribed, and coded. In addition to the interviews, each mother completed a thirteen-page questionnaire that included a series of questions regarding child-rearing ideas and practices as well as demographic information. The interview schedule and survey questionnaire are in Appendixes A and B.

Although this small sample is not a cross-section of American mothers, it includes women of many different backgrounds. First, I selected mothers from four categories, according to their class positions and their circumstances as either paid working mothers or stay-at-home mothers. In the end, I spoke with ten middle-class paid working women, ten working-class and poor paid working women, nine middle-class stay-at-home mothers, and nine working-class and poor stay-at-home mothers. Their household incomes ranged from under $10,000 a year to over $90,000; the median income of the working-class and poor mothers was $25,000, and the median income of the middle-class mothers was $75,000. Those who worked for pay included a retail sales clerk, a waitress, a secretary, a switchboard operator, a cosmetologist, a doctor, a real estate agent, a journalist, a psychiatrist, an office manager, and a physical therapist. Of the middle-class mothers, all but five had finished college; nine had completed a master's, a doctoral, or a professional degree. Of the working-class and poor mothers, all but one had received a high school diploma or completed a GED (General Equivalency Diploma), half had had some college education, and one was a college graduate. Six of these women were Latinas, two African-Americans, two Asian-Americans, one explicitly identified herself as an Italian-American, and the rest were white (with no specific ethnic identification mentioned). There were sixteen Catholic mothers, nine Protestants, three Jews, two Mormons, one Jehovah's Witness, and seven mothers who claimed no religious affiliation. They ranged in age from twenty-one to forty-two; the median age was thirty-one. Some had only one child; others had as many as four. The median was two. Five were single mothers, the rest were married. Three had become mothers as teenagers.

The small size of my sample coupled with the snowball technique means that these results cannot be claimed as representative or wholly generalizable. However, there are reasons to believe that the ideology of mothering these women espouse is not limited to this small group. Despite the diverse backgrounds of these women, they tended to share a specific set of ideas about good child rearing. Additionally, in the course of my interviews I reached the point where I was able to anticipate what mothers would say before they actually spoke the words, indicating that the mothers I had talked to had provided me with a sense of the central patterns in the logic of child rearing (see Glaser and Strauss 1980). Lending further credence to my analysis is the fact that the ideology of mothering that I uncovered through these interviews turned out to be one that closely matched the ideology of mothering developed historically and elaborated in the best-selling child-rearing manuals. A final test of the value of my interpretation of the contemporary ideology of mothering will be the extent to which the readers of this book come to recognize these mothers as women they might know, and to experience what Rubin (1976: 13) calls the "aha experience."

It is with a story from one of these mothers, whom I call Rachel, that I begin this book. Chapter 1 explores a disagreement between Rachel and her boss in order to lay out the problem that the remainder of the book will address. This disagreement serves to highlight both the difficulties faced by paid working mothers and the clash between the logic of good mothering and the logic of good business practices. The ideas of Rachel and her boss thus serve as stand-ins for two very different ways of looking at the world.

Chapters 2 and 3 provide the background for my analysis of contemporary mothering. Chapter 2 charts the historical construction of contemporary ideas regarding child rearing, childhood, and mothering — tracing them from the swaddled infants of the European Middle Ages to the rise of permissive child rearing in the 1930s. Chapter 3 continues by examining the approaches of the three top-selling authors of contemporary child-rearing manuals: Dr. Benjamin Spock, Dr. T. Barry Brazelton, and Penelope Leach. All three of these authors make it clear that they consider mothers primarily responsible for raising children. All three recommend methods that place the child's needs first, expect a deep emotional commitment on the part of the mother, and assume that the mother will dedicate her time and energy to attending to the child's needs and desires at each stage of development. Given that the majority of today's mothers buy and consult such manuals, and given that the majority of those mothers are now working for pay, these findings are striking.

In the remaining chapters I present the words of contemporary mothers. Chapter 4 explores diversity among mothers, examining differences among individual women as well as the more systematic differences that follow from social-class background. Chapter 5 moves from differences to similarities, outlining the central tenets and overall logic of appropriate child rearing as it is elaborated by mothers themselves. Chapter 6 considers the important question of how paid working mothers and stay-at-home mothers make sense of their respective positions. Although there are various reasons to expect that mothers who stay at home would be more committed to the ideology of intensive mothering than their paid working counterparts, I show that the differences between these two groups of mothers are far more complex and that both groups share a deep commitment to the ideology of intensive child rearing.

Chapter 7 concludes by attempting to untangle the social roots of the para-doxical persistence of the ideology of intensive mothering. Ultimately, I argue that the ideology of intensive child rearing persists, in part, because it serves the interests not only of men but also of capitalism, the state, the middle class, and whites. Further, and on a deeper level, I argue that the ideology of inten-sive mothering is protected and promoted because it holds a fragile but none-theless powerful cutural position as the last best defense against what many people see as the impoverishment of social ties, communal obligations, and unremunerated commitments.

Like all books, this one has many authors. First, there were all the mothers who lent their time, their energy, and their concern in attempting to explain to me how they understood the task of mothering and its significance. Their contribution was invaluable.

Then there were all those who raised me to be a sociologist, whom I treat here in alphabetical order. Bennett Berger taught me the sociology of culture, encouraged me to reapproach the social world as a critical outsider, and of-fered me the treasure of his ironic humor and his loyal friendship. Rae Blum-berg gave me the courage and the strength to make my feminism a part of my sociology; her warmth and support helped me to stay the course without losing sight of the goals and the struggles we share. Dick Madsen (by example more than prescription, since Dick is never one to press his ideas on anyone) taught me the framework of interpretive social analysis and the importance of building a humanist sociology, and cared for me in the same deep and honest way that he cares for the world. Bud Mehan patiently and persistently pushed me to probe the depth of the meaning of social constructionism, provided me with a crucial role model through his own commitment to overcoming social injustice, and was always available to buy me coffee, listen to my complaints, and offer his reassurances. Jeff Weintraub's teachings on classical social theory and the development of modern Western societies were the ultimate source for much of what is written here. He is personally responsible for the title of this book as well as many of what I think are its best lines. Jeff was and is both my harshest critic and one of my most unflagging and generous supporters. For all this, and to each of these people, I am eternally grateful.

I would also like to acknowledge my friends and colleagues who, through their emotional support and intellectual energy, helped to make this book possible. Laura Miller was with me on this from beginning to end; she agonized with me over each step of the process, talked me through every argument, and read every draft. She stayed inside my head and constantly nourished my soul. And she knows just how much I appreciate it all. Phyllis Baker mentored me through the early stages and was always there to remind me that it is the thinking together, the talking together, and the caring for one another that really matters. Sarah Corse gave me her friendship at a time when I felt lost in an unfamiliar wilderness, and she read through all the final drafts, offering both comfort and insightful criticism. And there were those who read all or part of the manuscript in one or more of its incarnations and provided generous comments: Barbara Risman, Cynthia Truant, Rachel Klein, Cameron MacDonald, Elizabeth Long, Alan Wolfe, and Paul Kingston. I also wish to thank all the others who both inspired and cared for me over the long haul—especially Babette Convert, Kozy Amemiya, Tia DeNora, Evan Adelson, and Danny Paight.

Then there was the editor sent from heaven, Gladys Topkis. For all those who know her I need not say more; for those who don't, eat your heart out.

The University of Virginia Summer Grants Program provided me with a much-needed summer dedicated to nothing but writing. My manuscript editor, Karen Gangel, impressed and overwhelmed me with her amazing attention to detail, and her kind and patient support made a tedious process almost enjoyable.

Many thanks are also due my husband, Tom Ehlers. I can't actually thank him for raising this "baby" with me, but he did do much to ease the process. I can thank him for all the times he did the dishes and went to the grocery store and folded the laundry and cooked the dinner and watered the plants even though it wasn't his turn. I can thank him for fixing the leaking roof in my study. I can thank him for providing the window that allowed me to ponder nature in those moments when I was too stuck or too tired to go on. Throughout, his own vision and artistry were a constant source of inspiration and a reminder that stretching one's imagination could help one access the breadth and significance of a multitude of different perspectives. And his love, of course, has sustained me.

For giving me the gift of a second father, one with a golden heart, an open and inquiring mind, and an irresistible, slap-stick sense of humor, I thank my step-dad, Donald Sudkamp. Finally, from the depths of my heart, I smother with kisses, shower with flowers, and promise an endless supply of frozen yogurt desserts to my beloved mother, Doris Hays Sudkamp — without whose mothering I would never have made it this far.

The Cultural Contradictions of Motherhood

Why Can't a Mother Be More Like a Businessman?

The Trouble with Rachel

Rachel is a successful professional woman with a demanding, well-paying job, a marriage she considers egalitarian, and a two-year-old daughter.[1] She told me the following story with measured rage. When her daughter was so ill as to be hospitalized, Rachel felt compelled to stay at her bedside "every second." The child's life was not in danger, Rachel explained, but she needed her mother's love and reassurance. Rachel's boss, on the other hand, needed Rachel for an important assignment and simply could not understand why Rachel had to be at the hospital all the time. Although Rachel's boss is a woman and therefore, Rachel implied, should have been sensitive to this situation, she is also a childless woman. Lacking empathy for Rachel's position, her boss was, as Rachel put it, "resentful and angry." Still Rachel refused to leave the hospital room. Her daughter was sick; she needed her mother — no one else would do.

It is clear to Rachel that her child is far more important than any work assignment, and she believes that everyone *should* understand that. People like her boss are simply ignorant and selfish, she tells me: "They have no conception at all of what it means to raise children; they just don't understand." To Rachel, the point of view of her boss is wholly unreasonable; the requirements of appropriate child rearing are self-evident, sacred, and untouchable.

But her boss's point of view might also be described as a sensible and rational one. Didn't Rachel understand that this assignment had to be completed right away? Couldn't Rachel's husband, sister, or mother stay with the child? Surely there were nurses as well. Or, even more cynically, this workplace manager might have inquired, "Is the child worth the cost?" Given that the child is neither a productive family member nor one bringing money into the household, from a certain point of view it would appear unclear what Rachel had to gain by maintaining her bedside vigil. Weren't the returns on Rachel's job much more tangible? And didn't she risk losing the next possible promotion by failing to follow through on her professional responsibilities? Certainly any self-respecting businessman would know better than to spend so much of *his* time comforting a sick child.

Rachel's unsympathetic portrait of her boss, and my cynical extension of it, may or may not be accurate, but the self-interested, calculating, cold-hearted behavior attributed to her is not that far-fetched. Though her attitude may seem strange with reference to children and family life, in the larger world her attitude does not seem strange at all: not only does it correspond to a scholarly portrait of a "rational actor," it also matches a commonly held view of human behavior in general.[2] According to this widely shared logic, any rational individual would seek to maximize her own interests (particularly her interests in material gain) without regard to the interests of others. Rachel's boss, then, would naturally attempt to manage her employees in the most efficient and profitable manner, since her own salary and career advancement depend upon it. And since Rachel is also clearly committed to pursuing a career, she does seem to be acting irrationally by devoting herself to her child at the expense of her paid work. From a hard-nosed outsider's point of view, Rachel appears morally and emotionally overinvested in her daughter and, without major changes, it seems that she will be facing the "mommy-track," her career permanently sidetracked by her commitment to mothering (Schwartz 1989). Given the higher status and greater material gain associated with career success, why does she choose to dedicate herself to a notion of appropriate child rearing that seems to put the child's needs above her own?

The contradiction Rachel faces between her commitment to her work and her commitment to her child is not just an individual problem; it is part of a larger cultural contradiction. In C. Wright Mills's terms, what Rachel experiences as the "personal troubles of milieu" are in fact closely connected to the "public issues of social structure" (1959:8). Rachel experiences these troubles, in part, because she is one of many mothers now in the paid labor force who must meet the dual demands of paid work and child care. More important, Rachel experiences these troubles because she shares with others a particular *perception* of those demands, one that is linked to contradictory cultural images of mothers who selflessly nurture their children and businessmen who selfishly compete in the paid labor force. To put it another way, Rachel's understanding of the logic of child rearing is connected to the cultural conception of women's private sphere in the home, and her boss's understanding of the logic of paid work is connected to the cultural conception of men's public sphere in the larger world. As an individual, Rachel is pulled between these two spheres.

The cultural contradiction between home and world has a long history, while the personal contradiction Rachel confronts as a mother and a career woman is a relatively recent historical phenomenon. Over the past two hundred years, Western society has been juggling the contradictory logics of appropriate behavior at home and appropriate behavior in the outside world. This tension, however, has been partially managed by attempts to maintain a clear ideological and practical separation between life at home and life in the outside world, with women responsible for one sphere and men responsible for the other.[3] In accordance with this, the public ideology of appropriate child rearing has urged mothers to stay at home with their children, thereby ostensibly maintaining consistency in women's nurturing and selfless behavior. But in reality the wall between home and world has always been structurally unstable and insufficiently high, and over the past fifty years the integrity of its construction has been increasingly threatened by the ever-greater number of women who have climbed over it to participate in the paid labor force.

The paradoxical nature of the situation this creates comes out most clearly against the contrast of the 1950s, the era of suburban life, domestic bliss, the "feminine mystique," Dr. Spock, and "momism." At a time when there were far fewer mothers of young children in the paid labor force than there are now, and when more American families than ever before were able to realize the middle-class family ideal, mothers' intense emotional attachment and moral commitment to their children seemed less contradictory. Today, however, when well over half of all mothers are in the paid labor force, when the image of a career woman is that of a competitive go-getter, and when the image of the family is one of disintegrating values and relationships, one would expect a deemphasis on the ideology of child rearing as labor-intensive, emotionally absorbing women's work.

Since 1950, the number of employed women with young children has more than quadrupled: 58 percent of mothers with children under six years of age worked in the paid labor force in 1993 as compared to 12 percent in 1950.[4] While no social consensus has been reached regarding the desirability of women with young children working outside the home, there has been a general acceptance of this trend (Greenberger and O'Neil 1990; Weiner 1985). In this social context, white, middle-class women in particular have become more and more committed to pursuing careers.[5] Many of these women are entering the paid labor force not just reluctantly, or out of necessity, but because they *want* to. And when they choose a career over a job, they make a long-term commitment to a path that does not allow them to come and go at will but instead requires ongoing dedication to life in the world outside the home.

Under these conditions one might expect that women would fully assimilate the logic of the marketplace, that the barrier between home and world would completely crumble, and that the rational calculation of self-interest would lead all of us to perceive child rearing as a fairly simple task. Yet the commitment to emotionally demanding, financially draining, labor-consuming child rearing seems to be thriving. Like many other women faced with this burdensome contradiction, Rachel does not choose to give up one commitment for the other; she juggles both. For Rachel, appropriate child rearing is not an ideology but a given, a matter of what is natural and necessary—there is simply no question of ignoring the child's multifaceted needs.

However, this form of mothering is neither self-evidently natural nor, in any absolute sense, necessary; it is a social construction. Child-rearing ideologies vary widely, both historically and cross-culturally. In other times and places, simpler, less time- and energy-consuming methods have been considered appropriate, and the child's mother has not always and everywhere been the primary caregiver. The idea that correct child rearing requires not only large quantities of money but also professional-level skills and copious amounts of physical, moral, mental, and emotional energy on the part of the individual mother is a relatively recent historical phenomenon. Why, then, does Rachel persist in her commitment to intensive mothering?

Arlie Hochschild (1989) provides another version of this question in her book on two-career families, *The Second Shift*. She asks: Why has the cultural revolution that matches women's economic revolution stalled? When rapid industrialization took men out of the home and placed them in the factory, shop, or office, a corresponding ideological revolution encouraged women (middle-class white women, especially) to *want* to tend the home and care for the children. Hochschild argues that we now need a new ideological revolution encouraging men to want to cook, clean, and nurture children, and encouraging employers and the state to want to provide for child care, job sharing, and parental leave.

But what Hochschild suggests—that we shift the focus from intensive mothering to intensive *parenting*—is only a partial solution to the contradiction between the demands of home and work, and one that does not begin to address the larger cultural contradictions. If men and women shared the burden that Rachel now bears primarily, the larger social paradox would continue to haunt both of them and would grow even stronger for men. Given the power of the ideology of the marketplace, a more logical (and cynical) solution would be an ideological revolution that makes tending home and children a purely commercial, rationalized enterprise, one in which neither mother nor father need be highly involved. Why don't we convince ourselves that children need neither a quantity of time nor "quality time" with their mothers *or* their fathers?

After all, from a cold and calculating point of view, the ideology of intensive mothering seems to contradict the interests of almost everyone. Paid working women[6] might like to avoid the extra work on the "second shift," stay-at-home mothers might enjoy a bit more free time, capitalists surely want all of their paid laborers' energy and attention, and husbands might prefer the career promotions of a woman who dedicates herself to bringing home the bacon. Such propositions are not so outlandish when we think about how powerful utility-maximizing assumptions are in modern society. If I were a Martian who had just landed in the United States, I might notice that the primary activity of the society seemed to be the instrumentally rational pursuit of self-interested material gain in a situation of limited resources. Most of the humans appear to be engaged in attempts to buy low and sell high, calculating the best possible gain and systematically pursuing it in the most efficient manner, individualistically competing with others for available resources all the while. Nurturing, moral mothers, constantly attentive to the needs and desires of another who has little tangible to offer them in return, seem quite out of place.

Of course human infants require a certain amount of physical care. Cultures around the globe and throughout time seem to have taken into account that children are not prepared to enter the adult world until at least age six or seven (Rogoff et al. 1976; Weisner and Gallimore 1977). But modern American mothers do much more than simply feed, change, and shelter the child until age six. It is that "more" with which I am here concerned.

Why do many professional-class employed women seem to find it necessary to take the kids to swimming and judo and dancing and tumbling classes, not to mention orthodontists and psychiatrists and attention-deficit specialists? Why is the human bonding that accompanies breast-feeding considered so important that elaborate contraptions are now manufactured to allow children to suckle on mothers who cannot produce milk? Why are there aerobics courses for babies, training sessions in infant massage, sibling-preparedness workshops, and designer fashions for two-year-olds? Why must a "good" mother be careful to "negotiate" with her child, refraining from demands for obedience to an absolute set of rules? Why must she avoid spanking a disobedient child and instead feel the need to explain, in detail, the issues at hand? Why does she consider it important to be consciously and constantly attentive to the child's wishes? Why does she find it necessary to apologize to the child if she somehow deviates from the code of appropriate mothering? Why is it important to have all possible information on the latest child-rearing techniques? Why must she assure herself that prospective child-care providers are well-versed in psychological and cognitive development? Surely all these activities consume massive amounts of time and energy. Why would a woman who has the opportunity to gain so much more from focusing on her professional responsibilities choose to believe in the need for these intensive methods?

Intensive Mothering

Rachel is, without a doubt, a dedicated mother. Although she considers herself a feminist and has a fine, well-paying career with much room for advancement, a career that would be understood as meaningful and enriching by any standard, and one that consistently demands a good deal of her time and intellectual energy, she remains committed to what I call intensive mothering. She has juggled her schedule and cut back her hours so she can spend the maximum amount of time with her daughter, Kristin. And Rachel is very careful to choose the correct "alternate mothers" to care for Kristin while she is at work. Kristin now attends a preschool three mornings a week where cognitive and physical development is stressed but not, Rachel explains, at the expense of playtime. For the remaining hours that Rachel is at work, Kristin is cared for at home by highly qualified, credentialed, female child-care providers.

Rachel is active in La Leche League and for twelve months breast-fed Kristin on demand (against the advice of her pediatrician and friends). She also participates in a mothers' play group, made up of professional-class women who first met at an exercise class in which mothers and their babies jointly worked to strengthen their physiques. These women now collectively take their same-aged children on regular outings.

Rachel reads to Kristin daily. She takes her to ballet class and swimming lessons weekly. Every Thursday (the one weekday that Rachel is not working for pay) is designated "Kristin's day": Rachel works until midnight once a week in order to make this special day possible. And this day is just for Kristin: all activities are centered around Kristin and Kristin's desires.

Rachel's self-conscious commitment to intensive child rearing also appears in her belief that there is no such thing as a bad child: "If you love your child, your child is good. If a child acts badly, it's probably the parents who are to blame." It is crucial to avoid corruption of the child's goodness and the child's innocence, and parental love is the primary ingredient for the maintenance of these virtues. Appropriate parental love, Rachel reminds me repeatedly, includes the conviction that a mother should be, as Rachel is, ready to "kill and die" for her child.

Rachel has "smacked" Kristin only once. It was a particularly bad day, she explains, and Kristin was terribly fussy and demanding. Rachel hit her "once on the butt" when her behavior became too much to bear. However, she emphasizes, "I know I didn't hit her hard because I was *so* in control." Control is important to Rachel since every action of mothering is understood to have potentially damaging consequences. And Rachel is clearly sorry she hit her child. The incident required numerous subsequent discussions with the two-year-old: "We talked about it a lot afterwards," she continues, "you know, how mommy lost it, she was stressed. And I've never done it since."[7]

Rachel tells me that her husband is just as concerned with Kristin's happiness and development as she is. They regularly discuss the stages Kristin is going through, he reads and plays with Kristin frequently, and, in Rachel's account, he shares equally in housekeeping and child-rearing tasks. He is, Rachel says, "protective and possessive" of Kristin. But the person Rachel most often talks to about child rearing is a female friend, and it is Rachel, not her husband, who takes Kristin to her lessons, chooses her caregivers, participates in the play group, and cuts back on her paid work hours to make time for "Kristin's day." Further, Rachel stresses that "the money from my salary goes to vacations and things for the house and Kristin's education and that sort of stuff." In Rachel's rendition, then, a mother's salary (not a father's) pays for the enhancement of family life and the requirements of socially appropriate child rearing.

Rachel's love for her home and her child is so powerful that it frequently spills over into her paid working life. At the office, she tells me, "our desks are shrines to our children and our marriages." Nonetheless, Rachel strives to retain a clear sense of the distinction between home and work: "I try to separate the two as much as I can. They're two different worlds." She continues: "My home is my private life, my child, my soul-mate. My nurturing side is there." Life on the job is public, cold, and uncaring; one needs to bring pictures and mementos from home as reminders of the warm and nurturing private side of life.

Does Rachel consider her child more important than her career? Absolutely.

I think human beings all have the desire just to bring another human being into the world, and raise another human being that's ours. To see a part of ourselves live on . . . I think that we all have that desire. Most of us do. And that desire is more enriching [than a career] for most people, to share our lives with another human being.

Rachel's ideas of appropriate child rearing can be understood as a combination of three elements—all of them interfering with her commitment to her job, and all of them in contradiction to the ideology of the workplace and the dominant ethos of modern society.

First, in Rachel's image of appropriate child rearing it is critical that she, as the *mother,* be the central caregiver. It is Rachel who must be at her child's bedside throughout the hospital stay; her husband is not even mentioned in this context. It is Rachel who must make room for Kristin's day. And it is Rachel who is ultimately responsible for Kristin's development. Men, apparently, cannot be relied upon to provide the same level of care. There is an underlying assumption that the child absolutely requires consistent nurture by a single primary caretaker and that the mother is the best person for the job. When the mother is unavailable, it is other women who should serve as temporary substitutes.

Second, the logic that applies to appropriate child rearing, for Rachel, includes lavishing copious amounts of time, energy, and material resources on the child. A mother must put her child's needs above her own. A mother must recognize and conscientiously respond to all the child's needs and desires, and to every stage of the child's emotional and intellectual development. This means that a mother must acquire detailed knowledge of what the experts consider proper child development, and then spend a good deal of time and money attempting to foster it. Rachel understands that this is an emotionally taxing job as well, since the essential foundation for proper child development is love and affection. In sum, the methods of appropriate child rearing are construed as *child-centered, expert-guided, emotionally absorbing, labor-intensive,* and *financially expensive.*

Finally, Rachel believes that a comparison of her paid work and her child-rearing activities is ludicrous. Not only is the child clearly more important, but a completely different logic applies to child rearing than to paid work. While Rachel's daughter may be a net financial drain, she is emotionally and morally outside the scope of market valuation: she is, in Zelizer's (1985) phrase, a "priceless child." Innocent and pure, children have a special value; they therefore deserve special treatment.

It is this fully elaborated, logically cohesive combination of beliefs that I call the ideology of intensive mothering. Although Rachel is a unique individual and her status as a white, middle-class career woman places her in a particular social category, I will show that this constellation of beliefs is held in common by many American mothers today. These ideas are certainly not followed in practice by every mother, but they are, implicitly or explicitly, understood as the *proper* approach to the raising of a child by the majority of mothers. In other words, the ideology of intensive mothering is, I maintain, the dominant ideology of socially appropriate child rearing in the contemporary United States.

The Cultural Contradictions

From the point of view of Rachel's boss and any self-respecting business-man — that is, from the point of view of self-interested, profit-maximizing util-ity — women's commitment to intensive mothering seems mysterious. While some might argue that the competitive, self-interested, efficiency-minded, and materialistically oriented logic of Rachel's boss is likewise mysterious to Rachel and other mothers, the fact is that the two ideologies do not hold equal status in today's society. For instance, many Americans would assume that it is human nature to be self-interested; almost none would claim that it is human nature to give priority to the needs and desires of others. The logic of Rachel's boss is thus far more powerful, and Rachel and other mothers are fully aware of this. On the other hand, some might argue that the two logics are benignly complementary when they are clearly separated and functioning smoothly in distinct contexts. In these terms, Rachel's emphasis on intensive child rearing makes sense in the context of her life at home or the context of a hospital room where her sick daughter lies, whereas her boss's logic makes sense in the context of a busy office and an important work assignment that is not yet completed. But this analysis neglects the unequal status of the two logics, ignores the fact that these logics cannot always be neatly compartmentalized and, most crucially, implicitly denies the fact that these are *opposing* logics.[8] In fact, Rachel and other paid working mothers are faced with the power of both logics simultaneously and are forced to make choices between them. In today's society, then, the strength and persistence of the ideology of intensive mothering seems mysterious for two related reasons — the first from the stand-point of paid working mothers, the second in terms of certain important trends in society as a whole.

Practically speaking, mothers who work in the paid labor force seem to be acting irrationally when they dedicate so much time and energy to child rear-ing, because this strategy is physically and emotionally draining — wearing them down with added demands on the second shift. At the same time, they face the contradiction of engaging in the self-interested pursuit of financial gain at work while simultaneously pumping vast resources into the appropriate rearing of their children. Many women find their take-home pay nearly wiped out by the costs of day care; others, like Rachel, regard their salaries as the means of ensuring their children's education and happiness. In those societies where children offer some return on this investment—serving, for instance, as the providers of social security in their parents' old age—this outlay of time, energy, and capital might make more sense. But in this society most children are, in fact, a net financial loss (Huber and Spitze 1988).

Furthermore, an employed woman faces the possibility of losing out on job promotions, endangering her current position, and decreasing her material returns because of all those days spent at home comforting sick children, all those hours spent arranging for day care, dental appointments, birthday parties, shopping for new shoes and toys, and all those mornings when she arrives with less than her whole "body and soul" to dedicate to the job. Additionally, there is the strain of maintaining the two roles that these women experience as they attempt to be cool-headed and competitive at work but warm-hearted and nurturing at home. Finally, for those women with careers (rather than simply jobs), we know that professional success offers far more status in American society than success as a mother. Why pursue the latter at the expense of the former?

These practical contradictions faced by individual mothers are all related to a larger contradiction in society as a whole. The strength of the ideology of intensive, nurturing, moral motherhood is in tension with what many have identified as the central trends in modern Western culture. The classical sociological literature portrays our society as one that values the efficient, impersonal, competitive pursuit of self-interested gain above all else. For Max Weber, the impersonality and efficiency of the modern West are constituted by the rationalization of social life. For Marx and Engels, the competitive pursuit of private gain is the result of the extension and intensification of capitalist market relations. And for Ferdinand Tönnies, both impersonal and competitive relations are a part of the larger historical shift from the gemeinschaft system of beliefs and relationships, grounded in custom, tradition, and particularistic ties of mutual obligation and commitment, to the gesellschaft system, grounded in commodification, bureaucratization, and impersonal ties of competitive exchange and contract.[9]

These classical social theorists believed that the ethos of rationalized market society would eventually penetrate every sphere of social life.[10] But for a long time it seemed that some spheres remained immune. Throughout the nineteenth and much of the twentieth century, the family, in particular, seemed to be organized around a different set of ideas and practices. Of late, however, a number of prominent scholars have argued that *all* spheres of life, including the family (and, by implication, the mothering that goes on within it), are now penetrated by the utilitarian pursuit of personal profit that has long dominated the larger society.

For Heilbroner (1988), this invasion of rationalized market relations takes the form of the "implosion of capitalism," as the norms and practices of the capitalist marketplace find their way into areas of life where they had not been before. For Bellah et al. (1985), this invasion is evident in the growing prominence of the language of "utilitarian individualism," as all of social life is increasingly perceived and discussed as if it were merely a collection of individuals who calculate the most efficient means of maximizing their power and material advantage. Polanyi (1944) would concur, emphasizing the historically unprecedented nature of societies such as ours where "the motive of gain becomes a justification for action and behavior in everyday life" (30). And Sahlins (1976) echoes these analyses in his treatment of the ubiquitous nature of the ideology of "practical reason" in Western capitalist societies: when the market economy becomes the primary producer of cultural logic, he argues, all human behavior, in all spheres of life, comes to be pictured as that of *homo economicus*.

Many feminists seem to agree, as they portray the contemporary family as one in which members calculate the efficiency of various family strategies and compete among themselves for power and material resources (e.g., Allen 1983; Bentson 1984; Blumberg 1991; Gordon 1988; Hartmann 1981a, 1981b; Peterson 1983; Polatnick 1983; Rapp et al. 1979). At the same time, other scholars emphasize the participation of the modern centralized state in this invasion: the bureaucratically organized, impersonal state, they say, continues to usurp and control more and more aspects of what were once private family matters (e.g., Bane 1976; Donzelot 1979; Foucault 1978; Lasch 1977; Rothman 1989). What all these analyses have in common is a vision of self-interested individuals struggling for power and profit, in the family as elsewhere.

In concrete terms, this means that the family is invaded not only by public schools, the courts, social service workers, gardeners, housekeepers, day-care providers, lawyers, doctors, televisions, frozen dinners, pizza delivery, manufactured clothing, and disposable diapers, but also, and more critically, by the *ideology* behind such institutions, persons, and products. They bring with them, in whole or in part, the language and logic of impersonal, competitive, contractual, commodified, efficient, profit-maximizing, self-interested relations. Family members, theoretically, are not the least bit immune to this ideology — in their homes, as everywhere else, they are, more and more, simply looking out for themselves.[11] Women's "abandonment" of the home to seek more lucrative employment might alternately be interpreted as a result or a cause of this invasion.

Given the invasive logic of the larger society, one would expect mothers to consistently act like good capitalists or bureaucrats, consciously calculating the most efficient means of raising children — that which would offer them the highest personal returns based on the least amount of effort. This, after all, would not only make their lives easier but should, theoretically, constitute the most socially valued and socially appropriate method.

In determining the most efficient and least costly means of raising children, it would appear that mothers have a wealth of alternative ideologies to choose from. Western history and the practices of other cultures provide examples of child-rearing methods that are far less demanding than Rachel's, and just as well accomplished by a variety of persons other than parents.[12] Furthermore, there are contemporary ideas that might serve the needs of employed mothers and society as well. As Rachel's boss might suggest, more independence for the child could help to develop her character, and more weekly chores rather than ballet lessons might better prepare her for adulthood.[13] The examples modern mothers offer of "bad" parents are also indicative of the forms that simpler parenting might take. There are women, mothers told me in dismay, who leave their kids in day care from six in the morning until seven at night and hire someone else to pick them up at the end of the day. There are people who think children should be seen and not heard. Even worse, there are parents who regularly (and carelessly) spank their children when they are disobedient. There are parents who wear earplugs through the night to avoid being disturbed by their young babies. And I was told the story of a mother who, faced with a fussy child suffering from colic, first strapped him into a car seat and then placed him in a closet. These are surely efficient methods of dealing with children, so why do many mothers consider them not only socially inappropriate but downright evil and unconscionable?

The ideology and practices of appropriate child rearing are socially constructed. Logically speaking, shouldn't the present ideal of intensive mothering be reconstructed to fall more reasonably in line with the needs of paid working mothers and the ideology and practices of society as a whole? In the case of child rearing, at least, the implosion of capitalism and the invasion of gesellschaft relations are apparently incomplete.

Cynical Questions

For Rachel and many other mothers I have talked to, questioning the logic of intensive mothering is the cynical response of selfish, ignorant, and insensitive persons. Women who stay at home with their children rather than work for pay might attribute this response to those professional working men and women who disdainfully inquire, "You're *just* a housewife? How do you fill your time?" Rachel and other employed mothers might recognize it as the response of certain types of men and childless career women who ask, "Why do you *bother* so much about your kids when there's more important work to be done?" But for many mothers, children are clearly more important. They deserve and require far more than minimal physical care.

As a sociologist, I here join the selfish, ignorant, and insensitive. Cynical questions are crucial to cultural sociology. That is, it is important for sociologists to critically examine aspects of the culture of everyday life that are so sacred, so deeply held, so taken for granted as to remain generally unquestioned and regularly treated as common sense. Such ideas and practices often point to something crucial in social life. Notions of appropriate mothering fall into this category.

To make problematic that which is sacred is to understand it as neither natural nor given but as a socially constructed reality.[14] Understanding the socially constructed nature of ideas and practices must begin with the recognition that there are alternative ideologies available, no matter how much these may grate against our deepest sense of what is right and natural. To say that ideas and practices are social constructs does not mean, however, that they are therefore either infinitely malleable or somehow unworthy. Neither the ideology represented by Rachel nor that represented by her boss is more or less "correct" in any absolute sense, nor is either of these ideologies superficial and transitory. The point is that neither is natural, inevitable, or *inherently* more rational, worthy, or valuable. Further exploration is necessary to understand why these ideas rather than others have come to be socially chosen and socially valued. With reference to naturalized ideas like the ideology of intensive mothering, an exploration of their social roots becomes all the more necessary, precisely because its social grounding is so deeply hidden.[15]

There may be many interesting arguments regarding the natural or biological bases of intensive mothering, arguments that trace, for instance, a mother's commitment to her child to the fact that she produces estrogen and milk.[16] But there are layers upon layers of socially constructed elaboration and reinforcement of this "natural" base. Although women do get pregnant and lactate, and may even experience some animal-like instinct to protect and feed and thereby preserve their offspring, this makes up a only a minuscule portion of what is understood as socially appropriate mothering. Mothers all over the world get pregnant and produce estrogen and milk, yet ideas of appropriate child rearing vary widely. It is the socially constructed *meaning* of pregnancy and lactation that is important; it is the ideas and practices attached to childbirth and child rearing that constitute the culture of socially appropriate mothering.

Many American mothers (and fathers) would argue that their child-rearing ideas and practices flow from the love they "naturally" feel for their children. And it is true that one can find fairly consistent evidence that parents have always and everywhere experienced a strong emotional response to their young. But that emotional response has not always and everywhere been understood as "love," and it has led to widely varied practices in the history of American society and in cultures around the globe. The ideology of intensive mothering is a very specific and highly elaborate set of ideas that goes well beyond any simple emotional response to children. The beliefs and practices that follow from a mother's feelings toward her child, in other words, are no more natural or inevitable than those that follow from a mother's lactation.

The same logic can be applied to notions of the "natural" requirements of children. There seems to be no question that children need not only physical sustenance but also some level of emotional and cognitive nourishment in order to thrive. Studies have made clear, however, that the requirements of children do not "naturally" lead parents to approach child rearing in any particular way (e.g., Kagan 1986; Mead 1962; Rogoff et al. 1976; Scheper-Hughes 1987, 1992). And, beyond these minimal requirements, the methods of child rearing that will *best* serve the needs of children are also ambiguous. Although some would argue that current methods of child rearing are the right methods or the most effective methods for preparing children for contemporary society, others would disagree.[17] Given this, I will simply bracket claims to the correctness of the methods proposed by the ideology of intensive mothering and focus my attention on understanding why they are considered correct (and natural) by so many.

Deeply entrenched as it is, the ideology of intensive mothering that Rachel represents, just like the ideology of the marketplace that her boss represents, has not gone wholly unquestioned. As Berger (1991) points out, once cultural ideals that have been taken for granted are contested, they become ideologies. Such ideologies then become matters of public debate, each side attempting to make a claim to truth and righteousness. Their status as "common sense" is lost. The arguments of Rachel and her boss, however, are almost never deployed explicitly and systematically. Rarely is self-seeking completely championed; rarely is nurturing motherhood completely debunked; and just as rarely is it suggested that the whole of society would operate more effectively if it followed the logic of Rachel's child rearing. Rather, the argument between Rachel and her boss tends to take the form of debates over the participation of women in the labor force, the fate of "family values," the proper responsibilities of fathers, and the effects of day care. It seems that few would dare to question intensive child rearing in a straightforward manner, just as few would absolutely oppose the logic of efficiency and self-interest. Nonetheless, ambivalence and tension are apparent, and the cultural ideal of appropriate mothering is potentially called into question. It is therefore no longer a cultural given, it is instead an ideology.

To examine such an ideology within the tradition of the sociology of knowledge means to critically analyze its context, carriers, and content. What are the social contexts in which these ideas arise and persist? If ideologies are the result of a historical conversation in which each generation shares ideas and argues with members of future, former, and present generations, then it makes sense to examine the similarities and differences in the worlds in which those generations reside — in terms of both the framework of relations between groups and the ideas and practices that are accepted as appropriate.[18] Who, exactly, are the primary proponents of these ideas, and what is their position in the social hierarchy? Since some people will likely be more attached to certain ideas than other people will, information on the gender, class, race, education, religion, and other social characteristics of the carriers of ideas allows us to speculate on why these particular persons might find these particular ideas attractive and important. Finally, it is crucial to examine the content of the ideology: its logic, its component parts, and the meaning it holds for its carriers. Ideologies, in other words, must also be taken seriously on their own terms.

The purpose of such an analysis, then, is not to debunk ideologies as "mere" strategies used by their carriers in struggles for material and status advantage, nor to dismiss them as "mere" reflections of some absolute set of structural requirements in a given context. Rather, the point is to fully explore the content and logic of such ideologies, to place them in their context, and to locate their carriers as a method of understanding why certain ideas come to achieve salience over others, in certain contexts, among certain groups of people.[19] In these terms, while neither the ideology of Rachel nor that of her boss can be taken at face value, it would be equally inappropriate to see either as simply "mistakes" in need of correction; the logic of both sets of ideas speaks to crucial aspects of social life.

Rachel's Story and Beyond

Perhaps the context of social change caused by the entrance of large numbers of middle-class mothers into the paid labor force and the invasion of the family by the ideas and practices of impersonal, competitive, self-interested gain has created a space in which the cultural ideal of motherhood becomes a debatable ideology. As a carrier, Rachel might be understood as attempting to deny the social tension, while her boss may be attempting to define a new road ahead. Both tend to use their ideas as weapons — Rachel claims her boss is ignorant and insensitive, her boss views Rachel as simply irrational. Sociologically speaking, both are equally naive: Rachel assumes her ideas speak to the "natural" propensities of mothers and requirements of children; her boss assumes that an instrumentally rational approach should "naturally" take precedence. Rachel appears sentimental; her boss appears blindly selfish. Yet both Rachel and her boss continue to cling to the content of their contradictory ideologies, treating them not only as a means of legitimating what they actually do but also as important guides for what they *should* do.

Rachel emphasizes nurturing qualities and a sense of personal obligation to others. Her boss emphasizes utilitarian concerns and a calculating cost-benefit analysis of individual advantage. Rachel's story exemplifies the sacred status of motherhood. Her boss's response represents the potential breakdown of that status. Both arguments are historically constructed ideologies that include a whole set of assumptions about human nature and the appropriate framework for social life. That the two contradictory ideologies coexist in contemporary society highlights the tensions that have developed between the demands of work life and the demands of family life, between the historically constructed images of warm, nurturing mothers on the one side and cold, competitive career women on the other, between the call for a revival of "family values" and the call for greater workplace efficiency, and between the impersonal pursuit of self-interested gain in the context of a competitive market system and the empathic pursuit of nurturing personal relations in the context of a system of mutual obligations and commitments. These two ideologies are expressions of what are, arguably, the two central cultural frameworks in contemporary Western society. And the opposition between these two ideologies highlights not only the paradoxical nature of contemporary ideas about child rearing and motherhood but also a central recurring tension in society as a whole.

It is these tensions that I intend to explore by analyzing the historical context of changes in ideas about child rearing and the family, the different carriers of child-rearing ideologies, both past and present, and the content of the ideology of appropriate mothering as it is represented in popular child-rearing manuals and as it is expressed by mothers themselves.

Although I feel very close and much indebted to a number of modern-day mothers, through much of this book I take a distanced and apparently cold-hearted stance toward the ideology of socially appropriate child rearing that many of them hold dear. But I do so only because this is the best way I know to pry the ideology loose from its naturalized and sentimentalized moorings. It is not my intention to degrade or dismiss current notions of appropriate child rearing, to imply that mothers are somehow suffering from "false consciousness," or to suggest that we should (or could) simply dispense with the ideology of intensive mothering as if it were a bad joke. I am convinced that ideas of appropriate child rearing follow from sincerely felt responses, that they are rational and reasonable in this social context, and that they are an indication of deeply entrenched and deeply experienced, socially generated needs, interests, and concerns. At the same time, however, I want to avoid the unreflective valorization of intensive motherhood. The purpose of this book, in other words, is not to endorse or attack current methods of child rearing but to uncover the logic of the ideology of intensive mothering, clarify its historical emergence, demonstrate its persistence, and speculate on the reasons it remains so powerful.

There are a number of potential explanations for the power and persistence of the ideology of intensive mothering. Many have argued that modern ideas of appropriate child rearing are the result of progress in knowledge regarding children's needs that follows from natural parental love. Others claim that present-day paid working mothers are increasingly calculating their self-interest and setting aside notions of intensive child rearing as they focus their attention on career advancement. Still others emphasize the ways in which unequal power in society accounts for what contemporary mothers say and do.

Each of these arguments provides important clues. But, taken alone, they are insufficient for making sense of the complex reality that underlies the ideology of intensive mothering. Certainly, there is no question that women love their children and that there is, in fact, more information available on children and child rearing than there once was. But the specific ideas and practices that follow from this love and information are neither self-evident nor based in nature; they are a socially constructed reality. And there is no question that mothers are engaged in what may be perceived as self-interested utilitarian attempts to retain or achieve middle-class status for their children and themselves, to cast their position either as participants in the paid work-force or as stay-at-home mothers in a favorable light relative to their counterparts, and to organize their lives in manageable and efficient ways. But there is little indication that most mothers are choosing to ignore their children when more lucrative options present themselves. Further, there is no question that women's relative lack of power largely explains their role as the primary caregivers for children. It accounts for the fact that stay-at-home mothers are burdened with a socially devalued and potentially isolating position at home, while employed women are saddled with a "second shift" of domestic chores and child-rearing duties and are hindered in their attempts at career advancement. These forms of subordinating women ultimately benefit not only men but also capitalism and the modern state. Nonetheless, there is something more in what these women do and say.

While the contemporary ideal of intensive mothering involves the subordination of women, it also involves their *opposition* to the logic that subordinates them. As I will show, the historical construction of intensive mothering demonstrates that its early blooming was directly connected to the ideological separation of public and private spheres, a separation according to which the values of intimate and family life stood as an explicit rejection of the values of economic and political life. The arguments of best-selling contemporary child-rearing advisers and, more importantly, the words of present-day mothers make it clear that this remains a powerful and deeply evocative distinction. The relationship between mother and child continues to symbolize, realistically or not, opposition to social relations based on the competitive pursuit of individual gain in a system of impersonal contractual relations. In pursuing a moral concern to establish lasting human connection grounded in unremunerated obligations and commitments, modern-day mothers, to varying degrees, participate in this implicit rejection of the ethos of rationalized market society.

The argument between Rachel and her boss, then, is symptomatic of a larger struggle in modern society. Although this struggle was not initiated by present-day mothers, they have become some of the primary persons who must cope with the problems it engenders. Given its deeply rooted nature, it is also certain that this conflict will not be won or lost in battles waged by individual mothers. In the final analysis, the argument between Rachel and her boss is indicative of a fundamental and irreducible ambivalence about a society based solely on the competitive pursuit of self-interest. Motherhood, I argue, is one of the central terrains on which this ambivalence is played out.

2

From Rods to Reasoning
The Historical Construction of Intensive Mothering

Images of children, child rearing, and motherhood do not spring from nature, nor are they random. They are socially constructed. Their natural quality is refuted not only by their variance across persons and places but also by their ever-changing character. And these variations are largely explained by the fact that ideas about child rearing, like all ideas, bear a systematic and intelligible connection to the culture and organization of the society in which they are found.

Appropriate child rearing in many (if not most) cultures means looking after the small child until it reaches the age of six or seven, at which point the child is considered ready to participate in some respects in the world of adults (Weisner and Gallimore 1977). Caring for the child during that early period generally does not involve an explicit, self-conscious concern for the child's psychological or cognitive development — it simply means making certain that the child is protected from physical harm and has enough food and clothing to ensure its survival. And when economic, political, demographic, medical, or cultural conditions make child survival precarious, many cultures develop strategies that provide for the survival of some of the family's children by ignoring the needs of the others, through practices of selective neglect, abandonment, or even infanticide (Scheper-Hughes 1987). But whether minimal physical care is provided for every child or not, such care is never understood as *all* that appropriate early child rearing entails; different cultures develop distinct and elaborate rituals for handling the young (see Mead and Wolfenstein 1955). The point is that the strategies and the rituals vary — no particular configuration follows automatically or naturally from blood ties or from a universal and absolute definition of the needs of children.

Significantly, and in contrast to the contemporary American ideology of intensive child rearing, there is also no reason to believe that mothers (or parents) must be the persons who raise the children. Margaret Mead writes, "Primitive materials . . . give no support to the theory that there is a 'natural' connection between conditions of human gestation and delivery and appropriate cultural practices. . . . [The] establishment of permanent nurturing ties between a woman and the child she bears . . . is dependent upon cultural patterning" (1962: 54). Nor is it true that individual mothers usually take primary responsibility for raising the children. In a standard anthropological sample of 186 contemporary cultures, individual mothers are the principal caretakers of children in only 20 percent of the cases (Weisner and Gallimore 1977). In most societies, the rearing of small children is shared among women, or among women and older children.[1]

Furthermore, in most cultures young children are economic assets. Children as young as age two may be encouraged to take on simple tasks, and by age six they are considered able, for instance, to take full responsibility for the care of their younger siblings, buy and sell at market, milk cows, carry wood, clean house, fetch water, and prepare meals, while also becoming apprentices in farming, crafts, or shopkeeping (Whiting and Edwards 1988).[2]

If children are economic assets in many societies, why are they not so considered in our society, particularly given our emphasis on economic productivity and efficiency? If cooperative and sibling caretaking is the norm in many social circumstances, and if American mothers today want or need to seek employment in the paid labor force, why can't they leave their young to the cooperative care of others? For example, couldn't school schedules be staggered to make older children available to care for their younger siblings? And couldn't otherwise unproductive retirees join the older children in caring for the little ones? Some of the reasons Americans today find such suggestions bizarre can be understood through a historical analysis of the social construction of child-rearing ideologies in the West.[3] Although much of Western history followed a pattern of cooperative child rearing and the treatment of children as economic assets, over the past two hundred years, I will show, what we find is the step-by-step development of the ideology of intensive mothering.

The image of intensive mothering, just like the image of children as economic assets, is a historically constructed *cultural model* for appropriate child care. Conceptions of appropriate child rearing are not simply a random conglomeration of disconnected ideas; they form a fully elaborated, logically cohesive framework for thinking about and acting toward children.[4] Implicitly or explicitly, such cultural models not only supply ideas about who children are, what their rearing entails, and who should raise them but also describe why this model is the best one for children, adults, and the society as a whole.[5] The model of intensive mothering tells us that children are innocent and priceless, that their rearing should be carried out primarily by individual mothers and that it should be centered on children's needs, with methods that are informed by experts, labor-intensive, and costly. This, we are told, is the best model, largely because it is what children need and deserve. This model was not developed overnight, however, nor is intensive mothering the only model available to present-day parents.

Each historical period, within any particular geographic region, offers a number of cultural models for appropriate child rearing.[6] Over time, older models are discarded and fade from historical memory, and new models arise in new social contexts. Yet it is important to recognize that the full range of all possible models is never readily available to the public imagination. A framework for caretaking by older, independent siblings, for instance, is apparently not currently available in the United States, nor is a framework available for ubiquitous day-care centers run by older children and retirees. At any given time and place one particular model tends to take precedence over all others. American mothers and fathers, just like parents of other times and places, are likely to recognize this dominant model of appropriate child rearing and feel pressed to adopt or reject it in whole or in part.

What follows is a sketch of the changing character of models of parenting in the developed West. It cannot be a full portrait, for it must neglect many of the details and much of the diversity in child-rearing ideas and practices. My primary focus is on middle-class notions of appropriate child rearing. Although this model has never been followed in practice by the majority of parents, the model of the white, native-born middle class has long been, and continues to be, the most powerful, visible, and self-consciously articulated, while the child-rearing ideas of new immigrant groups, slaves, American Indians, and the poor and working classes have received relatively little positive press.[7] Further, although I focus on a single model and carve up the history of child rearing into historical periods, I want to make it clear that the history and social construction of ideas of appropriate child rearing and mothering actually occur as an uneven process. History does not provide convenient partitions between periods, and the child-rearing models available at any given time regularly include subordinate models that later disappear or themselves become dominant.

Within these boundaries, this chapter is meant to demonstrate both the variable nature of child-rearing ideas and their increasingly intensive qualities — from the earliest discovery of childhood innocence in Western Europe, through the religiously grounded model of the American Puritans, the nineteenth-century valorization of mothers, and the turn-of-the-century establishment of expert-guided child rearing, to the dawning of the permissive era. In each period, I demonstrate, further pieces were added to what has today become a fully elaborated vision of intensive mothering. And over time, I argue, more and more mothers adopt ever greater portions of this model. Thus the history of ideas about child rearing in the United States is not, as some would have it, a series of "pendulum swings" (e.g., Beekman 1977; Cable 1975) but rather a story of the increasing intensification of child rearing. This historical analysis also makes it clear that little of what we think of as crucial to appropriate child rearing today is an absolute or biological necessity.

From Ignoring the Frightening Child to Focusing on the Innocent Child

I recently received a birth announcement in the style of a movie poster picturing the child as a kind of King Kong. Demanding and monstrous in its stance, the diaper-clad infant towers over its cowed parents, threatening to destroy their peaceful home. From a consideration of the historical literature, it seems to me that parents have always feared their infants and young children somewhat. After all, small children are strange and fragile beings. They look and act not at all like adults, they cry for unknown reasons, they suck at and even bite their mothers' breasts, they are uncoordinated, they get sick easily, their demands are incessant, their appetites appear endless, and their excretions seem inhuman. Although we poke fun at such fears, it is quite possible that they produced many different child-rearing beliefs and practices historically and cross-culturally.[8]

Certainly such concerns were evident in Europe in the Middle Ages. Adults found children demonic, animalistic, ill-formed, and physically fragile. Many educators reminded parents of the child's natural propensity for evil, picturing children, for instance, as "gluttonous animals" or as demons who attempted to drain their mother's lifeblood as they bit at her breasts (Badinter 1981; Hunt 1970). If left to their own devices, it was believed, these demonic creatures would harm not only others but also themselves. For example, if not restrained by tight swaddling clothes, it was thought that an infant might "tear off its ears, scratch out its eyes, or break its [own] legs" (Stone 1977: 115).[9]

The practices following from this attitude toward children also included administering opium to troublesome children and treatment through alchemy. Whipping was the normal method of discipline (Beekman 1977; Hardyment 1983; Stone 1977). Playing with the child involved, among other things, the custom of "tossing" infants, which physicians regularly warned against since it potentially resulted in breaking the children's bones (DeMause 1974). When small children were not being fed, drugged, whipped, or tossed, they were often simply ignored.

The attention to children that was absolutely required to maintain their physical health was considered an onerous task preferably left to someone else. Any subordinate would do. Small children were frequently abandoned or, if the parents could afford it, boarded out to be cared for by others. The practice of using paid wet nurses was particularly common among the middle and upper classes, though many of the children sent off to wet nurses would die of disease, starvation, or neglect, and many who survived would never see their parents again (Badinter 1981; Boswell 1988; Shorter 1977; Stone 1977). Women were the primary caretakers of most children simply because women were low on the scale of the great chain of being. The more "valuable" children of aristocrats, by contrast, were often cared for by males (Ariès 1962; Hunt 1970). Certainly there was no belief in a maternal instinct that led mothers to protect and nurture their young. Child rearing, unlike childbearing, conferred neither honor nor status on those who performed it.

The relationship between parents and children, like the relationship between husband and wife, reflected the same hierarchy and demands for deference to one's superiors that was required throughout society (Stone 1977). Women obeyed their husbands and children obeyed their parents, just as subjects obeyed their king and believers obeyed their God. As Badinter puts it, "Until the seventeenth century there was the continual refrain: The father was to his children what the king was to his subjects and what God was to men — that is, what the shepherd was to his flock" (1981: 17). But, Badinter continues, the shepherd did not directly herd his sheep; he relied on the sheepdog. In this scenario, fathers were the shepherds, mothers were the sheepdogs, and children were the sheep, lowly and stupid yet valuable when they were ready for market. Just like different sheep, different children (including siblings) were treated in different ways, depending on the extent to which they were thought to be future assets for their parents (Badinter 1981; Stone 1977). Those who were strong and well equipped for later work, those who were expected to bring large dowries, those who would establish advantageous political alliances through marriage, and those who would one day be important members of court were given more attention than their less valuable counterparts. But as children, all were relatively worthless; it was only with adulthood that they could achieve social value.

Very young children were therefore ignored as much as possible until they appeared more adultlike in their behavior (Ariès 1962; Hunt 1970). Most were provided no special clothes, and none were given special toys or spaces for play. Many were left in the hands of servants, from whom they seem to have been barely distinguished. When young children died, as vast numbers of them did, there was no public grieving and there were no headstones to mark their graves (Ariès 1962; Shorter 1977; Stone 1977).

By the age of six or seven, children in the European Middle Ages were considered mature enough to become "apprentices" in adult work, worship, play, street life, and court.[10] They were routinely sent out to work in other households as servants or apprentices in a craft (Ariès 1962; Hunt 1970; Laslett 1984; Stone 1977). In other words, by that age children were no longer considered troublesome wards or frightening demons; instead they were more or less valuable members of adult society, and were expected to behave in a manner befitting their parents' social rank.

Although some historians have concluded from these facts that parents simply "did not care" and, in fact, "did not love their children very much" (Shorter 1977: 204, 1974: 595), it seems quite possible that adults in the Middle Ages felt a good deal of affection and concern for their children. This affection and concern were probably mixed, however, with socially constructed fears of the child's demonic qualities and socially maintained status concerns regarding the inappropriate and lowly behavior of affectionately cuddling, caring for, or playing with a young child. (One would, after all, want to avoid a public display of fondness toward an animal or a demon.) As Ariès points out, parents may well have felt affection for their children, but no one "admitted that these feelings were worthy of being expressed" (1962: 49). There was, in addition, the related problem that so many young children died before they reached adulthood (e.g., Ariès 1962; Boswell 1988; Shorter 1977). Under such conditions, investing one's time and emotion in these strange and fragile beings was simply impractical, and the socially developed ideologies and rituals of child rearing helped to legitimate and reinforce this reality.

The cultural contradictions of motherhood that I have described did not yet exist at this time. The ideology of child rearing flowed directly from the values, beliefs, and hierarchical organization of society as a whole. The treatment of small children followed from their dependent and relatively useless state. Parents (including mothers) spent only as much time, energy, and money on children as children promised to give in return: as soon as they were able, the young were obligated to contribute to the family's subsistence, wealth, or status and were enlisted in the armed protection of the family and community. As adults, these progeny were expected to fulfill the same obligations for their aging parents. One could argue that parent-child relations followed the same patterns that governed all spheres of life: affection mixed with aggression and fear, and mutual obligations and commitments mixed with the pursuit of personal advantage.

In the seventeenth and eighteenth centuries western European views of children and child rearing began to change, first among the bourgeoisie, then among the aristocracy. For this small portion of the population an ideology slowly emerged in which childhood was understood as a special and valuable period of life — particularly with reference to the child's newly discovered "innocence." Evidence of the new value attached to childhood includes the special clothing made for children, the toys and books created solely for children, the special schools built for children, the growing popularity of family portraits, and the special caskets made for those who died young (Ariès 1962; Badinter 1981; Shorter 1977; Stone 1977). Further, the flogging of children was increasingly opposed, the words *mama* and *papa* were more commonly used, more and more mothers began to breast-feed their own infants, the use of swaddling clothes was gradually abandoned, and public figures began boasting of their own domestic virtues on their tombstones (Stone 1977: esp. 246).

At the same time it was determined that the now-innocent bourgeois or aristocratic child was in need of protection from the ways of the larger world. These children were increasingly separated from life on the streets, from the company of their elders, and from members of the lower classes. Child-rearing advisers urged parents to remove servants from their households to avoid corrupting the children. And specially valued middle-class children were no longer sent out early in life to work as apprentices; they were instead protected at home or sent off to school (Ariès 1962; Matthaei 1982; Stone 1977).

The focus of prominent philosophical works on child rearing shifted as well. For instance, John Locke's *Some Thoughts Concerning Education* (1693) argued that children should be educated in reason, by means of strict discipline in the early years and by means of friendship as the children grew older (Calhoun 1973; Greven 1973), thus making it clear that early childhood training was crucial to future character development and that parental love had a place in the later training of a child.[11] But the real forefather of current child-rearing advisers was Jean-Jacques Rousseau. In his popular novel *Julie* (1761) and his widely read study of childhood education, *Emile* (1762), Rousseau portrayed the child as a sacred, "noble," and innocent being. Appalled by the widespread use of wet nurses, the offhand attitude of fashionable women who either ignored their children or spoiled them, and the uneducated parents who demanded obedience from children without understanding the stages of childhood, Rousseau argued that child-rearing practices should follow from the development of the child's inner nature rather than from adult interests and that children should be cherished, treated with love and affection, and protected from the corruption of the larger society (Rousseau [1761, 1762] 1964; see also Cleverly and Phillips 1986; Stone 1977). With this, the child's status as an innocent was formally codified.

It is in this context and among these carriers that an early form of the cultural contradictions of child rearing first appeared. Although child rearing was not yet equated with mothering and the ideological separation of home and world was far from complete, there was a clear disparity between the behavior considered appropriate in the larger world and the behavior considered appropriate with reference to children. Certainly the bourgeois bureaucrat or entrepreneur would have experienced a tension between the way he treated his children and the way he behaved with his clients. Traditional rules of deference would have made any attention to a lowly child seem especially out of place in aristocratic life. And innocence was surely not a respected characteristic among the adult population in general. Yet the value placed on children and childhood innocence during this period is manifested in the separate spaces and activities provided solely for children and is highlighted by Rousseau's notion that the child should be protected from the "deceit, vanity, anger and jealousy" of the larger world ([1761] 1964: 36).

Nonetheless, these new ideas about the value and innocence of childhood were not extensive in seventeenth- and eighteenth-century Western Europe. Although the toys, books, schools, portraits, breast-feeding, and caskets provide strong evidence that children were claiming a special place, this was true only among the relatively small portion of the population made up of wealthy merchants, the squirarchy, and the aristocracy. Even among these groups, it is hard to say just how many parents actually put into practice the child-rearing advice of Locke, Rousseau, and others like them.[12] In the American colonies, there was little evidence of the development of such beliefs and practices among the early Puritans.

Patriarchy, Community, and God-Guided Child Rearing

In late seventeenth- and early eighteenth-century New England we find no notion of childhood innocence, no protected place for children, no separate children's toys or games. Small children continued to be dressed in swaddling clothes, subjected to floggings, and sedated with opium (Beekman 1977; Hardyment 1983). But there was a belief in early childhood as a special and distinct stage—it was the stage when the child needed to be "redeemed" through strict discipline (Demos 1970; Wishy 1968). The young child was not ignored but consciously molded by means of physical punishment, religious instruction, and participation in work life.

For Puritan New Englanders the purpose of such early obedience training was to overcome the "sin nature" of the child. The young child's inherent sinfulness, they believed, took the form of self-will—and self-will was considered blasphemous.[13] Thus, the now well worn phrase "spare the rod and spoil the child" had an explicitly religious meaning when it was first preached by the evangelist John Wesley in this era (Cleverly and Phillips 1986; Greven 1973). It was only after the sinful child's will had been quashed through the use of the rod that the child could be trained in appropriate obedience to God, parents, and work.

The properly obedient Puritan child not only demonstrated its God-given grace but was also an economic asset.[14] For early Protestants, these economic and religious concerns were closely connected. Beyond a religious conversion and absolute obedience to God and patriarch, a crucial sign of the child's salvation was the child's commitment to hard work (Beekman 1977; Greven 1973; Hardyment 1983; Stone 1977). Failure to work was treated as a moral failure. The proper child, then, was a willing and obedient participant in the "family economy." According to this system, "As soon as they could pluck goose feathers or dry spoons, children were also servants" set to work on the family farm or at the family business (Ulrich 1982: 157). A child at play not only met with disapproval but was also treated as a legal offender. Insubordinate and idle children, just like adults, could be sentenced to public whipping or public confession (Cable 1975; Kessler-Harris 1982).[15]

The primary guide for child rearing was the Bible, supplemented by the sermons and speeches of church and community leaders. Of the few child-rearing manuals that were available, most were written by Puritans and all were addressed to fathers or parents, never to mothers (Degler 1980; Stone 1977).

The patriarch ruled the home and demanded obedience from both women and children. It was fathers who provided discipline and moral supervision, since theirs was the voice of reason and moral fortitude. Women, on the other hand, were thought to be particularly susceptible to "passions" and "affections," and given to "indulgence" and "excessive fondness" (Demos 1986: 45). The firm hand, strong will, and cool head of the patriarch were considered essential to counteract such maternal indulgence, the fear of which was pervasive (Ryan 1985; Ulrich 1982).

Wives were valued for their fertility but not for their child-rearing abilities (Ulrich 1982). Having many children was understood as beneficial in economic and religious terms, but how children were reared depended more on the authority of the church, the community, and the male head of household than on the particular methods of the mother. Children not big enough to work were watched by older sisters as often as by mothers (Kett 1983). Once children were old enough to help, a mother served as the overseer of their labor in the household, making little distinction between servant children and her own offspring — all were treated as subordinate workers in the family economy (Matthaei 1982; Ulrich 1982). A good mother was thus a good sheepdog, in Badinter's terms. Her task was to keep the children in line; ultimately she obeyed the shepherd, and it was he who decided on the path and destination of the flock.

Outside of Puritan New England, other cultural models of child rearing were in use. For American Catholics, for instance, breaking the child's will through physical punishment was not an absolute necessity since the child's sin could be expunged through baptism and other sacraments. Smith (1983) argues that planter families of the Chesapeake Bay actually demonstrated great affection toward their children and were permissive in their child-rearing practices. White children in the South, far from being condemned for their indolence, were provided with their own slaves to serve as personal servants and playmates (Hardyment 1983). And though the mothers of these slave children were reduced to mere breeders in the eyes of their masters, for the short time that they retained control over their children and for the brief moments of the day when they were allowed to nurse them or rest with them, African-American slave women seem to have indulged their children with affectionate nurture (Birns and Hay 1988; Jones 1985). Further, many parents took an approach that was quite similar to the utilitarian one of the European Middle Ages: Cott cites as typical of women in small agricultural towns the mother who, busy with boarders, livestock, and tanning hides, "considered her own two children 'grown out of the way' and 'very little troble [*sic*]' when the younger was not yet weaned" (1977: 58).

Nonetheless, to the extent that the Puritans are considered central in the making of American ideology, one might understand theirs as the dominant cultural model of the prerevolutionary era. And in Puritan child rearing the cultural contradictions of motherhood had not yet emerged. For these settlers, there was no sharp separation or moral opposition between home and world, children held no special value and could claim no special virtue, and the ideology of child rearing did not require an unremunerated commitment to nurturing the young: mothers and children, just like fathers, were expected to be productive members of the family economy, integrated participants in the community, and obedient servants of God.

The Making of the Moral Mother

It would certainly be hard to imagine a modern-day mom like Rachel following the methods of the Puritans: obeying her husband's rules for appropriate child guidance, swaddling, whipping, or feeding opium to Kristin when she was fussy, expecting her to behave like a working apprentice by age six, and punishing her if she was indolent. It would be far less difficult, however, to picture Rachel as a nineteenth-century mother. In fact, a number of the crucial portions of the contemporary ideology of intensive mothering appeared in the late eighteenth and early nineteenth centuries.

For the middle-class urban dweller during that period, ideas of appropriate child rearing shifted dramatically. To the extent that this group set the standards of appropriate behavior, the value of childhood was formally "discovered" in the United States perhaps a century later than in Western Europe. The young child was, in Wishy's (1968) terms, no longer seen as an agent of sin in need of redemption but was instead proclaimed an innocent "redeemer." Increasingly, motherhood was valorized, parents went to great lengths to prolong the period of childhood innocence, and affection suffused the mother-child relationship. Labor-intensive techniques of ongoing psychological manipulation intended to instill conscience replaced the rod and externally imposed discipline. And by the second half of the nineteenth century child rearing was synonymous with mothering. The overall image of both was one of pervasive sentimentality mixed with purity, piety, and patriotism.

This process may have begun in the fervor of the revolutionary period, when urban middle-class women attempted to cast themselves as "republican mothers" with an important role in socializing the republic's future citizens (Kerber 1986).[16] While traditional views held that women epitomized the dependence, irrationality, and thirst for luxury that would lead to the corruption of the republic, these women struggled mightily to demonstrate their capacity to raise virtuous citizens for the new nation. Since women, they argued, were entrusted with raising the children while the men were busying themselves in politics and industry, women should be educated for their role — trained in reason, taught to overcome their frivolity and their passions, and set to the task of conscientiously rearing little George Washingtons.[17] Meanwhile, evangelical preachers were proclaiming that the home, and the women and children within it, stood as a moral counterpart to the corruption of the outside world (Cott 1977; Ryan 1981). In no time at all, this movement culminated in what has variously been called the "cult of domesticity," the "cult of true womanhood," and the "Domestic Code": women, safely protected within the domestic enclave, would provide moral and emotional sustenance for their husbands and children and thereby participate in creating a more virtuous world (Cott 1977; Sacks 1984; Welter 1966).

With this, a mother's role in child rearing began to take on new importance. The status of the mother depended increasingly on her careful rearing of a small number of children rather than on her fruitfulness.[18] No longer were fathers the shepherds and mothers the sheepdogs. Mothers, and only mothers, now moral and pure, were the shepherdesses, leading their flocks on the path of righteousness.

Not surprisingly, during this era one also finds the earliest representation of mothers as the keepers of morality. The active participation of middle-class women in the creation of this portrait of moral mothers raising virtuous children was evident in the organizations they formed and the books they wrote and read. Throughout the century middle-class women formed a variety of reform groups—maternal, revivalist, social-purity, antislavery, and temperance—all connected to mothers' superior moral virtue (Cott 1977; Degler 1980; Gordon 1988; Ryan 1981, 1985; Stansell 1987). Maternal associations in particular proliferated in the 1820s and 1830s, and a number of them established nationally circulated mothers' magazines (Ryan 1985). During the same period there was an explosion of domestic novels (written largely by women) and of child-rearing manuals, now directed at mothers rather than fathers or parents, and written by mothers, educators, and doctors as well as the theologians who had earlier dominated the market (Degler 1980; Ryan 1985).

All this literature, as Ryan points out, was full of "flowery prose [that] imbued the home with gentle emotions" (1985: 30). The clichés "home is sweet" and "there's no place like home" originated in this era (Cott 1977: 63). And this sweet home was understood as primarily the creation of sensitive and emotional women. The simultaneous valorization of home and motherhood was summed up in the words of Mrs. Beecher: "The roots of all pure love, of piety and honor must spring from this home. . . . No honor can be higher than to know that she has built such a home . . . to preside there with such skill that husband and children will rise up and call her blessed is nobler than to rule an empire" (Stendler 1950: 125). To rule this empire, a woman's "passion" had to be repressed, but her "affections" were now understood as a positive and crucial force for the good of all.[19]

At the same time that women were coming to be seen as more virtuous, educable, and pure, children were increasingly portrayed as innocent, "angelic missionaries" (Ryan 1985: 103). Uncorrupted by the outside world, small children promised to make that world a kinder and gentler place. The concern with childhood innocence and its preservation was highlighted not only by the language of domestic advice books and novels but also in the proliferation of toys, games, and books designed exclusively for children. It was further reflected in the concern over precocity and harsh school discipline. Mrs. Lousia Barwell's *Infant Treatment* (1844), for example, argued that "weakness and disease" arose from a "premature use of the brain," and the press in the 1850s cited widespread fears that children were being overworked in schools, going "insane" from too much study (Beekman 1977; Hardyment 1983; Ryan 1985).

Above all, the rise of the ideology of childhood innocence among the native-born middle class was clearly demonstrated by the decline of the putting-out (apprenticeship) system (Margolis 1984; Ryan 1981). Children were no longer seen as little workers; instead, they needed to be protected against the outside world. In 1855 in Utica, New York, for instance, a full 80 percent of the fifteen-to twenty-year-old progeny of professional and white-collar fathers were kept out of the labor force.[20] Unheard of fifty years earlier, this practice was now considered necessary not only to allow for further education but also (as the *Mother's Monthly Journal* of 1838 would have it) to keep children "from encountering prematurely the seductive wiles that the wicked world [would] be sure to throw around them" (Ryan 1981: 168).

In the molding of such an innocent child, the goal was to develop the child's conscience (see Cable 1975; Ryan 1985; Stendler 1950).[21] There was little sign of the Puritan belief in self-will that needed to be broken or of the Lockean position that the child's reason needed to be carefully developed; the focus was clearly on bringing out and maintaining the child's Rousseauian inner goodness. In line with this, methods of discipline began to shift from forms that relied on physical punishment to instill obedience to forms that relied on the withdrawal of love to instill self-control (Rodgers 1980; Sears 1975).[22] Herman Humphrey, in *Domestic Education* (1840), proclaimed, "Affectionate persuasion addressed to the understanding, the conscience, and the heart, is the grand instrument to be employed in family government" (Ryan 1985: 50). The development of the child's morals, manners, delicacy, religious faith, and virtuous citizenship were all contingent upon such affectionate persuasion.

The middle-class child's successful internalization of the demeanor necessary to his or her future position was thus understood to be wholly dependent on the intensity of the mother-child relationship. *Mother's Magazine* in 1833 described a mother's appropriate response to her son's misbehavior: "I would not smile upon you, I should not receive your flowers, but should have to separate you from my company" (Ryan 1981: 159). Such methods could be effective only if the emotional bond between mother and child was quite strong.

Although the development of a child's conscience was thus grounded in maternal affection, the content of that conscience relied on the mother's careful attention to the appropriate socialization of her progeny and her own example of moral purity. One mother expressed it this way:

> Nothing but the most persevering industry in the acquisition of necessary knowledge — the most indefatigable application of that knowledge to particular cases — the most decisive adherence to a consequent course of piety — & above all the most unremitted supplications to Him who alone can enable us to resolve & act correctly — can qualify us to discharge properly those duties which devolve upon every Mother. (quoted in Cott 1977: 89)

In other words, according to the logic of this emerging ideology of appropriate child rearing, the good mother must not only lavish affection on the child; she must also be constantly vigilant in maintaining her own virtue and using the proper methods to instill like virtue in her child. All this, of course, was not only emotionally absorbing but also labor-intensive.

Appropriate child rearing remained a self-conscious moral enterprise as it had been for the Puritans, but for the urban middle class, portions of the cultural model had changed dramatically. Although the father was still the ultimate authority, the mother now had a much larger and more valued role to play in shaping the child. The good child was still one educated in morals — exhibiting honesty, generosity, orderliness, and piety — but the method of education had changed from demands for absolute obedience to the expression of love and the threat of love's withdrawal. The affection once condemned as maternal indulgence had thus become a central and positive force in appropriate child rearing. And the child who was once an economic asset was now provided an extended period of protected education. No longer a sinful creature in danger of burning in hell, the child was celebrated as an innocent and pure being who promised to redeem the world.

This period marked a critical turning point in the social construction of valorized motherhood and childhood innocence. It also set in place a number of important building blocks for the ideology of intensive mothering. Child rearing came to be understood as a task that was best done primarily by the individual mother — without reliance on servants, older children, or other women. The mother was instructed to bring all her knowledge, religious devotion, and loving capacities to bear on the task, and she was urged to be consistently affectionate, constantly watchful of her own behavior, and extremely careful in guiding the child. Child rearing had become expensive as well: the child not only needed the right toys, books, and clothes but also had to be kept out of the paid labor force and supported through school. It had become part of a mother's duty to keep her children walled off from the market and market valuation.

This period in American history corresponds to a time of massive changes in political life and the dramatic expansion and extension of capitalist markets. Increasingly, the factory system replaced the family farm and the family business, wage labor replaced the family economy, production was moved outside the household, and women's domestic work was distinguished from men's wage work (Cott 1977; Matthaei 1982; Zaretsky 1976). These changes marked the separation of public and private spheres of life, not only by physically separating home and workplace but by ideologically separating those spheres. Although the public realm was understood as cold, competitive, and individualistic, the home was valorized as warm, nurturing, and communal, explicitly pictured as a haven, a refuge, and a sanctuary, and contrasted to the world outside in the same way that heaven was contrasted to earth. Women, of course, were understood as the keepers of this haven.[23]

The ideology of appropriate mothering that accompanied this ideological separation of home and world was useful to various social groups. As more and more men left their homes each day for the factory, shop, or office, they may have been glad to entrust the rearing of the children to their wives; it would simultaneously spare them from that time-consuming task and eliminate much of women's competition in the paid labor force. Meanwhile, as factories replaced family farms, urban middle-class women became less economically useful and were therefore well served by new claims that their domestic contributions were crucial (Collins 1971a, 1985; Degler 1980; Watt 1957). The growing middle class also solved a number of problems with this new cultural model. As parents became increasingly unable to enforce discipline through the passing on of family-owned land, mother love and affection could provide an alternate incentive for children to "stay in line" (Greven 1970; Philipson 1981). Since the middle-class child's future was no longer determined simply by the social position of the father but, rather, depended upon the child's performance as an adult, the child's schooling and the methods of child rearing that promised to create independent and self-motivated adults became more critical (Matthaei 1982; Ryan 1981). The new ideology of domesticity also served as a central symbol for the distinctive identity of the American middle class, providing them with a claim to moral superiority over both the frivolous rich and the promiscuous poor (Cott 1977; McGlone 1971; Ryan 1985).

At the same time, in a rapidly changing world that in many respects appeared alien and corrupt, the focus on women's moral, nurturing role explicitly represented, as Cott points out, a protest against the "contagion" of "pecuniary values," and the home that women maintained was widely understood as "a redemptive counterpart to the world" (1977: 68, 98). This ideological separation of home and world and the early form of the ideology of intensive mothering that went with it marked the beginnings of the cultural contradictions of motherhood. The world was increasingly thought to be dominated by impersonal relations and the competitive pursuit of self-interested material gain, yet within it the tiny enclave of the family was to operate according to an opposing logic. The boundaries of that enclave were surely fragile.

Although these circumstances placed intensive mothering in a precarious position, the cultural contradictions of motherhood were probably far less pronounced than they are today, for two reasons. First, middle-class women as well as children were understood as appropriately living their lives outside the market economy. According to *Ladies' Magazine* in 1830, these women and children were completely "removed from the arena of pecuniary excitement and ambitious competition" (Cott 1977: 67). A significant part of this separation from "pecuniary excitement" was the absolute prohibition against "proper" (native-born, white, middle-class) married women working for pay (Weiner 1985). Thus, unlike today's paid career women, these mothers did not face questions of where to focus their time and energy — all their attention was appropriately directed toward domesticity — nor did they confront contradictions in seeking social status for themselves, for their best chance at status was clearly in the domestic sphere.

Second, the socially constructed ideology of intensive mothering was not yet complete in this period, its logic was not immediately assimilated by every middle-class mother, and its reality remained quite distant for large portions of the population. Some nineteenth-century child-rearing advisers still found it necessary, for instance, to inveigh against the use of swaddling clothes, opium, and the rod, and others continued to urge that children be trained to absolute obedience and submission (Beekman 1977; Hardyment 1983; Sunley 1955). At the same time, the fear of maternal indulgence persisted, and notions of women as lacking in reason lurked in the background. One child-care book suggested that mothers curb their affections and put children on definite feeding schedules; another denounced the "exaggeration of the sentiments and nature of maternal love"; and yet another accused mothers of inappropriately giving children the breast "whenever they cry" (Ryan 1985: 99). Thus, while an ideology of sentimentalized mothering may have been recognized by the urban middle class, there was no consensus among the child-rearing experts of the day and, as we shall see, there is some question about how many middle-class mothers actually spent their days protecting their children's innocence and carefully molding their children's character. More important, vast numbers of people were clearly outside the influence of this ideology. For the rural population, child-rearing practices probably followed the older methods of the family economy. For the poor, immigrant, and working-class populations in the cities, as I will show, there was little separation between public and private spheres, children remained little workers, and their toiling mothers had scant time to be gentle nurturers.

The Uneven and Incomplete Rise of the Mother's Empire

One might well ask just how much time nineteenth-century middle-class and affluent women actually devoted to raising their children and keeping their homes. After all, according to the *American Ladies' Magazine* in 1833, a good middle-class home had "a nurse for the infant, a nursery maid for the small children, [and] a governess for the eldest daughter" (McGlone 1971: 302). Those families that could afford it also hired someone to do the cooking, cleaning, and laundry. In fact, domestic service was the single largest occupation for women in the nineteenth century, employing 30–50 percent of women who worked for pay (Degler 1980; Dudden 1983). This meant that in 1855, for instance, about one-fifth of Boston families had a full-time live-in servant, and there was one servant for every four households in Buffalo and New York City (Dudden 1983). In the cities of the South the numbers were even higher. In Richmond in 1880, for instance, there were nearly 450 household workers (servants, cooks, and launderers) for every 1,000 households (Hayden 1981: 15).[24] The vast majority of these servants were women, and most were black or foreign-born (Sutherland 1981).[25] All this might lead one to question both the white, middle-class woman's commitment to child rearing and the ability of less affluent women to gain the status that went with intensive, patriotic, and pious motherhood.

Since these domestic servants were employed by the middle and upper classes, who considered such service a requirement for the running of a proper home as well as the maintenance of their class status, one might be tempted to argue that the nineteenth-century advice on mothering was simply hot air. Such advice, after all, held that children should be kept away from servants, who might taint their character and overindulge them. Yet it seems that many of these children did not spend much time in the loving arms of vigilant "moral mothers" but instead were under the care of immigrant or black domestics. Not until 1918 do we find a *Ladies' Home Journal* editor noting that the postwar generation of children would be the first to be raised "exclusively" by their mothers (Cowan 1976: 153).[26]

While many nineteenth-century middle-class mothers were thus ignoring much of the labor-intensive work of child rearing, it is true that a good nursemaid was considered particularly hard to find (even more so than a good housekeeper). She had to be intelligent, moral, interested in domestic pursuits, and not given to nightlife. Mothers still considered it their job to oversee the work of such caregivers and often would not allow them to discipline the child in any way (Dudden 1983; Sutherland 1981). In this sense, we could guess that the nineteenth-century rhetoric regarding appropriate child rearing was internalized by many middle-class mothers, though incompletely.

Further, one might wonder about the child-rearing ideas and practices of the domestic servants themselves, as well as their working-class and poor sisters. The home, apparently, was not *their* empire. And their children were probably far from innocent.

From Stansell's (1987) portrait of tenement life in New York City in the first half of the nineteenth century it appears that native-born working-class and immigrant populations in the cities still operated according to the rules of the family economy.[27] That economy, however, had become a wage-based one: the urban setting meant that it was nearly impossible to grow one's own food or keep one's own animals, so men, women, and children all went out to work at jobs that were often temporary and always paid low wages. Women in this context were surely not "angels of the hearth" free to dedicate themselves to conscientious child rearing, home decorating, and philanthropy. Not only did such women engage in wage labor and piece work, tend street stalls, and take in boarders; they were also held responsible for doing the laundry, mending, cooking, canning, and cleaning for their own households (Kessler-Harris 1982; Stansell 1987; Weiner 1985). Many such women remained single, and many others were left to raise their children alone. To cope with this situation they formed networks of reciprocity, helping each other out with child care, domestic labor, and subsistence on a regular basis.

Among this population there was no separation of home and world, public and private. Life was lived on the streets, at the taverns and bawdy houses, or on the front stoop. Paid work was often undertaken inside the home, and the same rules of conduct applied in all spheres of life. Just as there was no notion of women's purity or gentility, so there was no notion of childhood innocence, of protecting children from the "contagion of pecuniary values," or of carefully molding the child's conscience. Older siblings continued to be considered acceptable child watchers (Zelizer 1985). These same children were expected to work as soon as they were able: if they could not find work for wages or in street selling, they were sent out as scavengers to forage for the family necessities in the city streets (Matthaei 1982; Stansell 1987).

In the nineteenth century, then, working-class women did not independently develop an ideology of domesticity or a particular consciousness of themselves as mothers. They formed no reform societies, no maternal or evangelical associations. While middle-class women had managed to portray themselves as reasonable, pure, and virtuous, working-class women continued to be publicly understood as foolish, immodest, and devious (Kerber 1986; Stansell 1987).[28]

It is a paradox that contemporary theorists claim that the children of the middle classes are trained in independence while the children of the working classes are trained in obedience (Lynd and Lynd 1956; and see Kanter 1978; Kohn 1969; Komarovsky 1962). From a historical point of view one might guess just the opposite. The working-class children of New York were surely far more independent than their middle-class counterparts. From a young age they lived in the streets as hawkers, scavengers, and thieves, worked in shops and factories as apprentices and laborers, performed domestic chores, and served as independent caretakers for their younger siblings. Wage labor, in particular, assured their early independence from their families of origin. And all seem clearly more independent than their closely supervised middle-class counterparts, who were guarded against the streets and sustained in the domestic enclave while their innocent childhood was being prolonged.

Part of the solution to this paradox can be derived from an understanding of the struggle of working-class parents. They were faced with the difficult task of encouraging their children's sense of obligation and responsibility to the family unit against the lure of independence offered by the streets and wage labor. Unlike middle-class parents, those of the working class could not offer in return a comfortable, commodious home full of warmth and affection and protected from the harsh world outside, and they could not offer a future position in the family business to their sons or a reputable marriage to a well-bred female child. To keep their children in line, the only means available to working-class parents during this period was reliance on traditions of family responsibility and the application of external discipline. The unintended consequence of such discipline, of course, would have been to prepare these children for obedience in the factory, store, or workshop.

Thus, even though working-class children may have, practically speaking, achieved independence from their families of origin at earlier stages than children in the middle class, the middle-class focus on conscience and internalized self-discipline could well have made those children more psychologically independent. And this would also explain why family relations for members of the working class in the nineteenth century "harbored little explicit, articulated tenderness" (Stansell 1987: 77). Their financial status and their consequent need to rely on externally applied discipline and older, more utilitarian traditions of the family economy meant that they simply could not "afford" it.

Meanwhile, throughout the nineteenth century philanthropic organizations, women's reform societies, and middle-class women employing domestic servants did their best to impose middle-class visions of proper child rearing on urban working-class and poor families (Finkelstein 1985; Gordon 1988; Ryan 1981, 1985; Stansell 1987). Middle-class mistresses repeatedly attempted to reform their servants by admonishing them to dress conservatively and to curb their "promiscuous" public life, particularly their leisure pursuits.[29] Among the many social reform agencies, one prominent male-run philanthropic organization geared to eradicating poverty attempted to solve the problem of the "irredeemable" urban poor by sending their children to good Christian farm families out West, where they would work as laborers. (Although these placements were supposed to be voluntary, many children were simply taken off the streets and called orphans; their parents never saw them again.) The tactics of women's reform societies were a bit softer. They tried to get children off the streets by making the child's employment or school attendance a prerequisite for financial aid, and they established organizations meant to train poor and working-class women in appropriate domestic pursuits and to "civilize their character" (Dudden 1983; Gordon 1988; Stansell 1987).

But there is reason to believe that many such middle-class efforts at persuasion were futile. Although the outright removal of children from the home would certainly have disrupted a working-class family's efforts to raise the children, attempts to civilize the mother's character seem to have had little impact. Middle-class mistresses appear to have been relatively ineffectual, since many of their domestics continued to dress in fancy clothes, visit the dance halls, and cavort about town (Stansell 1987). And, as Gordon (1988) shows, working-class women found ways to use social reform agencies for their own purposes at the same time that they devised ways to subvert middle-class attempts to set the standards for financial assistance. Working-class women continued to rear their own children and behave in their own neighborhoods according to the codes of the working classes. Such mothers worked for their economic sustenance, and for them there was little distinction between the behavior considered appropriate at home and at work. Their children continued to perform domestic chores, including sibling caretaking, and continued to be sent out to scavenge and "huckster." Early wage labor for these children was still the hope of their parents (Stansell 1987).[30] In other words, though working-class women may have had knowledge of the cult of the home and the emerging ideology of child rearing that attended it, intensive mothering was not an everyday experience for them, either as women or as members of the community of working poor.

The Doctor Knows Best

Toward the end of the nineteenth century middle-class child-rearing ideologies took a somewhat curious turn. A mother's instincts, virtue, and affection were no longer considered sufficient to ensure proper child rearing. She now had to be "scientifically" trained. With the growing belief in child rearing as a science, mothers' status as valorized, naturally adept child nurturers was diminished at the same time that affection and sentimentality lost favor. The fear of maternal overindulgence rose once again, and the explicit concern with the development of the child's moral character was replaced with what was considered a more scientific emphasis on behavioral training. The mother now had to do more than set a good example; she needed to keep abreast of the latest information on child development and to practice the methods the experts suggested.

This was the era of strict scheduling, regularity, and letting the child "cry it out" rather than calming him with affectionate nurture. This is an ideology of child rearing that is clearly within our historical memory. Many of us had mothers or grandmothers who were admonished to refrain from picking up their infants when they cried, told to set rigid schedules for the child's feeding, changing, sleeping, and playing, and urged to establish elaborate bookkeeping systems to track bowel movements and childhood diseases.

The child had lost the status of pure innocent and was instead considered full of dangerous impulses. These, however, were not judged the impulses of a demon but rather the inherent propensities of a child: to masturbate, to suck its thumb, and to dominate its parents (Wolfenstein 1955). Although one might argue that the fear of the child had reemerged during this period, parents were told they could overcome these dangerous tendencies and shape the child into an acceptable adult using techniques of precise scheduling, detached handling, and behavior modification.

The prominent child experts of this era were Drs. Luther Emmett Holt, G. Stanley Hall, and John Watson. All were interested in making child rearing a scientific enterprise; none thought it should be left to untrained mothers. In *The Care and Feeding of Children* (1894) Holt established a regularized curriculum for feeding children and asserted that a mother who responded to her baby's cry by rocking or carrying the infant was inappropriately "indulgent." The behavior of children, Holt claimed, should be fully regimented by the age of three or four months; infants under six months should not be played with, cuddled, or given pacifiers (see Cable 1975; Ehrenreich and English 1978; Margolis 1984). Hall, in *Youth: Its Education, Regimen, and Hygiene* (1904), similarly argued that maternal affection was insufficient: women had to be educated for motherhood, and of course only experts could provide the proper knowledge. With this in mind, Hall founded the popular Child Study movement and advocated the careful scientific study of each stage of child development. Watson also considered untrained women overpermissive, incompetent caretakers and, in his *Psychological Care of Infant and Child* (1928), suggested that mothers' overindulgent and irrational techniques be replaced by Pavlovian ones — namely, conditioning the child by rewarding good behavior and punishing bad behavior (Cleverly and Phillips 1986; Lomax, Kagan, and Rosenkrantz 1978; Margolis 1984). Echoing Holt, he wrote, "There is a sensible way of treating children. . . . Never hug and kiss them, never let them sit on your lap. If you must, kiss them once on the forehead when they say good night. Shake hands with them in the morning" (quoted in Ehrenreich and English 1978: 204). All these authors believed that women in general and mothers in particular were irrational and emotional, but they also implied that, with careful expert guidance, it *might* be possible to educate them.[31]

This type of advice was echoed elsewhere. In social work, Gordon (1988) documents a shift from concern over fathers who were cruel and immoral to a new emphasis on the reform of untrained mothers. Mothers' magazines changed their focus as well, moving from articles on sentimental child-rearing techniques to ones concerned with child welfare legislation, or ones proclaiming the importance of scheduling the child and warning of the dangers of "smother love" (Margolis 1984; Stendler 1950). The popular *Infant Care* of the U.S. Children's Bureau similarly advised mothers of the 1920s to stick to strict schedules and to remember, for instance, that "toilet training may be begun as early as the first month" with the goal of establishing "absolute regularity" (Vincent 1951: 205).[32]

It is hard to say how many middle-class mothers actually followed such advice — how many refrained from picking up their wailing babies, used Pavlovian techniques to assure proper behavior, or kept precise records of their children's bowel movements and vomiting episodes. Certainly some did, if the Holt-inspired National Congress of Mothers, with clubs throughout the nation and an estimated 190,000 members in 1920, was any indication (Rothman 1978; Zelizer 1985). One might also guess that many other middle-class mothers, if they failed to maintain the records in their baby books or found themselves comforting unhappy infants, probably felt guilty about it.

All this emphasis on scientific methods in child rearing was accompanied by a more general surge in the importance attached to children. This is the era Zelizer (1985) focuses on to document what she calls the "sacralization of childhood." During this period, she writes, adoption rates rose, especially for pretty, affectionate, economically useless girls. At the same time children's insurance — meant to cover the cost of child funerals — became popular, especially among working-class parents. Further, the accidental death of children began to be treated as a "new and alarming social problem," and a number of wrongful-death suits were filed. In determining the dead child's worth in such cases, the court began to replace earlier calculations of the child's future wage-earning capacity with a new emphasis on sentimental criteria. The process of sacralizing innocent children that had begun over one hundred years earlier was thus further solidified, and its logic embraced by a much larger portion of the population.

This was also the time when the U.S. Children's Bureau was initially established (in 1912) to monitor the working conditions of children. The bureau quickly expanded its operations to include the publication of *Infant Care* — the best-selling government pamphlet of all time (Ladd-Taylor 1986; see also Sears 1975; Takanishi 1978; Zelizer 1985).[33] During this same period an increasing number of child labor laws were enacted, the juvenile court system was established, and stricter compulsory schooling laws were enforced. The kindergarten movement bloomed, the Playground Association of America was formed to promote playgrounds as a "supervised alternative to the moral hazards of street life," and settlement houses maintained by reform-minded middle-class women in working-class neighborhoods proliferated (Cavallo 1976; Hayden 1981; Rothman 1978; Takanishi 1978; Zelizer 1985).[34] This busy era also marked the opening of the "century of the child" and the federal establishment of "Mother's Day" (Margolis 1984).

The development of scientific child-rearing techniques, the enforcement of compulsory schooling and child labor laws, and the founding of the U.S. Children's Bureau, the kindergarten movement, playground associations, juvenile courts, and settlement houses were all closely connected.[35] Two related social phenomena highlight this connection and may in part explain the shift in ideas about appropriate mothering. On the one hand there was increasing concern with the effect on the nation of the exponential rise in the number of new immigrants, the growing ranks of urban poor, and the striking increase in labor unrest.[36] On the other there was a new belief in the possibility of discovering scientific, technical, expert-guided, and state-enforced solutions to such social ills (see Bellah et al. 1985; Cavallo 1976; Finkelstein 1985). New ideas about children, child rearing, and motherhood, it could be argued, grew out of these same national concerns and this same confidence in scientific solutions.[37]

This was the Progressive Era. Experts, it was thought, could iron out the wrinkles of race and class conflict and could provide technical solutions for all social problems. The mania for scientific management was a symbol of the logic of this era. In the case of mothers, the growing prestige of expert knowledge and the assumption that science could solve all social ills was combined with the old fear of maternal overindulgence and the new concern to regulate immigrants and the labor force.[38] The resulting child-rearing ideology was an expert-guided, scientifically structured method of disciplining mothers and children in the service of the nation's greatness. And the state, more boldly than ever before, got into the act.

The majority of reforms defined as measures to protect the young, I would argue, can largely be understood as attempts at scientific, technical solutions to the problem of the child-rearing methods of the "permissive" poor, working-class, and immigrant populations.[39] Middle-class children, after all, were already attending school and staying out of the workforce and off the streets. Certainly playgrounds, compulsory schooling, and child labor laws were not necessary for them. While middle-class mothers were urged to become more scientific and conscientious in the training of their young, and many eagerly engaged in such behavior, it is also important to recognize that most of the state-enforced reforms during this period were directed elsewhere.[40]

These reforms had particularly dramatic consequences for poor and working-class families. Reformers had tried to persuade or compel these groups to veer toward middle-class domesticity throughout the nineteenth century, but this time they had the force of the state behind them. It is therefore no surprise that efforts to alter the way poor and working-class parents raised their children became more successful during this period. Compulsory education and child labor laws, in particular, clearly disrupted the family economy of the working class (see Matthaei 1982). Although many young children of the working class continued to earn their own money by running errands, doing housework, and baby-sitting (Zelizer 1985), their contributions to the family economy were trivial in comparison to what a child's paid labor had provided previously.[41] Further, keeping children in school meant the loss of sibling caretakers.[42] It is no coincidence, then, that during this era working-class women's labor patterns began to change. Whereas they had once sought paying jobs when their children were young and had left the labor force when those children were old enough to work for pay, the new laws signaled the beginning of the opposite trend — working-class women began to stay at home when their children were young and to seek paid work at the time their children first went to school (Weiner 1985).

What all this meant was that more and more women were initiated into this early form of the culture of intensive mothering. Child labor laws and compulsory schooling were coupled with powerful efforts to solidify the family-wage (male-breadwinner) system. At the same time an increasing number of protective labor laws excluded women from certain kinds of work and cut back their hours so that their employment would not interfere with their mothering role.[43] These combined actions seem to have gradually resulted in the assimilation of a form of the cult of domesticity among working-class women.[44]

Such efforts clearly included oppressive attempts by the state to control volatile populations. The ideologies of experts such as Hall, Holt, and Watson might also be understood as a form of disciplining *all* women, who were considered potentially insubordinate and clearly insufficient as mothers (Donzelot 1979; Lasch 1977; Platt 1977). At the same time, the native-born middle class once again claimed an identity superior to that of the working class and poor. Men, as before, were spared the drudgery of domestic chores and the danger of women's competition in the paid labor force. Middle-class women also stood to gain from this new cultural model: it did, after all, promise to elevate their child-rearing and domestic duties to the status of a scientific profession (Ehrenreich and English 1978; Hayden 1981).[45]

But the changes in the cultural model of appropriate child rearing during the Progressive Era involved more than oppression and the pursuit of status or financial gain. The rising adoption rates for girls, the judicial valuation of children by sentimental criteria, the popularity of *Infant Care,* the establishment of the National Congress of Mothers, the Kindergarten Association, juvenile courts, Mother's Day, and the rest all demonstrated a profound belief in the importance of mothers and children. And although the methods of strict discipline and rigid scheduling may seem harsh to many mothers today, at the time they indicated a deep concern with appropriate child rearing (see Finkelstein 1985; Platt 1977). In this sense, the protest involved in the separation of home from world persisted and, one could argue, spread its net wider. To the extent that reform efforts directed at the poor, the working class, and immigrants were successful, *all* women and children would be protected from the corruption wrought by the larger social emphasis on impersonal, competitive, commodified, profit-maximizing, self-interested relations.

At first glance this era may seem a bit out of place in a history that otherwise appears as a straightforward march toward the valorization of nurturing motherhood, the exaltation of childhood innocence, and increasingly child-centered child rearing. In fact, however, it not only marks a conspicuous rise in public concern for appropriate child rearing but also signals two related trends in child-rearing ideologies that would outlast the relatively short-lived fad of strict scheduling and behavior modification (which was most powerful from about 1910 to 1925). First, the so-called experts would continue to dominate child-rearing advice. Second, the explicit focus on the child's moral character was replaced by an equally explicit focus on the more scientific categories of emotional, behavioral, and cognitive development.[46] Both of these changes demonstrated an increasing concern that children be properly reared and a declining faith that mothers could handle the task without training and guidance. From that time forward, not only would scientific knowledge be applied to the task of raising children, but experts (social workers, judges, medical practitioners, and others) would henceforth have the right to intervene if the child was seen as somehow endangered.[47]

Thus, the ideology of appropriate mothering was further intensified in this period. A mother's reliance on experts did not make her job easier. She had to know all the latest information on physical, emotional, and cognitive development. She had to keep a tight rein on displays of affection. She had to be consistently attentive to her child's stage of development in order to do her job properly. And she had to be objective, detached, and insightful in responding to her child's needs. The child, as the symbol of the nation's future, was clearly in the foreground.

Although it is clear that changes in child-rearing ideas during this era fit with the larger social context, the cultural contradictions of motherhood were also further solidified and extended. Intensive child rearing and the ethos of impersonal, competitive relations in the pursuit of individual gain remained in tension. Even though most white, middle-class mothers remained outside the labor force, they were nonetheless asked to become efficient but unremunerated scientific managers in the home. And although efforts to reform poor, working-class, nonwhite, and foreign-born mothers were not an overnight success, child labor laws and compulsory schooling meant that many working women began to experience the contradictions in their daily lives. These women, however, had little voice or power, and their predicament received little public attention.

During this period the language of the state and the marketplace had entered the home in the form of an emphasis on professionalization and technical efficiency, thus signaling an invasion by the ethos of impersonality and utilitarian calculation. Theoretically, this invasion could have led to an instrumentally rational solution to the problem of the inefficient and costly system of leaving potentially productive mothers in homes where they (perhaps unscientifically) reared just two or three youngsters. John Watson himself had sug-gested that children would be "finer and happier" if they were *not* raised by their own parents.⁴⁸ But few people seem to have listened. Instead, the em-phasis on innocent children and emotional, nurturing motherhood quickly returned — this time, with further elaboration and even greater strength.

The Permissive Era

The ideology of permissive child rearing that dominates contemporary advice and provides the cultural model used by Rachel and other present-day mothers had its beginnings in the 1930s. By the mid-1920s detached handling, strict scheduling, and behavior modification had lost favor, and by the end of the Depression two-thirds of the child-rearing articles in *Ladies' Home Jour-nal, Woman's Home Companion,* and *Good Housekeeping* were emphasizing a mother's love and affection as the central factors in child development and arguing that babies should be allowed to establish their own feeding and sleeping times and styles (Stendler 1950). Indicative of this trend, *Infant Care* in the 1940s warned mothers that "unvarying obedience is not desirable" and "training should not come too early or be too strict" (Vincent 1951: 205).

The primary objective was no longer the rigid behavioral training of the child to meet adult requirements; nurturing the child's inherent goodness was again the goal. But this was no simple swing of the pendulum. Although the family had become child-centered in early nineteenth-century America — in the sense that children became the center of familial attention — child rearing was then perceived as guided by parents, in line with *adult* interests. Not until the "permissive era" did child rearing become child-centered in the sense of being explicitly determined by the needs and desires of (innocent) *children.* To put it another way, throughout the nineteenth and early twentieth centuries the explicit goals of child rearing were centered on the good of the family and the good of the nation; the emphasis was on the importance of imprinting adult sensibilities on children from the moment of birth; and it was the making of a proper adult that was understood as the basis for training the child. By contrast, the most striking feature of permissive-era advice is the idea that the natural development of the child and the fulfillment of children's desires are ends in themselves and should be the fundamental basis of child-rearing practices.

With this, the conception of a child-centered family takes on a new mean-ing. Not only is home life centered on children, but child rearing is guided by them. The child (whose needs are interpreted by experts) is now to train the parent. It is at this point, and within this ideological framework, that the recommended methods of child rearing become fully intensified: not only have they become expert-guided and child-centered, they are also more emotionally absorbing, labor intensive, and financially expensive than ever before. All this money, time, and attention has as its goal not economic productivity or the nation's greatness but the protection and preservation of the child's natural innocence, affection, purity, and goodness.

The child-centered nature of appropriate child rearing was documented in the most influential child-care book of that decade, Anderson and Mary Aldrich's *Babies Are Human Beings*, published in 1938 (Cable 1975). Elaborating on the necessity of affectionate and nurturing mothers who adjusted their behavior to the needs of their children, the Aldriches wrote,

> To give the baby all the warmth, comfort, and cuddling that he seems to need; to meet his wishes in the matter of satisfying and appropriate food; to adjust our habit-training to his individual rhythm; and to see that he has an opportunity to exercise each new accomplishment as it emerges; these are the beginnings of a forward-looking programme in mental hygiene. (quoted in Hardyment 1983: 215)

In fact, this book contained many of the central elements of present-day child-rearing advice. Following the teachings of Arnold Gesell, the Aldriches believed that it was a mother's job to understand each child as an individual, to be attentive to the child's wants and needs, and to follow rather than force the child's development. The foundation for this child-centered method, it was argued, was a mother's love; because she loved her child, she would necessarily allow the child's needs and desires to determine her own behavior. Such mothering was therefore considered, in Gesell's words, a "natural aptitude" (quoted in Ehrenreich and English 1978).

It was also during this period that the categories of psychological and cognitive child development that had first come into vogue in the Progressive Era were elaborated in the works of Sigmund Freud, Erik Erikson, and Jean Piaget. These theories in turn were popularized in child-rearing literature. Children's tendencies to masturbate, suck their thumbs, and attempt to dominate their parents, for instance, were now understood as Freudian "drives" and thereby interpreted as natural and relatively benign urges. *Infant Care*, for instance, no longer treated these tendencies as dangerous and in need of correction but instead understood them as harmless or positive (Wolfenstein 1955).[49] Erikson brought his own interpretation of Freud into child-rearing advice with his outline of childhood in terms of the ego qualities appropriate to each developmental stage and emphasized the importance of psychologically stable mothers in securing healthy child development (Lomax, Kagan, and Rosenkrantz

1978). What Freud and Erikson did for the child's psychodynamic stages, Piaget did for the cognitive ones. Every child, according to Piaget, goes through a series of preset cognitive stages; good parents, like good educators, recognize and build upon these stages (Cleverly and Phillips 1986). Taken together, the popularized versions of these theories suggested that parents needed to guard against a wide variety of childhood fears and anxieties by carefully fostering a basic sense of trust between parent and child, that infancy and early childhood were the stages most critical to the child's overall development, and that good parents would "naturally" want to acquire further knowledge of cognitive and emotional development in order to prepare themselves to meet the child's needs during those early stages.[50]

At the same time that more and more child-rearing manuals were espousing intensive methods, manuals in general were becoming the primary source for child-rearing information. Given the now-lofty status of scientific knowledge, expert advice was increasingly preferred to the advice of grandmothers and members of the extended family. At the same time, geographic mobility and the further nuclearization of the family made the advice of extended-family members less and less accessible (Degler 1980; Litwak 1960a, 1960b; May 1988). So more mothers began reading books on how to rear their young.

The early decades of the permissive era also brought forth the paradoxical simultaneous emphasis on the absolute necessity of a mother's loving nurture and the fear of maternal overindulgence and overprotection. The critical importance of maternal affection was documented not only by Erikson but also, for instance, in Anna Freud's studies of the detrimental effects on infants who were separated from their mothers in wartime nurseries, in Harry Harlow's research on young monkeys who bypassed food to seek out substitute maternal figures, and above all in the highly popular and widely disseminated "maternal attachment theory" of the British psychoanalyst John Bowlby (see Dally 1982; Ehrenreich 1989; Eyer 1992). In 1951, Bowlby proclaimed,

> What is believed to be essential for mental health is that the infant and young child should experience a warm, intimate and continuous relationship with his mother (or permanent mother-substitute) in which both find satisfaction and enjoyment. . . . A state of affairs in which the child does not have this relationship is termed "maternal deprivation." (Bowlby 1952: 11)[51]

Mother love was clearly considered crucial. On the other hand, the old fear of maternal overindulgence remained. This was expressed, for example, in Philip Wylie's best-selling advice book *A Generation of Vipers* (1942), which described mothers as "vipers" who "infantilized" their progeny; in Dr. David Levy's *Maternal Overprotection* (1943), which defined overprotection as a "disease" with identifiable symptoms; and in Dr. Edward Strecker's *Their Mothers' Sons* (1946), which blamed overweening mothers for the psychological disorders he found among army recruits. Completing this portrait was the "maternal rejection syndrome" — considered the cause of a variety of childhood disorders ranging from autism and speech retardation to psychotic development — which, like maternal overprotection, was yet another way in which mothers were said to express their "unconscious hostilities" (Ehrenreich and English 1978; Margolis 1984). Summing up this argument was Lundberg and Farnham's *Modern Woman: The Lost Sex* (1947). Nearly half of all mothers, they wrote, were either "rejecting, over-solicitous, or dominating" (Margolis 1984: 260). According to this logic, one mother's overweening love for her child and another mother's rejection of hers were simply two sides of the same problem: women who seemed pathologically determined to keep their children tied to psychological apron strings.[52]

Together, these theorists of maternal attachment and maternal hostility seemed to say that while maternal affection was absolutely necessary and natural, it could easily slide into dangerously unwholesome forms. Maternal omnipotence was stressed, and women were either held responsible for all that was good in children and morally desirable in society or blamed for their children's individual psychological disorders and the larger social ills that resulted from them. Given the centrality of the maternal role, it was implied, mothers had to be carefully guided in order to negotiate the tortuous road between neglect/rejection and overprotection/overindulgence.

Coming out at a time when these concerns were at their height was the work of the pediatrician Dr. Benjamin Spock.[53] His *Baby and Child Care* (1946), which incorporated the psychoanalytic theories of Freud and Erikson, the recapitulation theory of Hall, and the stage-theory and child-centered approach of Gesell and the Aldriches, dominated the literature as no other child-rearing manual ever had.[54] Spock combined knowledge of physical and psychological child development theories with information on the practical details of daily physical care. In many respects the book served as a trouble-shooting guide for problems in each of these areas, with a masterful index and table of contents. And if the book wasn't enough, there was Spock's constantly repeated suggestion to "consult your doctor," the local expert. But his most widely recognized piece of advice comes from the first line of his book, a piece of advice that was echoed throughout the volume: "Trust yourself. You know more than you think you do" (1946: 3).

By its very form, however, this detailed, step-by-step instruction manual implicitly denied the natural, commonsense, trust-yourself approach that Spock claimed. In a deluge of advice, the book made it clear that a mother required the aid of experts to recognize and appropriately respond to each of the child's developmental stages and all of the child's needs. Without such help, it suggested, the mother would be at a complete loss in the day-to-day care of the child.[55]

Overall, Spock's recommendations centered on the crucial importance of child rearing that was grounded in maternal affection, that followed from the child's development, and that allowed the child ample room to express its wants and needs. Even though a great deal of knowledge, time, and patience was required to properly understand the child's development and interpret its needs, Spock portrayed the process as a pleasurable one. Raising children is pleasurable, he implied, first, because children are inherently good and friendly and, second, because mothers are naturally loving and empathic. These two beliefs were the ultimate basis for his claim that mothers should "relax," "trust themselves," and "enjoy" the process of child rearing.

Nonetheless, Spock was apparently unable to guide mothers along the fine line between maternal rejection and maternal overindulgence or to appropriately train children (via mothers) to develop the behaviors necessary for their adult social roles. Twenty years after his book was first published, Spock was charged with responsibility for the moral failure of the generation then coming of age; after all, it was argued, these children had been raised according to the permissive practices Spock advocated.[56] It was his recommendation of maternal indulgence, Spock's detractors claimed, that produced spoiled, hedonistic children lacking the moral fortitude that leads to hard work and self-denial. Spock's advice had allegedly created a generation of self-centered consumers and narcissistic troublemakers with no respect for authority (see also Ehrenreich 1989).[57]

There is no question that Spock was far more permissive than the behaviorists who had preceded him. He did, by and large, urge mothers to allow children to set their own feeding and sleep schedules; he did advise that loving affection should replace the Watsonian handshake; he did argue for less rigid discipline; and he did believe that mothers should follow the child's lead rather than demand adult behavior. Yet through all the attacks on his permissiveness, Spock's child-rearing advice survived. Just as the emphasis on maternal bonding, the fear of maternal overindulgence, the centering on the child's needs and desires, the stress on the child's psychological and cognitive development, and the belief in the importance of experts persist, so too does the popularity of Spock's child-rearing manual.[58]

Thus, American history's most intensive model of mothering emerged shortly before World War II and, if Spock's continuing popularity is any indication, has maintained its dominance ever since. During this same era more middle-class married women and mothers entered the paid workforce than in any previous period. More women than ever before were therefore personally experiencing the cultural contradictions of motherhood in their daily lives — asked to be warm, unselfish, and nurturing as mothers at the same time that their paid work took place in an environment where individualistic competition for private gain was valued above all else.

After the war a great deal of effort was expended to suppress the contradictions thus created. The media, government, and business seemed particularly interested in urging "Rosie the Riveter" to cheerfully quit her job and return home; the "feminine mystique" told women that their ultimate fulfillment would be derived from their work as loving wives, nurturing mothers, and faithful keepers of the home; and programs like *Leave It to Beaver, Ozzie and Harriet,* and *The Donna Reed Show* were filling television screens with compelling images of familial satisfactions (Campbell 1984; Coontz 1992; Kessler-Harris 1982; Weiner 1985). But these attempts to suppress the cultural contradictions of motherhood by portraying the domestic sphere as women's proper place were, in many ways, unsuccessful.

This postwar portrait of suburban domestic bliss is too simple. In fact, many Rosies didn't go home, others were forced to against their wishes, and many mothers found themselves less than fulfilled in their struggles to mimic June Cleaver (see esp. Coontz 1992). Although vast numbers of women were forcibly ejected from paid work, particularly manufacturing jobs, many remained in the paid workforce, and still others sought employment in the sex-segregated labor market for the first time. In fact, the rate at which women entered paying jobs after the war was the same as the rate at which they entered it during the war. Mothers in particular were seeking paid employment in record numbers (see Goldin 1990; Kessler-Harris 1982; Milkman 1987; Weiner 1985).[59]

Yet despite the entry of mothers into the paid workforce, the ideology of intensive mothering persisted. It survived Betty Freidan's (1963) famous attack on the "feminine mystique," widespread concern with "momism," the condemnation of Spockean methods, and feminism's "second wave" of activism, which included the proliferation of literature damning the family as an oppressive institution. Indeed, the ideology of intensive mothering has only grown more extensive and elaborate in the present day, when the trend toward mothers' participation in the paid workforce is undeniable and the logic of the market and bureaucracy are increasingly invading the home. In the face of such challenges, this ideology maintains the distinction between home and world and treats children as innocents who must be protected from market logic. What this means is that the cultural contradictions of motherhood are now more pronounced than ever before.

3

"What Every Baby Knows"
Contemporary Advice on Appropriate Child Rearing

What Every Baby Knows is the title of a child-rearing manual by the pediatrician T. Berry Brazelton. In many ways this title epitomizes current notions of appropriate parenting. Child rearing today is, more than ever before, child-centered — it follows not from what every parent knows (needs or wants) but from what every baby knows (needs or wants). This, as we have seen, is the approach that has come to be called permissive. And this, I will show, is also the approach found in most of today's top-selling child-rearing manuals. In fact, the three most popular child-rearing advisers recommend not only child-centered child rearing but a fully elaborated model of intensive mothering.

According to a 1981 study, 97 percent of American mothers read at least one child-rearing manual, and nearly three-quarters consult two or more manuals for advice on how to rear their young (Geboy 1981). Exemplifying this, Dr. Spock's *Baby and Child Care* (1985) has sold 40 million copies in its six editions, outselling all other books in the history of publishing with the single exception of the Bible (Hackett 1967; "At S & S" 1992). Two of Spock's major competitors are T. Berry Brazelton (whose *Toddlers and Parents* has sold 400,000 copies, and *Infants and Mothers,* 315,000) and Penelope Leach (whose most popular book, *Your Baby and Child,* has sold 1.5 million copies) (Lodge 1993). Together these three authors make up the best-selling triumvirate of child-rearing advisers (Chira 1994; Lawson 1991).[1] They are also the most widely read authors among the mothers I surveyed and interviewed. Considering the ubiquity of these books, an examination of their contents is surely in order.[2]

What follows is an analysis in the tradition of the sociology of knowledge that treats the images of childhood, mothering, and child rearing presented in these manuals as a reflection of the historically constructed ideology of socially appropriate child rearing. This analysis begins with the assumption that the methods of child rearing that Spock, Brazelton, and Leach recommend, and the view of mothers and children they convey, did not arise spontaneously in the minds of these authors and is not a measure of some absolute and timeless truth, but is instead a reflection of a specific cultural model that was constructed socially, over time, under particular circumstances.

In reporting this model from a social-constructionist position, I am not attempting to degrade or dismiss it; nor is it my intent to endorse it. While a dispassionate (or childless) outsider may be tempted to attack the prescriptions of Spock, Brazelton, and Leach as overzealous or overly demanding, the insider (or parent) is likely to understand the recommendations of these authors as flowing from knowledge and concern for what is best for children. I want to avoid taking either of those positions. The point of the following analysis is to clarify the logic of child-rearing ideas as it is outlined in these manuals and to thereby make explicit a set of beliefs that, though in apparent contradiction to the ethos of the larger society and the practical needs of paid working mothers, is nonetheless quite powerful.

These manuals, of course, cannot tell us all we need to know about the ideology of mothering in the United States today. There is no direct correspondence between what the manuals advise and what mothers and parents actually think, say, and do (see Mechling 1975; Zuckerman 1975). As many sociologists of culture have pointed out, different people make use of culture in different ways (e.g., Berger 1981a; Hebdige 1979; Radway 1984; Swidler 1986).[3] Yet these best-selling child-rearing manuals are in themselves an important source of information. The popularity of these particular manuals, rather than others, indicates that they have struck a chord with readers and evidently supply what many parents perceive as the necessary and appropriate information and guidance. At the same time that they reflect the prevailing views of many parents, the wide distribution of these books and the regular appearance of their authors in the national media also mean that the ideology they espouse potentially affects the ideas and practices of contemporary mothers. Thus, we might guess that the material presented in these manuals is an approximation of the dominant cultural model of raising children.

At first glance, these three child-rearing advisers appear quite distinct. Spock's manual (1985) is an encyclopedia of child care, with answers to every question that parents might ask a pediatrician (or their own mothers, fathers, or best friends) — and more. Over half the book is dedicated to practical advice for parents on such topics as the supplies needed for the newborn, the pros and cons of breast-feeding, the elements of a good diet for infants, the symptoms of illness, and instructions on first aid. The rest of the book provides step-by-step advice on how to understand and respond to the child's behavior at each stage of its development.

Brazelton, on the other hand, offers anecdotes. Most of his books center around four or five families, tell the stories of their child-rearing practices and problems in the context of their varied lives, and demonstrate how their pediatrician, Dr. Brazelton, helps them cope. This format means that no one of his books is a comprehensive guide to raising children and that each book contains less advice than it might if it treated parenting in more general terms. But Brazelton is quite prolific, and if all the reader's concerns are not covered, he or she can simply buy another Brazelton book — or read Brazelton's syndicated newspaper column or watch one of his widely distributed videos or tune in to an episode of the numerous television series he produces and in which he stars.

Leach, a British social psychologist, self-consciously writes her books from the child's point of view. She supplies detailed information on the infant's and older child's physical makeup, behavioral habits, psychological states, and cognitive abilities at every stage up to age five. This emphasis allows Leach to provide the reader with more specific information than the other two authors on what she considers the "scientifically" discovered facts of child development. She suggests that parents, armed with the knowledge of what children in general tend to want and need, can make more informed decisions regarding their own unique children.

I would further characterize Brazelton and Spock as friendly neighborhood pediatricians (with extensive knowledge of child behavior, physiology, psychology, and cognitive development) who assume that the reader wants to be told precisely what to do. Leach, on the other hand, treats parents as competent professionals who simply want to learn the facts, weigh them, and make their own reasoned judgments based on observations of their own children. Unlike the others, she does not remind her readers to visit pediatricians or child guidance centers for more specific advice on child behavior. With the single exception of medical problems, she assumes that reading her books will provide parents with all the information they need.[4]

Although the format and focus of these books vary, all three share a set of assumptions about the elements of good child rearing. The child is, as Spock puts it, "born to be a reasonable, friendly human being" (1985: 3). Small children know what they want and will ask for only what they need. A good parent is therefore guided by the child's desires. In line with this tenet, fostering the child's inherent goodness and self-discipline is considered far preferable to the use of restraint and externally applied discipline. Parental affection is central, they say, both as a motivation to empathically meet the child's needs and as a basis for encouraging the child's internalization of discipline. This is an enjoyable process, since parental love and affection for the child come "naturally." Nonetheless, parents need expert advice, particularly on the developmental stages children pass through. And children require a tremendous amount of individualized attention — especially in terms of psychological nurturing and cognitive stimulation. Children of different ages, stages, and temperaments simply cannot be treated in the same way.

All in all, Spock, Brazelton, and Leach demand what I have called intensive mothering. First, they assume that child care is primarily the responsibility of the individual mother. Second, the methods they recommend are child-centered, expert-guided, emotionally absorbing, labor-intensive, and financially expensive. Finally, they clearly treat the child as outside of market valuation: children are sacred, innocent, and pure, their price immeasurable, and decisions regarding their rearing completely distinct from questions of efficiency or financial profitability.

The Mother Is Primarily Responsible

In their early days Spock, Brazelton, and Leach each assumed that *mothers* would raise the children, and their original manuals referred to mothers almost exclusively.[5] The most recent U.S. editions, however, are addressed in an egalitarian fashion to "parents." The authors tend to be conscientious in their use of pronouns: Leach claims to use "she" to refer to the caregiver and "he" to refer to the child *only* for the sake of convenience and consistency, while Spock and Brazelton try to switch back and forth between "he" and "she" when speaking of parents and children. All these authors, at one time or another, proclaim the mother's equal right to paid work. How, then, can I claim that their books are directed primarily at mothers and that they assume the individual mother is the primary caregiver?

First, it is important to recognize that mothers are the primary consumers of these books. All the mothers I spoke with who used child-rearing manuals personally chose and purchased most of them. Similarly, nationwide nearly half of bookstore customers for children's books are mothers; fathers account for less than 10 percent (Roback and Maughan 1995).[6] These authors (and their publishers) are well aware of these facts, and they are also aware that over half of all mothers with small children have paying jobs. Combined, this knowledge may well account for both their attempts to use gender-neutral language and their underlying assumption that the primary child raisers will be mothers.

Second, all these authors argue that consistent nurture by a *single primary caregiver* is crucial. Day-care centers, preschools, spouses, and baby-sitters may help out, they admit, but the child needs to bond with an *individual* adult (e.g., Brazelton 1983b: 56; Leach 1989: 196; Spock 1985: 45). In demonstrating who they believe this individual caregiver must be, a few examples will have to suffice.

Spock, for instance, seems to undermine his use of gender-neutral pronouns when, in his latest edition, he suggests that the "parent" buy "a new dress" or go to the "beauty parlor" if child rearing is giving (him or) her the blues (1985: 32). Further, when Spock writes, "The mother (as if she didn't have enough to do already!) has to remember to pay some attention to her husband" (1985: 33) yet finds no reason to make an equivalent comment about fathers, he clearly informs the reader who is expected to do the child rearing and who is actually responsible for the emotional well-being of all family members. Spock also participates in gender stereotyping. Just as he implies that women like to go to beauty parlors and buy new dresses, he also makes it clear that men are "virile," that the father is the "head of the family," and that husbands are interested in sports, fishing, camping, ball games, and reading the newspaper after a hard day at the office (1985: e.g., 31, 34, 389–90). Implicit in such characterizations is the additional stereotype of women as nurturers and, by extension, those best suited for raising a child.[7]

Similarly, Brazelton did not bother to change the title of one of his most widely read books in its 1983 revised edition: it continues to be called *Infants and Mothers*. Brazelton further contradicts his self-conscious attempt to promote egalitarian parenting when he makes such statements as, "Mothering is too complex and instinctive to teach" (1983a: 42). In considering the social pressure for women to seek paid careers, Brazelton reinforces this notion of maternal instinct:

> We may be ignoring . . . a *deep-seated drive* in women — a strong feeling that their primary responsibility is to nurture their children and their spouse. It may be unfair to expect a woman to be the fulcrum of her family; but it has always been so, and women feel it *instinctively*. (1983b: xviii, emphasis mine)

Instincts and drives, of course, are immutable; women, Brazelton thus suggests, *inevitably* take primary responsibility for the well-being of their children.

As for Leach, even more telling than her use of gendered pronouns are her constant and explicit references to what *mothers* should do: the "mother meets and anticipates [the child's] needs," the "mother gets up cheerfully in the night to feed her baby," the "mother wants to help father avoid a rough and tumble game," "mothers have to learn to interpret their infants' cries," and "mothers spend a good deal of time . . . expanding their children's telegraphese into sentences" (1989: xx, 62, 383). Yet Leach never seems to feel the need to tell us what *fathers* should do. And when Leach writes, "Few fathers are in a position to receive their baby's first attachment because mundane matters like jobs prevent them from being that ever-present, always-responsive person" (1986: 122), she manages to simultaneously valorize motherhood, assert its intensive nature, and inform us who is expected to stay at home with the children. Leach further underlines this belief when she writes, "In an ideal world no woman would ever have a baby unless she really knew that she wanted to spend two or three years being somebody else's other-half" (1989: 196). There is no doubt that Leach assumes full-time mothering.

Not surprisingly, then, Leach never treats at any length the issue of mothers who work in the paid labor force.[8] Spock and Brazelton, however, have both made additions to their earlier works that consider the position of paid working mothers.[9] Although these additions are meant to encourage paternal participation, in fact they continue to present mothers as the primary child rearers and fathers as additional "help." Brazelton, for instance, notes that "even when a father can *fill in* for just a few hours, the baby will have more sense of belonging and an opportunity to know him, and the mother will be less stretched" (1983a: xxvii, emphasis mine). When Spock writes, "The father *may* be home in time to give the bath before the 6 pm or 10 pm feeding" (1985: 203, emphasis mine), he similarly implies that fathers are merely extra help. Suggesting that even in the case of paid working mothers the mother-child bond remains far more crucial than that between fathers and children, Brazelton claims that "whenever a mother returns to work, her baby will likely regress" and elsewhere adds that such a mother "feels so torn and grieved at losing part of her baby's day that she feels less than adequate" (1983a: 61; 1983b: 83). One wonders why the father's "return" to paid work does not seem to lead to the child's regression or to invoke paternal feelings of grief and inadequacy.

Clearly, these authors have not escaped the assumption that individual mothers are primarily responsible for raising children. Although one may be tempted to "forgive" them, since, after all, they are living in a world in which mothers *do* generally take primary responsibility, this is not the point. It is not a question of whether Spock, Brazelton, and Leach are responsible for creating this state of affairs; the fact is that they participate (intentionally or unintentionally) in reproducing it.

Intensive Methods

These manuals also reflect the ideology that appropriate child rearing requires intensive methods. First, the authors portray raising children as an emotionally absorbing experience. Affectionate nurture is considered the absolutely essential foundation for the proper rearing of a child. Leach believes that "the most important thing one can give a child is genuinely unconditional love" (in Lawson 1991), Spock argues that children need loving nurture "just as much as [they] need vitamins and calories" (1985: 3), and Brazelton claims that children who are not allowed to experience full emotional attachment to an adult in the early stages of infancy may later be unable to establish human relationships at all (1983b: 56).

For these writers, maternal love and affection are not only vital, they also come naturally. Leach writes, "Whatever your mind and the deeply entrenched habits of your previous life may be telling you, your body is ready and waiting for him. Your skin thrills to his. His small frame fits perfectly against your belly, breast, and shoulder" (1986: 34). For Leach, then, a mother is naturally thrilled to cuddle her child, even if her mind seems to tell her otherwise. Spock also consistently refers to parental instincts toward loving nurture,[10] and Brazelton, as I have noted, explicitly claims that "mothering is instinctive." In fact, he writes, parents are "programmed with a whole set of 'reflex' responses" that leave them "geared to lavish affection on the child" (1983a: 42, 11, 2).

The methods of child rearing suggested by these authors are also clearly child-centered. Not only is the child understood as extremely important and the center of familial attention, but the child is also the person who *guides* the process of child rearing. The mother's day-to-day job is, above all, to respond to the child's needs and wants. Spock is considered the central proponent of this permissive ideology in his recommendation that parents should "follow [the] baby's lead" (1985: 200), but Brazelton and Leach actually have even more pronounced views in this regard. Brazelton highlights the notion that "every baby knows what is needed" and will show "a sensitive parent" just what to do (1987: 3). Good parenting, he argues, follows from attention to the child's cues and requests. And while Spock actually warns that "the more parents submit to their babies' orders, the more demanding the children become" (1985: 249), to Leach (1986) submitting to the child's orders is the *only* logical approach, since she believes there is a "natural harmony of interests" between mother and child.[11] According to Leach, if you give the child what the child wants and needs, the child will be happy and you will be happy; if you don't give the child what the child wants, the child will simply keep asking for more and more, and both of you will be frustrated and upset. Mothers must therefore "anticipate wishes which [the baby] can barely recognize let alone formulate" (1989: xvii).[12] Such parenting requires extreme sensitivity, since children are not always articulate about what (they know) is needed.

To properly decipher and appropriately respond to a child's needs, a mother must take action on a number of fronts, all of which make for child rearing that is labor-intensive. The first task is to acquire knowledge of what the experts know to be the changing requirements of children as they pass through the stages of development. For these thinkers, there are a multitude of developmental stages. Brazelton (1983a), for instance, breaks down the stages of infanthood month by month, whereas Leach's (1986) most popular manual cites 0–6 months, 6 months to 1 year, 1 to 2½ years, and 2½ to 5 years as significant stages. Each of these must be further subdivided in terms of physical, psychological, and cognitive development. Knowledge of these stages and their subdivisions is considered essential to good parenting.

In all these works the primary method for ensuring the child's healthy psychological development is the parental love that fosters the child's self-esteem and sense of emotional security. But there is no consensus among these authors regarding the methods required to ensure the child's proper cognitive development. The practices of parents who are overly concerned with their child's intellectual development have received a great deal of attention in the popular media, particularly the methods espoused by Glen Doman's Better Baby Institute that are mimicked in images of flash-card-toting parents in movies such as *Baby Boom* and *Parenthood*. Such parents spend much time, energy, and money attempting to awaken the genius that is said to be inherent in each and every child. However, both Spock and Brazelton make it clear that they find these practices extreme, that pressuring the child to be "intellectually clever" is a mistake, and that the real foundation for cognitive development is a parent's attention to the child's emotional development (e.g., Spock 1985: 20–21; Brazelton 1983b: 122). This position does not mean they believe one should ignore the child's intellectual growth; they simply want to counter what they consider an overzealous approach. Leach, on the other hand, seems quite concerned with the making of an intellectually "better baby." In her extended treatment of the importance of teaching the child language, for instance, she writes,

> Talk as much and as often as you can directly to your child. . . . Let the toddler see what you mean, by matching what you do to what you say. . . . Let the

toddler see what you feel by matching what you say with your facial expression. . . . Help your child to realize that all talk is communication. (1986: 355)[13]

In other words, according to Leach if mothers wish to assure their child's proper cognitive development, they must be attentive not only to the quantity and quality of what they say but also to their facial expressions while they say it. Making certain that the child receives enough communication of the right kind, of course, requires constant individualized attention.[14]

Nonetheless, these advisers do not consider knowledge of the child's cognitive, emotional, and physical development and the generally appropriate responses to each age-graded stage sufficient to prepare the mother to respond correctly to her own child's needs and desires. She must also learn how to interpret the particular behavior and peculiar needs of her child, moment by moment. Brazelton, for instance (speaking of the first week of the child's life), warns the reader that "overstimulation can be very demanding" while the lack of stimulation can be "devastating" (1983a: 32). Elsewhere he adds that "without the advantage of a stimulating, individualized environment in infancy, a child's future development will be impaired" (1983a: xxvii). The only way to determine precisely the *correct* amount of stimulation is to watch the baby at every moment, interpret its behavior, and analyze its requirements at that particular time.[15] Leach also brings out this point in stressing the importance of learning to "read" the baby's cry. Babies, she writes, can cry for a number of reasons: it may be from fear, an encounter with the unexpected, or a sense of helplessness, anger, or frustration. The good mother will conscientiously "decode" the cry, determine its specific cause, and provide an appropriate solution (1986: 235). Of course anyone who has ever listened to a wailing child recognizes that one would do anything to stop it, but the point here is that these authors imply that mothers, to do their job properly, must be gathering data, and analyzing data, constantly.

Good parenting also requires the understanding that all children are unique individuals. Spock is always careful to remind the reader that "every baby's pattern of development is different" (1985: 4). Brazelton points out differences among children and categorizes their expected needs and wants according to their character (active, quiet, or average) as well as their birth order (firstborn, middle, or youngest). At the same time, he stresses that such categories are only the first step toward understanding the more complex differences among individual children. And all this means, as Leach suggests, that the good mother should raise her child not "by the book" but "by the baby" (1986: 16).

The parent is thus provided with a complex map of children's needs, all of which must be attended to carefully and consistently. First, there are the age-graded developmental stages. Second, there are the subdivisions within these stages of physical, psychological, and cognitive development. Third, there are the different circumstances that influence children's developmental stages and therefore require different parental responses. Fourth, there are the general distinctions among types of children. Finally, there are the characteristics unique to each child. All these elements must be kept in mind by the good mother who (naturally) wants to provide the appropriate response to her child. In practical terms, this means that the conscientious mother not only should spend a great deal of time educating herself as to the latest knowledge on childhood development but also should invest even more time (and money) on a daily basis attempting to appropriately apply that knowledge to her child.

Further indicating the labor-intensive character of present-day child-rearing advice are the recommended methods of discipline. In line with the emphasis on responding to children's needs rather than enforcing parental desires, all these authors recommend the careful molding of the child's self-discipline as opposed to demands for compliance to an absolute set of rules or the use physical punishment. Like the child-rearing advisers of the nineteenth century, Leach refers to this process as the development of the child's "conscience" (1986: 434).

All these authors consider the use of physical punishment a mistake. Brazelton makes it clear that "physical punishment should be the very last resort" (1987: 63). Spock feels that such punishment is completely unnecessary, adding that the "American tradition of spanking may be one cause of the fact that there is much more violence in our country than in any other comparable nation" (1985: 408). Leach seems to concur. "There is nothing good to be said of physical punishments," she writes, since a "gradual and gentle exposing of the child to the results of his own ill-advised actions is the only ultimate sanction you need. Any other kind of punishment is revenge and power-mongering" (1986: 440).[16]

By and large, discipline is to be accomplished by "setting limits" for the child, providing a good example in one's own behavior, and giving the child the love that will make her want to internalize those limits and those examples as her own (e.g., Spock 1985: 249; Brazelton 1983b: 168; 1987: 64; Leach 1986: 434). As Spock puts it, since children have an "intense desire to be as much like their parents as possible," the "main source of good discipline is growing up in a loving family" (1985: 406).

Although Spock makes this sound simple, it is not. If the parents' example is crucial, then such parents must constantly monitor their actions — never exhibiting any type of inappropriate behavior lest the child make it his own. And even if the parents' example is (miraculously) perfect, the child might still pick up bad behavior elsewhere. In this case, the parent might turn to Leach's suggestion and attempt to "gradually and gently" expose the child to the results of his inappropriate behavior. But, in practical terms, this advice also means that the primary caregiver must expend much energy to assure that this exposure process goes smoothly, must put up with a great deal of frustration (and fear) as the child experiences the consequences of his actions and must, above all, suffer patiently through the child's (temporarily?) bad behavior.

In addition, the good parent will set limits. As Brazelton puts it (in a curious turn of phrase that nonetheless captures the logic of instilling self-discipline), "The most critical thing we can do for a child is to let her learn her own limits by setting them and helping her to live up to them" (1987: 54). Of course the full elaboration of such limits generally requires a verbal child, which leaves a few years of the child's life during which the parent is potentially without recourse beyond the command of no! More important, since physical punishment is taboo, it cannot serve as a sanction when the command of no proves inadequate or when more verbally competent children overstep their limits. According to the logic implied by all these authors, love is the *sole* foundation of good discipline. It is the bond of love that leads the child to want to make his parent's limits his own limits. It is the carefully managed temporary withdrawal of loving attention, then, that serves as the central form of punishment. And this means that proper disciplinary techniques are emotionally absorbing as well as labor-intensive.

Finally, it is suggested that setting limits for the verbal child requires reasoning with the child. Leach elaborates on this process. First, the mother should recognize that it "is an insult to your child's intelligence to tell him to do something without telling him why." And "telling him why" is not enough; you should also consistently "let your child join in the decision-making process." This means that you must give the child a chance to provide "reasonable arguments" and should always be willing to allow your mind to be changed by such arguments (1986: 435, 442–43). Anyone who has ever tried to thus negotiate with a three-year-old knows that it requires a tremendous amount of time and effort. There is no question that demanding absolute obedience to a strict set of rules and backing up these demands with the threat (and reality) of physical punishment would make the parent's job much easier.[17]

A further example of the intensive character of appropriate child rearing that is particularly illuminating in the context of the cultural contradictions of contemporary motherhood is the treatment of nonparental child care. Given mothers' increasing participation in the paid labor force and the widespread use of day-care facilities, these advisers all spend some time considering the issue of child-care arrangements. While Spock, Brazelton, and Leach all argue that it is critical for the primary parental caregiver to stay at home with the child for at least the first several months (up to the first three years),[18] they recognize that at some point both parents may be working outside the home, thereby necessitating alternative care. Spock prefers, however, that both parents cut down to less than full-time jobs or dovetail their work schedules so that one parent can be with the child at all times (1985: 49). And Leach believes that day-care facilities established to serve full-time paid working parents are in *all* cases bad for kids; for Leach the only form of nonmaternal care that should ever be considered is a part-time preschool (and this, she tells us, is only appropriate when the child is "ready") (1986: 392).[19]

All these authors recognize, however, that in *some* cases nonparental child care will be required. But even in this situation, the list of appropriate concerns is virtually endless. First, all three authors recommend a child-to-caregiver ratio that the average mother would have tremendous difficulty finding, let alone affording: for Spock there should be "not more than four children under age five, nor more than two under age two" (1985: 49); for Brazelton, more than three babies to one adult is a problem, and four toddlers to one adult is the "upper limit" (1983b: 90, 120); for Leach, even three babies to one care-giver is "unmanageable" (in Lawson 1991). And the mother must, of course, make sure that the basics of safety, cleanliness, and proper nutrition are attended to. But this is just the beginning. For Brazelton, mothers must also find day-care arrangements where the children are treated as individuals, where stimulating experiences are provided, where the staff are ready and willing to adjust to differences among children, and where the caregivers are well paid (1983b: 119). Leach additionally urges mothers to seek programs where the children are "happy and busy," "talk freely," and are given a "choice of activities" and where the caregivers "really like small children" (1986: 395). Spock believes that having someone come into the home or placing the child in a home setting is preferable to using a commercial center. He also feels it is essential to find child-care providers who are "affectionate, understanding, comfortable, sensible, [and] self-confident" and provide the "responsiveness to the child's questions and achievements that good parents naturally give" (1985: 48–51).[20] Certainly such advice makes the search for appropriate day care difficult, time-consuming, and expensive.

Once proper alternative care is found, the mother's job is not over. Spock tells us that it is critically important for mothers to "take great care in observing the way a prospective caregiver or family day care parent takes care of their children and other children over a period of several weeks" (Spock 1985: 50); Brazelton suggests that the good parent will work with the caregiver to plan the child's day each and every morning (1983b: 174). Additionally, the mother should never be late in picking up the child, should always watch for signs of the child's unhappiness, should consistently talk to the child about the events that took place while she was away, and should occasionally "spy" on the day-care provider to make sure things are going well. If the parent should find the day-care situation less than perfect, the long, hard, and expensive search for proper child care begins anew.

Of course there are many good reasons to be concerned about the quality of child-care arrangements today. And most mothers would agree, in principle, with most of the recommendations these authors offer in this regard. But there is also no question that this long list of appropriate concerns contributes to the demanding character of contemporary child-rearing advice.

Throughout such discussions of child nurture, childhood development, proper discipline, day care, and other related matters, these authors also make it clear that expert guidance is crucial. This expert advice is, of course, provided by the books themselves. Spock and Brazelton additionally urge parents to make use of child-guidance clinics, child psychologists, social workers, and their child's doctor whenever necessary (e.g., Brazelton 1987: 38, 264; Spock 1985: 83, 493–94).[21] Leach dedicates a separate book, *Babyhood* (1989), to providing the expert-informed theoretical background for her more widely read instructions.

Finally, it should be clear that these recommended methods of child rearing are financially taxing. Although these authors rarely refer to the expense of child rearing, it is clearly implied in much of what they say. Attending to the basics of providing for the child's general health, safety, and physical comfort is just the beginning. Since a child's desires can be quite far-reaching, "following the child's lead" and responding to all her needs and wants can be extremely costly. And the importance of assuring proper cognitive and psychological development means that parents are implicitly urged to buy the right toys, provide the right learning experiences, take the child on the right outings, and offer the child swimming and dancing and judo and piano lessons.[22] When extra expert advice is needed, parents must also incur the expense of child psychiatrists, child development specialists, and child guidance clinics. One must also take into account the lost wages of the parent who stays at home with the young child and the financial drain on parents who must cut back their paid work hours in order to dovetail their schedules and make sure that they have the maximum amount of time to spend with their progeny.[23] When both parents are working for pay, the child-care arrangements they use must be "the best," their adult-child ratios low, and their workers well-paid. All of this seems to require a bottomless pocketbook.

In sum, the methods of mothering these authors recommend are extremely intensive, as is demonstrated in their attention to every detail and their concern for every consequence. What these methods add up to is child-centered, expert-guided, emotionally absorbing, labor-intensive, and financially expensive child rearing.

The Ideology of the Sacred Child and Its Contradictions

Not only do these child-rearing manuals reflect the belief that mothers are primarily responsible and that the appropriate methods of raising children are intensive, they also reflect the belief that children are sacred and should be cherished for their innocence, purity, and inherently loving and trusting nature. These authors participate, in other words, in what Zelizer (1985) has called the "sacralization" of the economically "worthless" but morally and emotionally "priceless" child. And by doing so, they not only implicitly deny the logic of self-interested market relations but explicitly *reject* that logic.

From a historical and cross-cultural point of view it is important to begin with the fact that the children described in these books are certainly not treated as productive laborers. In fact, their future wage-earning capacity is never mentioned. What is to be valued is the child's goodness. And the child's goodness is derived from the child's purity and innocence. This, in turn, is a marker of the child's distance from the "corrupt" modern world. "Naturally friendly" children who "mean well" and should be welcomed with "unconditional love" are not the individualistic competitors one encounters in the world of paid work; they are affectionate and caring others who can be trusted without question.

Not only do these advisers treat children as outside of market logic, they also portray child rearing as a practice that stands in opposition to the self-interested, competitive pursuit of personal gain. In other words, just as the "nature" of children stands in contrast to the outside world, so the methods of child rearing contradict the practices of corporate enterprises and the centralized state. In child rearing, love is the foundation. One must "lavish affection" on the child, anticipate his every desire, and be constantly attentive to his unique characteristics and special needs. Yet love is certainly not the essential ingredient in the average business transaction. And any bureaucrat attending to the "unique" characteristics of the individual with whom he dealt would soon find himself without a job. But in child-rearing, giving freely of one's love, one's labor, and one's resources is the appropriate code of behavior; any self-serving concern for efficiency or profitability is condemned.

Most critically, it is important to remember that from a market perspective, time is money, efficiency is the watchword, and financial profit is the goal. Adults are simply more productive than children: their time is more valuable, and their labor more efficient and manageable. From this point of view, asking parents to pump copious amounts of time, energy, and money into children, without a thought to the efficiency of the methods or the profitability of the enterprise, is surely bizarre. But not one of the best-selling authors of contemporary child-rearing manuals considers such facts. The very *absence* of discussions of profitability or efficiency in these manuals speaks volumes on the special value placed on the child.

The authors of these manuals are explicit in articulating their belief that appropriate child rearing is in opposition to the behavior that is appropriate in the outside world. Although emotional distance and efficiency are appropriate in the workplace, Brazelton writes, "an efficient women could be the worst kind of mother for her children"; at home with her child, "a woman must be flexible, warm, and concerned" (1983b: xix). Mothers who work in the paid labor force must therefore learn to "switch gears" when they come home from their paid jobs, since the values that are applicable outside the home are destructive inside it. Spock similarly worries about the "focus on money and position" that prevails in our industrialized society, concerned that it tends to "foster rivalry" between people as they strive to acquire more money and more status than others. This, he argues, is clearly inappropriate in child rearing. According to Spock, the value of money and position cannot and should not compete with what he calls "the warm glow that comes from working cooperatively" (1985: 40).

In fact, I would call these child-rearing manuals hesitant moral treatises. All these authors' prescriptions for appropriate child rearing contain an underlying moral condemnation of impersonal, competitive, market relations and a celebration of the importance of caring for others. And appropriate child rearing, they imply, in its fostering of unselfish love, caring, and sharing, is not only important for the creation of the home as a haven in a heartless world but may ultimately lead to a positive transformation of society as a whole.

Leach makes it clear that child rearing is a morally grounded undertaking: "Unrealistic though this view of dedicated parenthood may seem, I make no apology for it. . . . There is a moral obligation to choose carefully whether or not to have a child. There is then a moral obligation to rear the children we do choose to have as well as we can (1989: xix)." And that moral obligation, as we know, involves selflessly giving much of one's time and attention to the unspoiled and unspoilable child. Leach also implies that the mother's moral obligation includes the creation of a haven against the potentially cold and cruel outside world. As the child grows up, she writes, he will always find security in this: "Because he has you; because you care and he knows that you care, his sadness need never be solitary; his despair need never be desolation. Whatever the world must do to him, he has a safe haven with you" (1986: 444).

The value of home as a protected haven against the impersonal pecuniary relations that dominate outside it also comes out in the authors' treatment of day care. Spock stresses the importance of choosing child-care arrangements that are homelike and condemns "the common [day-care] situation in which a person takes in many babies and small children with the idea of making as much money as possible, and with no idea of what children's needs are" (1985: 50). Leach disapproves of child-care centers established to serve paid working parents (as opposed to those established to serve child development), implying that the message sent by such parents — paid work is more important than the child — rubs off on the workers, so that "your child's happiness may not be of as much concern to them. . . . It will be assumed that he is there because he has got to be there rather than because you expect them to derive positive enjoyment" (1986: 393). In these ways the authors remind us that it is absolutely inappropriate to mix the pursuit of self-interested gain with the rearing of a child.

Appropriate child rearing, these advisers suggest, may also have larger implications for the good of society as a whole. For instance, Brazelton tells us that "the 'ME' generation is a blot on our society" (1983b: 182) and lets us know just what is at stake when he writes, "Our society may need a serious reevaluation — we are raising children to be highly individualistic, intellectually clever, and self-motivated — to the exclusion of caring about others around them" (1983b: 129). Raising children using proper methods and proper values, it is implied, may transform society by creating kind and sharing adults rather than selfish market competitors. Spock expresses like sentiments: "The child-centered, psychological approach," he writes, "can leave parents in a lurch unless it is backed up by a moral sense." And the moral sense Spock recommends becomes clear when he tempers his pessimism regarding today's "disenchanted world" with an optimism about the "only realistic hope" he finds: "to bring up our children with a feeling that they are in this world not for their own satisfaction but primarily to serve others" (1985: 19).

Even the emphasis on the natural quality of children and child rearing speaks to its caring and cooperative rather than impersonal and competitive character. It is implied that there is something unnatural, false, and therefore bad about life in the outside world, while that which is natural is good. The natural innocence of the child is one side of this, and the parents' natural love for their progeny completes the portrait. What is natural and good is the purity of love, caring, and sharing, untouched by what Rousseau called the "deceit, vanity, anger, and jealousy" of civilization ([1761] 1964: 36). Not only is this made clear in Spock's criticism of the rivalry that comes from struggles for money and position, in Leach's stress on the creation of a haven, and in Brazelton's condemnation of the "ME" generation, but both Spock and Brazelton also express this in their nostalgia for societies in which the market is not the central feature of social life. Brazelton speaks of Mayan Indians in southern Mexico, Spock speaks of "simpler" societies, and both focus on the natural quality of the extended and sustained contact these societies allow between mother and child, as well as the natural system of mutual support they provide between nuclear and extended families. In such societies, it is implied, warm and supportive relationships between people take precedence over competition and the pursuit of individual gain. And this value system is the appropriate one.

Child rearing is surely envisioned here as a moral enterprise. But unlike their predecessors in the eighteenth and nineteenth centuries, these child-rearing advisers often hesitate to state explicitly the goals of this enterprise, in part because they do not want to claim an absolute *shared* morality. Of the three, Spock is the most willing to clearly articulate his larger vision of the common good: throughout his book, he condemns injustice, urges the creation of caring and sharing children imbued with a strong sense of social responsibility, and speaks out against violence, war, racism against blacks, and the massacre of the American Indians.[24] Brazelton, as we have seen, is equally concerned to create a more caring world, but he also expresses a certain reluctance to elaborate on this concern beyond his particular area of expertise. This is evidenced in the following statement:

> Parents today search for values for their children. . . . Nuclear warfare, misuse of our resources, the breakdown of the family — all contribute to a kind of emptiness for parents. They are missing a set of sturdy values with which to indoctrinate their children. We [child-rearing advisers] know a great deal about child development, but *we don't yet know how to direct parents in their search for meaningful values* for their children. . . . What parents need instead is a respect for the importance of the child's personality and self-esteem, as well as a sense that they have values to impart. (1983b: 143, emphasis mine)

Although Brazelton is sure that fostering the child's self-esteem is a positive goal, in this instance he finds himself unable to name the other meaningful shared values that all parents should want to impart. But it is Leach who is the most hesitant of the three to make any claim as to the larger moral goals that are served by the proper raising of a child. The only goal she is willing to state (and this she does throughout the volume) is the "happiness" of mother and child.

Individual happiness becomes that elusive good upon which we can all agree. In fact, the permissive era has been identified with the trend toward what Wolfenstein (1955) calls "fun morality," where the central goal and prescription for both parent and child is to enjoy themselves. But fun and happiness are slippery concepts. As Varenne (1977) points out, although happiness is an individualistic notion, one experiences it in the context of relationships with others. Varenne therefore suggests that the concept of happiness "form[s] a bridge between the two poles of American culture" by emphasizing the importance of both individualism and community (1977: 185). In the case of these child-rearing advisers, happiness seems to be a code word for the sense of security, continuity, trust, and love that the mother-child relationship engenders. Although this happiness is understood as a property of the individual participants, to the extent that it is connected to notions of caring and sharing that are in opposition to the self-interested rivalry that dominates many other relationships, it takes on a larger significance.

Overall, each of these authors is certain that raising a child is one of the most important things one can do for society. Brazelton writes, "My bias is that a woman's most important role is being at home to mother her small children" (1983a: 173). Leach, in the context of a discussion of moral obligations, informs us that raising a child is "more worthwhile than any other job" (1989: xviii). For Spock, money and position are "meager substitutes" for the "joy" of child rearing, and "pride in our worldly accomplishments is usually weak in comparison" to the satisfaction that comes from raising our children to be "fine people" (1985: 40, 23). These authors here imply that child rearing is more worthwhile than paid work and thereby risk incurring the wrath of all of those readers who are also paid career women. They take this risk, however, in order to bring out the special nonmarket value of the child and the parent-child relationship.

In a similar vein, one might expect these authors to recognize the need to prepare children for their future roles and to therefore advise that children be simultaneously trained in the appropriate behavior for home *and* workplace. Yet Spock, Brazelton, and Leach never advise parents to teach their children to be competitive, efficient seekers of financial success. Implicit in this omission (particularly for Spock and Brazelton) is the belief that if we raise our children to be nurturing, caring, and sharing, they can one day help to make the world a better place. In short, these authors clearly suggest that the reason child rearing is so important is that it is meant to create both a protected space of security, trust, and close human connection, and people who are nurturing and generous rather than individualistic and competitive.

In all of this, the three most widely read child-rearing authors have fully elaborated the ideology of intensive mothering. First, despite their reluctance to claim shared moral values, they are not at all hesitant to portray child rearing as completely distinct from the self-interested pursuit of pecuniary gain, and children as completely immune from market valuation. Second, the unremunerated task of child rearing, they claim, is appropriately child-centered, expert-guided, emotionally absorbing, labor intensive, and financially expensive. Finally, the task of child rearing is considered primarily the responsibility of the individual mother.

The historical intensification of child rearing that these manuals represent means that the cultural contradictions of motherhood are more pronounced than ever before. In no previous period is the distinction between what is appropriate in relation to mothering and what is appropriate in the outside world at greater odds. The sacred character of the child is fully elaborated and articulated: nowhere does the language of impersonality, efficiency, and profit enter in. And all this is true at a time when the outside world seems to be influencing the world of the mother and child to an increasing extent — not only in terms of compulsory schooling, child labor laws, prenuptial agreements, surrogate contracts, frozen dinners, and diaper services but also in the form of mothers who spend much of their lives in a paid workforce where time is money, efficiency the watchword, and personal profit the goal.

Given these circumstances, why wouldn't the socially constructed logic of child rearing be reconstructed to one more in line with the ethos of instrumental rationality and profit-maximization so pervasive in modern societies? And why wouldn't the methods of appropriate child rearing be transformed so as to make the task simpler for the majority of mothers who are now working in the paid labor force?

One might be tempted to argue that this paradox is simply an illusion. After all, mothers are also listening to other advisers. Different models of appropriate child rearing coexist in any given time and place, and it is true that the current collection of child-rearing models includes some that differ from the top three sellers. Dr. James Dobson, for instance, in his widely read *Dare to Discipline* (1970), attacks permissive child rearing, urges greater strictness, advises parents to shape their child's will, and suggests that they seek guidance from God and the Bible.[25] The mass-market best-seller *Tough Love* is also far from permissive ("Childcare Bestsellers" 1991). In fact, many popular books have satirized today's child-rearing techniques, including two of the twenty-five nonfiction best-sellers of the 1980s: Bill Cosby's *Fatherhood* and Erma Bombeck's *Motherhood: The Second Oldest Profession* ("The Top 25 . . . " 1990). Nonetheless, I would argue that most popular child-rearing guides (including *What to Expect the First Year* and *How to Talk So Kids Will Listen, and Listen So Kids Will Talk*) as well as most popular parenting magazines

(*Parents, Parenting, Child*) include much the same advice as is found in the works of the three top-selling authors.[26] Given the ubiquity of this child-rearing advice, and given the status of Spock, Brazelton, and Leach, it seems plausible that they represent a reflection of the dominant cultural model of appropriate child rearing today.

The popularity of these manuals, however, tells one nothing about how present-day mothers interpret such advice or the extent to which women have made the ideology of intensive mothering their own. If the point is to understand the present construction of contemporary child-rearing ideas, one must listen to mothers themselves.

4

Sorting the Mail
The Social Bases of Variations in Mothering

Mothers are faced with a plethora of advice admonishing them to be at once nutrition experts, psychological counselors, and cognitive development specialists. Spock, Brazelton, and Leach, along with their coworkers in the advice business, tell mothers to be constantly attentive to the child's needs, to be alert to each new developmental stage, and to learn how to read the child's cries and to organize the child's play activities. If mothers fail in the task, other "experts" may charge them with child neglect, emotional abuse, and "toxic parenting" or denounce them for creating a "dysfunctional family" (Bradshaw 1990; Forward 1989). But are mothers listening?

Articulating a sentiment common to many mothers, one respondent told me that sorting through child-rearing advice is like sorting through the mail: "You take the junk mail and throw it away and you take the good mail and save it." The collection of available child-rearing ideas, in this sense, is like a pile of mail, and mothers pick and choose among the pieces of advice at their disposal. The issues then become: What are the sources of the "mail" mothers receive, and how do they determine what is junk and what is not? In other words, whose ideas are they listening to, and on what basis do they decide which ideas are worthy?

In this chapter I explore these questions. First, I show that mothers acquire information on raising children from a wide variety of sources. I then argue that mothers make selections among these sources and develop interpretations based on their social circumstances — including both their past and present social positions and their past and present cultural milieux. In sorting through advice, interpreting it, and deciding what is worthy, individual mothers therefore actively engage in reshaping the social ideology of appropriate child rearing. This process means that every mother's understanding of mothering is in some sense unique. It also means that there are systematic group differences among mothers that are grounded in their different social positions and different cultural worlds.

Although this chapter is primarily meant to acknowledge and highlight such differences among mothers, it is also meant to provide the beginning of a demonstration of important underlying similarities in child-rearing beliefs. Given that all mothers in the United States are ultimately exposed to a similar social universe, all share a recognition of the prevailing ideology of child rearing (though they may understand it only implicitly or partially). No matter how different the circumstances and beliefs of the mothers in my study, my interviews suggest that almost all mothers recognize and respond to this ideology — either by accepting it or, if they reject it in whole or in part, by feeling the need to justify that rejection. And this dominant model of child rearing is almost precisely the same model as is found in the manuals of Spock, Brazelton, and Leach. In short, American mothers recognize, interpret, sort through, and respond to the ideology of intensive mothering.

Interpreting Advice

Mothers frequently refer to the use of common sense and intuition in raising children — as if no special knowledge were required and as if many of their practices were grounded in some biological instinct. Although there is a sense of naturalness connected to such terms, there are many good reasons to believe that mothers are actually referring to learned behaviors. After all, common sense is clearly connected to ideas developed in interaction with other people, and intuition often refers to socially acquired ideas and beliefs that are so deeply held as to seem natural. It is therefore difficult to distinguish a "mother's intuition" from ideas arising from a woman's social role, a woman's upbringing, and the culture of motherhood. Given that the dominant model of appropriate child rearing is widely available in the culture at large and that many women begin to learn its central tenets long before they are mothers (and often before they are able to articulate or analyze them), it is not surprising that much of that model is so fully internalized that it seems a matter of intuition and common sense.

But alongside references to intuition and common sense, almost all mothers admit that they seek at least some explicit advice on how to raise their children. As I have noted, child-rearing manuals are one of the central sources of advice. More mothers treat manuals as their primary source of advice than any other source. All but two of the women I interviewed had purchased at least one child-rearing manual, and many owned three or more. Among these mothers, as is true among mothers in general, Spock, Brazelton, and Leach were the three most popular advisers.[1] But, as I have argued, these child-rearing manuals are subject to interpretation.

Although the best-selling authors present their advice as objective and scientific truth, most mothers let me know that they do not completely trust these so-called experts. First, expert advice, they tell me, frequently doesn't make sense; the basis for experts' recommendations is, after all, "just theory." Mothers complain, for example, that two different books will often provide "totally opposite theories," that the methods suggested regularly "just don't work," and that the books seem, at times, far too demanding and "idealistic."[2] Over and over, these concerns come out in such phrases as "you can't believe everything you read" and "the fact that it's printed doesn't mean it's true." Further, a number of women told me that they reserve the title of expert for mothers who have successfully raised a number of children themselves. As one mother proclaimed, "These [authors] don't even have children! And I'm not going to ask my neighbor for advice on cooking when I know she can't even fry an egg." More than once I heard the connected refrain "the proof's in the pudding." Finally, mothers often consider such expert advice inadequate because it cannot possibly take into account the wide variety among children. As one mother put it, "Your child doesn't always do what the books say." Summing up these concerns, another mother concluded:

> One gets a lot of information. We just automatically learn to filter the advice. You just sorta don't hear what you don't want. . . . To begin with, it helps to know if they have kids. Plus a lot of times the way information is collected in a study, it's not always typical of the average child. Children just come into the lab and they look at them. That's a very narrow thing. . . . But these books they really try to cover everything. I wouldn't want to put my head on the block for every single thing they said.

Additionally, some mothers, even if they think the advice they find in books is sound, just can't bring themselves to follow it. This mother, for instance, expressed her reliance on and trust in child-rearing manuals at the same time that she demonstrated her reluctance to practice all they preach:

> I wouldn't know how to treat a boy. But [I learn] from reading books, trying to get knowledgeable, not trying to rely on just myself all my life, reading books. In the books it says, 'try to treat 'em the same'. . . . But I don't want [my son] to grow up to be a faggot. [She laughs.] I wouldn't want him to be a wimp.

Further, mothers tend to read advice books selectively. Less than one-quarter of the mothers I interviewed said they read child-rearing manuals from cover to cover; the rest said they use them as reference books, picking out relevant portions as problems arise — for instance, when they need information on breast-feeding, potty training, sleep patterns, or discipline. Most mothers therefore consult these books primarily for suggestions on specific issues and not, as one mother stated, as overall guides on "how to raise my child or, you know, what to say or do to them."

Finally, as I have noted, mothers use a number of sources of information on child rearing. After child-rearing manuals, the second most frequently cited source of advice was one's own mother; the third was one's friends (especially those who are also mothers). And, along with pediatricians, paid caregivers, and other family members, these sources of advice are consulted constantly. Over three-quarters of the mothers reported talking to someone daily about their kids; nearly all the rest reported talking to someone weekly. But as is true with child-rearing manuals, mothers listen to such individuals selectively and interpret the advice provided. In short, they take both what they read and what they hear "with a grain of salt."

Another central source of information on appropriate child rearing, these mothers told me time and again, is a mother's reflections on her own upbringing. Women try to repeat the way their mothers mothered them to the extent that they experienced it as positive and struggle to avoid what they consider the mistakes their mothers made. Generally, however, mothers do not give any more credence to their own mothers' *explicit* advice than they give to the advice of manual writers, friends, and other family members. Mothers who offer too much unsolicited advice to their daughters are often considered busybodies, and their suggestions are often treated as inappropriate or far too old-fashioned to be taken seriously.[3]

Mothers often stated that the primary method they use for sorting all forms of child-rearing advice is the degree to which it fits with their own beliefs and circumstances and the needs of their own children. This position is expressed in statements such as "You kind of read and find what goes with your philosophy"; "I listen to it, and I'll make up my own decision"; "I think I look for the things that I agree with"; and "I believe what feels good with me." One mother, who was quite candid about her reasoning, declared: "A lot of the things that I do, or we do, are often reinforced by *Parents* magazine. So, of course, we continue to read that."

Mothers, in other words, are certainly not cultural dopes who unself-consciously mimic the child-rearing methods recommended by others. They actively respond to what they read, see, and hear, and they shape it in ways that make sense to them. The result is that mothers mother differently.

Nonetheless, mothers *do* buy and read child-rearing manuals, and they *do* constantly talk to people about raising their children. Even if they don't follow the advice offered, they do take note of it. Consequently, the ideas about child rearing they perceive to be their own are never entirely (or even largely) their own but are, instead, socially shaped. And that social process means that there is a strain toward a common model of child rearing.

A crucial indicator of this point is the fact that the central reason mothers seek advice, they tell me, is for "reassurance." In part, of course, this statement is meant to demonstrate that they don't take the advice they receive that seriously but are merely seeking confirmation of their own methods. When mothers seek reassurance, however, they are also looking for some evidence that the methods they use are the "right" ones. For instance, one mother tells me that, without advice, "you have no way of knowing anything [about] how to do it. Reading books and talking to people answers some of the questions so that you know that you're okay." Another, referring to a television program she had watched on child rearing, states: "It made me feel better. I guess I'm doing things right. But I need to hear it from somebody that I'm kind of following the right directions." Yet another speaks of reading the books because of the "reassurance that comes with that, that takes the focus off of you." When you read the books, she continues, "it's more 'this is a problem to be solved' [rather than] 'if you were only a better parent, if you only had a better child, this wouldn't be happening to you' — which I think a lot of people secretly worry about." Mothers ("secretly") worry about whether their methods are right and whether their children will be all right. To overcome this anxiety, they tell me that they "want to hear from somebody" that they are "following the right directions" because, as another mother adds, it "reaffirms that you're okay, and that your child will be okay."

The point here is that in order for advice to serve successfully as reassurance, it must to some degree match the practices and beliefs of the advice-seeker. In this sense, mothers are seeking affirmation that the ideology of appropriate child rearing is a *shared* one. And, by and large, it is. The information that is passed about in conversation and the information that has come to seem like common sense more often than not corresponds to the information found in magazines, on radio talk shows, in the pediatrician's office, and at the day-care center. And this is frequently the very same information found in the manuals by Spock, Brazelton, and Leach.[4] When mothers seek affirmation that they are using the right methods, then, the model of "rightness" they most often encounter is the model of intensive mothering.

Even though mothers do not consider every child-rearing adviser an expert, do not consider their advice infallible, and neither agree with nor heed all of it, they still, by and large, are confronted with and feel the need to respond to the dominant cultural model of child rearing—a model that makes individual mothers primarily responsible for raising children, that requires intensive methods, and that treats children and child rearing as sacred, pure, and appropriately uncorrupted by the selfishness and pecuniary values of the larger world. Before examining in greater depth the similarities created by this cultural schema, however, it may be useful to document the differences that arise as the different social circumstances of mothers shape their interpretations and responses to the dominant model of child rearing in distinct ways.

Mothers Are as Unique as the Children They Raise

Every mother's ideas about mothering are shaped by a complex map of her class position, race, ethnic heritage, religious background, political beliefs, sexual preferences, physical abilities or disabilities, citizenship status, participation in various subcultures, place of residence, workplace environment, formal education, the techniques her own parents used to raise her — and more (see esp. Glenn, Chang, and Forcey 1994). The impact of some of these social factors can be seen in the following four mothers. Although all the mothers I spoke to were uniquely shaped by diverse social factors, these four mothers were distinct from the majority of women I encountered. They were the outliers in my sample — their ideas about child rearing seeming to diverge sharply from the larger consensus among mothers. I profile them here not only because they provide examples of the social shaping of difference but also because, despite their differences, these mothers, like all the mothers I talked to, ultimately respond to the prevailing model of socially appropriate, intensive mothering.

Jacqueline is a hard-working, highly paid scientist and the mother of two. In a way that many mothers would find disturbing, if not shocking, Jacqueline repeatedly emphasizes the importance of money, discusses children as if they were animals, and talks of child rearing as if it were a scientific enterprise. Hers is the language of genetics, biology, contracts, cost-benefit analyses, professionalism, and instrumental rationality. The language of emotion, sacrifice, protection, and nurturance at first appears to take a back seat.

References to science infuse her talk. For instance, to explain the importance of information and guidance in raising children she says, "I think of gorillas," and goes on to elaborate on a scientific study of their nurturing capacities: "Gorillas, if they've been raised in captivity, away from any other social animals, they kill their newborn. They have to take lessons with their keepers on handling dolls. None of it's reflex." Here she suggests that mothers by nature would just as soon kill their young and therefore must be trained by their "keepers" to handle their own children. Yet Jacqueline also argues that mothering involves some animal instincts. The reason she set out to find a husband, in fact, was because she experienced a "burning biological drive" to have children. And in line with this biological emphasis, she tells me that one of the criteria she used to choose her husband was that "he comes from good genetic stock." After all, she explains, the character of children is almost wholly dependent upon their genetic makeup:

> There's a crap shoot that occurs at the moment of conception when all those chromosomes are whizzing around . . . and the mother's ability to change that, or modify it, is limited, extremely limited. If they come out with the wrong chromosomes, there's nothing you can do for them.

Mothering, then, seems secondary to the accidental combination of careening chromosomes.

Alongside her focus on science, genetics, and biology, Jacqueline's talk of contracts and cost-benefit analyses makes her quite unique. She "negotiated" a marriage contract with her husband that freed him from child-rearing responsibilities and included the hiring of a full-time, live-in nanny to be the day-to-day caregiver. Such an arrangement, they agreed, was far more cost-effective than having Jacqueline stay home. She did stay home to nurse her first child but found it very expensive:

> The first time cost me $20,000 in savings to nurse her for six months. That's what I burned through by staying home! I couldn't afford to do that the second time. You can think you're going to nurse for six months, but wait 'til you see what that costs when your salary isn't coming in. [She laughs.]

The choice between mothering and money, in this statement, seems clear.[5]

Yet Jacqueline ultimately follows many of the basic tenets of the ideology of intensive mothering. First, she considers herself as having the primary responsibility for raising the children. Her husband does not help with child care at all. He just "defers" to her on matters relating to the children, and she is generally satisfied with this arrangement since "he's completely oblivious to people's emotional needs" and therefore is not a qualified caregiver. Although the nanny cares for the children for more hours than Jacqueline does, Jacqueline puts a great deal of effort into spending "quality time" with the kids during the evenings and on weekends. In fact, she's quite sure that she "overindulges" them in order to make up for the time she spends away:

> I don't come home and put me first for those two hours. . . . I mean, I come home and act like I haven't seen them all day and meet their needs first. And so they have this expectation that when I'm there that I'm all theirs. . . . I work my day around their needs and not mine.

In stating so emphatically that her children's needs come before her own, Jacqueline demonstrates her sense that it is important not only to compensate for but also to justify the lack of time she spends with them. This concern is also apparent when she reminds me repeatedly that the paychecks she brings home are important precisely because they provide her with "the ability to give my kids everything I want to." These statements could be understood as rationalizations, but it is also true that what money can buy is, like her nights and weekends, something Jacqueline gives to her children with great sincerity.

Further indicating her dedication to her children, Jacqueline tells me that, although little can be done to change a child's genetic makeup, a mother must be committed to providing the child with all she can to supplement and shape those genes: "You *can* provide them with a margin," she adds to her earlier comment, "and we put an incredible effort into that margin." For Jacqueline, providing that margin includes giving her children what she describes as "a safe and secure but limited experience of the world that's enlarging at the right speed for that particular individual." In other words, innocent children need to be protected from the world, and it is a mother's job to ensure that they encounter that world in just the right increments.

Finally, although Jacqueline's scientific training and advice from her most trusted friend leave her certain that less indulgent methods would be better for her children and easier on her, she simply can't bring herself to use them. Speaking of the suggestion that she should handle her youngest daughter (who is "hell on wheels") by locking her in her room when she is "acting out," Jacqueline tells me that she cannot bear to punish her daughter in this way, insisting that the few hours they spend together are too important, even though she knows that such punishment can be quite effective: "It does work. I did enough behavior training on pigeons, rats, and monkeys as an undergraduate—this will work. But I'm a mom! There's too much empathy there." A mother's empathy, it seems, is sometimes simply more powerful than a mother's training in scientific methods. And in her experience of that maternal empathy, Jacqueline is surely not unique.

Thus, despite her talk of science and contracts and cost-benefit analyses, Jacqueline feels the strain toward child-rearing methods that are child-centered and informed by emotional responses and that call for an investment of far more time and money than she can ever expect to recoup. She also considers this work her responsibility as a mother, and she understands her task, in part, as one meant to protect sacred, innocent children. The tensions in her talk, therefore, mirror her dual roles as scientist and mother, just as they mirror the pushes and pulls she experiences between paid work and home. And in this she is also not unique. She tells me that if she won the lottery, she would *try* to stay home ("I crave the time I spend with them") but would probably find the need to do outside work, maybe in the public sector, where she could provide services and help for more people. Jacqueline thus expresses a real ambivalence regarding the culturally prescribed "choice" between the intensive mother's appropriate sacrifice for her children and the satisfaction, money, and status one can gain from work in the paid labor force. And this ambivalence is something that Jacqueline shares with many other paid-working mothers.

Margaret is also a middle-class mom, but her ideas are quite different from Jacqueline's. She is a stay-at-home mother who has two children and wants two more. She is also an evangelical Christian. She shows me the books of the child-rearing adviser Dr. James Dobson and gives me copies of *Focus on the Family,* a magazine published by Dobson's religious institute.[6] She schools her children at home to ensure that they receive the proper Christian education. Hers is the language of Christian values and of obedience to God and husband, a language that harkens back to the days of Puritan child rearing.

Margaret believes she has a personal relationship with God through Jesus Christ, and it is very important to her that her children also have this. Children are born with a sinful nature, she tells me, but this can be cleansed by asking Jesus to come into one's heart, as Margaret herself did at age three. In fact, her own three-year-old daughter recently made a "wordless book," which pictures the black of a sinful heart that prevents one from reaching heaven and shows the red blood of Jesus washing it clean. Later, the child saw an unwashed car and said, "You see that dirty car? Well, that's the way my heart was before Jesus came and washed it with his blood." Margaret tells me this story with great pride; she considers her child's awakening a measure of her own good mothering.

In accordance with Dobson's recommendations, Margaret thinks it is very important to teach young children that adults are in charge. She works hard to set limits for the kids: if they overstep those limits, she uses "time-out";[7] if they express "willful defiance," she spanks them with a switch. Margaret finds the switch very useful; if she applies it every once in a while, she tells me, the undesirable behavior dissipates: "Like my six-year-old, she very rarely requires a spanking. And I think it's because at three it was really established who was boss." Teaching kids obedience and, when necessary, using physical punishment to do so are part of what Margaret understands as the code of appropriate child rearing.

Although this set of beliefs places Margaret in a minority among mothers, in many respects her ideas about children and child rearing match the dominant model of intensive mothering. Where they do not, she feels the need to carefully justify her separate stance. Like Jacqueline, she considers herself primarily responsible for raising the children; in her case, this sense of responsibility extends to an absolute commitment to staying at home with them. Margaret had a good career before she had children, but she left her job specifically to raise the kids, and now she sees child rearing as her "calling." Her husband agrees. In fact, she says, "part of the reason we got married is that we share the value of the woman staying at home and taking care of the kids." Her husband spends far less time with the children than she does, but he works hard, she tells me, and "needs time for himself." Besides,

> women are just better at raising kids than men. A mom is really inclined to detail, detail, and really watching the kids closely, and dads don't. . . . Men are usually more one-track than women. Whereas I think a woman is more able to balance all these things at once. We can think about many things at once: missing tennis shoe over here, what are you going to cook for dinner, now we do this. He's more easy-going.[8]

In articulating this conception of the grounding of mothering in the differential natures and capacities of men and women, Margaret speaks for a number of other mothers.

Although Margaret's regular use of physical punishment as a primary means of disciplining her children marks her as distinct from most of the women I talked to (especially women of her class background), she blends this method with the more popular time-out, and she also feels the need to *explain* why she rejects what she understands as overindulgent, permissive methods. She tells me that parents have been far too permissive with children in the past few decades, that such methods have not worked, and that enlightened people like herself are therefore returning to older norms of child rearing. Speaking of the permissive era, she says,

Kids were treated like adults and not given much guidance, like there are no real values of right and wrong, you just make it up, and you decide for yourself. I just think kids lost a lot of guidance: no values, no sense of right and wrong. And I think we're seeing the result. We're seeing a very high teenage suicide rate and just a lot of very disturbed children.

For these reasons, she tells me, even Dr. Spock has now recanted much of what he once advised, and mothers should do so as well.[9] Children require moral guidance, and teaching them the difference between right and wrong, according to Margaret, must include teaching them that the parents' rules are best.

Margaret's rejection of permissive child-rearing methods does not mean, however, that she otherwise lacks a commitment to child-centered, expert-guided, emotionally absorbing, labor-intensive, and financially expensive mothering. Even in her explanation for rejecting permissive child rearing she makes it clear that children's needs and interests should take precedence over the needs and interests of adults. And, as her dedication to Dobson indicates, she considers expert advice crucial. Further, as her stay-at-home and home-schooling philosophies testify, she is firmly committed to providing her children with full-time, intensive care. Margaret is also certain that the reason women must be committed to such time- and energy-consuming practices is that children are more important than the pursuit of personal profit; the practices of child rearing, she implies, stand in opposition to the selfishness that is so pervasive in the world outside. Part of Margaret's commitment to Christian values, in fact, is founded in her belief that we have strayed too far from such appropriate family ideals. She tells me:

Well, I think we swung the pendulum to where women were encouraged to think about themselves. Self, self, self over everybody and everything, we went to the extreme of self, self. . . .

And I think a lot of kids feel like they're not important, they're not of value. And I think that's one thing that I want my kids to feel—they're valuable to us. They're more important than a new car, or mommy getting some job and having a lot more money to buy more clothes or something. They're more valuable than that.

In this elaborated expression of the opposition between the values of child rearing and the values of the marketplace, Margaret is certainly not unique.

Unlike Jacqueline and Margaret, Cindy is a working-class mother and a single mother. And, like 12.8 percent of mothers in the United States, Cindy had her child when she was a teenager (U.S. Bureau of the Census 1992: 68). She had wanted to go to college to learn to be an interior designer and had therefore made plans to put the child up for adoption—going so far as to negotiate with the couple she had chosen to be his new parents — but, as she puts it, "When I had him, I wanted him . . . 'cause he was part of me. I don't know, I just wanted him because he was my child, and he was part of my boyfriend." She dropped out of school and moved in with the child's father. The relationship didn't work out, and she now lives with a female friend and works full time as a clerical employee. Her son is three.

During the two years Cindy lived with her boyfriend, they were both heavy users of illegal drugs. They provided their son with little guidance and no special treatment. They simply took their son with them wherever they went, no matter what the hour, and otherwise let him do whatever he wanted to; there was, as Cindy puts it, "no structure." By the time she left her boyfriend, her son "was pretty wild, you know . . . he was having fits all the time."

Cindy is still not quite sure what she can provide for her son. Not only do the needs of children continue to be something of a mystery to her, but she is even less sure what she should do for a boy. Asked if she thought she might treat a daughter differently from a son, Cindy responds:

> I would definitely treat her differently . . . just taking her shopping all the time, dresses and, you know, you buy him bicycles and stuff. Boys don't really require . . . a lot of special, special attention like girls need. Boys can kind of do things on their own for some reason. I don't know what special attention [one would provide them]. Taking them to see dinosaurs? I don't know.

Although going shopping and going out to view dinosaurs are the only ideas she has about special activities for children, Cindy has learned a good deal about the code of appropriate child rearing since her early days as a mother. After she left her boyfriend and found a paying job, she moved in with her day-care provider, who began to teach Cindy how to talk to her son, how to cook nutritious meals for him, how to provide him with educational toys, how to give him rules, how to schedule him, and how to use time-out as a method of discipline. And this instruction, she thinks, has made a big difference. Although Cindy says that three years ago she wasn't ready to be a mom (especially because she "couldn't stand the way a newborn cries"), she thinks she's a good mom now, much more patient and willing to give him the time and energy she feels he deserves. She tells me, "If I had to get two or three jobs to support him, I would." She also says she'd like to be "the main one" taking care of the next child she has.[10] She continues:

> I want to make the sacrifices now. . . . I didn't like him at all when he was born, I didn't want to have anything to do with him, but I definitely do now. It's something I don't mind doing, for his happiness, I would do anything for him. His happiness is important because a kid's young childhood should be the

happiest time in their lives. Because when they get older they're going to have to deal with so much more stuff.

The stuff adults have to deal with, the stuff children need to be protected from, is, of course, the stress and strain of life in the harsh world outside the home. In this, Cindy demonstrates a knowledge of the ideology of the sacred child. And, in this, coupled with her understanding that a mother appropriately sacrifices on behalf of her children, Cindy is not alone.

Mecca is the one mother I interviewed whom the others would find the most difficult to understand. She was raised by her maternal grandmother in South America and came to the United States as a teenager. Her mother was Latina, her father black. She uses a Muslim name and is extremely proud of her African heritage. Mecca is currently living on welfare, although she hopes one day to open a "small boutique" (she's been to a modeling school and says she has "a very good sense about clothing"). She is the mother of three children, ranging in age from two to twelve. Each of her children has a different father. She lives with the children in a small apartment in a rundown neighborhood; her rent is partially subsidized by the state. Much of what Mecca has to say about child rearing can be better understood once this background is taken into account.[11]

Mecca reminisces nostalgically about the way things were in South America when she was growing up. Referring to her five-year-old daughter, she says:

> When I was her age, I knew how to cook. I knew how to wash clothes, but it wasn't a wash room, it was by hand. And I used to have to iron clothes. I used to iron my panty hose too. I used to iron everything. Like, when I was friends with my grandmother, there was a garden. I used to go get the vegetables in there and go get the eggs from the chickens. We used to go to market — it was, like, market day on Saturdays — and then you get a chick, and later on, well, that's your dinner. It was different, but it was good. . . . We didn't have no fancy clothes and stuff like that, but we did good.

Though life was hard, it was good. Back home in South America, kids were part of the family economy, participated in productive labor, and did not have time to get into trouble. In Mecca's opinion, such child labor and strict discipline are far preferable to the practices of spoiling children she now encounters.

Mecca also believes that men are appropriately the rulers of the home and that women should have little say in the matter. For instance, although she had always expected to have children eventually, her first child was not planned. She was taking birth-control pills, but her first husband was anxious to have children ("he wanted twelve kids"), so one day he just threw the pills in the garbage. Mecca says he was "just like the macho man" and told her, "Now you have to be pregnant." Following her divorce, Mecca wanted to go back to school, but her new boyfriend didn't like the idea. She therefore gave up her aspirations for continuing her education because "it was like, forget it — when it comes to men, there's no way to change their minds."

It is very important to Mecca that her children are "presentable." She is dismayed by other mothers who do not keep their children clean and well dressed. "They have to learn to be clean, because I don't want the kids to be like other kids, they're like broken [torn] pants and things like that." But more important than cleanliness is that the kids are well behaved. Mecca explains: "I'd rather have open doors than doors closing in my face just because of the kids, because the kids [don't] behave, because they're brats." People, Mecca believes, will "close doors" in her face, refusing to be in her company, unless her kids are well dressed, well mannered, and quiet.

In general, she thinks most mothers are far too lax with their children:

> Kids these days, they don't have no respect for the parents no more. A lot of the kids I've seen, they don't have no respect at all. . . . Right now these days, especially when it comes to child rearing, you can't even do anything to the kids. The way that trying to discipline them is like, well, if they cry, forget it, you're killing the kids. They [other mothers] let them do whatever they want. They let them have tantrums and everything . . . [but] I don't want to spoil my kids.

Permissive parents spoil their kids, while well-raised children mind their parents. Mecca's children, as I observed and as she told me, do not speak unless they are spoken to, and she is quite proud of that.

Her neighbors recently called the police to report Mecca as a child abuser. The detective who came to her apartment took her children to Child Protective Services, but the children have since been returned to her. Mecca explains:

> And they say I'm an abusive mother. And I go, "How can you say I'm an abusive mother when the only thing I want is to have my kids to be in a place where people can say, 'Wow, those kids, her mom did something good for their education'?" You know, well-mannered kids and things like that.

She says that the accusations are totally false, that her neighbors probably made the charge because they owed her five dollars and didn't want to pay her back or because they were just jealous that her kids were so well behaved. Yes, she concedes, she does spank her children regularly, but only to keep them in line; she does not believe that she is an abusive mother.

It would be difficult to characterize Mecca as an intensive mother. But she is also well aware that her practices differ from the norm. She feels, nonetheless, that her methods are superior to those of mothers who fail to correctly discipline their kids and can't stand to see them cry: her children, unlike theirs, are not spoiled and do not misbehave. Mecca is also particularly quick to compare her practices favorably with what she understands as those of other welfare mothers:

> Now, these days, a lot of mothers, they get the check and they go spend it on themselves, or they go buy a dress, or they go buy alcohol, and forget it. Just go to Pizza Hut and buy pizza for the kids, and forget it, they're ready. To raise these kids these days, you've got to make sacrifices. It's like, I don't get things for myself, but I get things for them. And I'd be the last one to satisfy myself. My kids don't have it, forget it, I don't have it.

Mecca, like Cindy, thus emphasizes her willingness to make sacrifices on behalf of her children. She is therefore a good mother, she says, not a "goody-goody-two shoes," not a "perfect mother," but a good, "normal" mother.

Although Mecca does not consider herself a perfect mother, she does understand many of the basic tenets of intensive mothering. She makes financial sacrifices on behalf of her children. She devotes a good deal of time and attention to making sure that her children are well fed, well dressed, and well behaved. She firmly believes that her children's well-being is far more important than her own convenience. And she expresses her desire to be a good mother. In all this, Mecca has much in common with other mothers.

These four mothers are surely unusual. They are different from one another, they are different from most of the mothers I talked to, and not one of them mimics precisely the model of motherhood proposed by Spock, Brazelton, and Leach. What makes these mothers unique is the same thing that makes all individuals unique — the particular configuration of their past and present social positions, practical circumstances, and socially generated beliefs, and the ways that these factors have led them to actively shape and reshape their lives, including their ideas about child rearing. Although these mothers were examples of extreme differences within my sample, much of what made them so has had an impact on other mothers as well. We know, for instance, that there are many American mothers who use the language and logic of their professions to make sense of children and child rearing, who make explicit the financial cost-benefit analyses that child rearing entails, whose distinct religious beliefs inform their child-rearing practices, whose particular childhood experiences have fundamentally shaped the way that they think about mothering, whose addiction to illegal drugs interferes with their ability to care for their children, and who are physically abusive in the treatment of their children. The four mothers portrayed here act as representatives of widespread variations in mothering. Yet, despite their differences, these mothers recognize the prevailing model of appropriate child rearing and have developed their views with reference to that model, as I have tried to show. Even the more widespread forms of individual differences among mothers, then, may hide basic underlying similarities. Further, both individual uniqueness and broad similarities can mask differences that are systematic for socially distinct *groups* of mothers. One central form of systematic differences among mothers follows class lines.[12]

Class Differences in Mothering

There are clearly noteworthy differences between the beliefs and practices of working-class and poor mothers, on the one side, and those of middle-class and upper-middle-class mothers, on the other. Given differences in their financial resources, their reference groups, and their cultural milieux, this is not surprising. The women in these two groups have different baseline standards for what "good" mothers should provide for their children as well as differential means and differing images of how to achieve what is best for them. For instance, although all these mothers want to spare their children future financial hardship, for working-class and poor mothers this leads to a tendency to stress their children's formal education, whereas middle-class mothers are more likely to be engaged in promoting their children's "self-esteem." In a connected way, working-class and poor mothers tend to emphasize giving children rules while middle-class mothers are busy providing their children with choices. And working-class and poor mothers are somewhat more likely to demand obedience from their children while their more well-to-do counterparts are more likely to negotiate with theirs.[13] But all these mothers, I will argue, share a set of fundamental assumptions about the importance of putting their children's needs first and dedicating themselves to providing what is best for their kids, as they understand it.

Eva is a working-class mom who lives with her husband and their two-year-old daughter on a military base. Her parents immigrated from Mexico when she was young, and both worked long hours on assembly lines while she was growing up. Eva is currently a clerical worker. Just as Mecca compares herself favorably with other welfare mothers, Eva compares herself favorably relative to other working-class mothers:

I think I'm a good mother because I sacrifice a lot for my daughter. I try to think of her future. And a lot of the things I see other people do, like, for instance, they'll go out to parties, get drunk, take drugs, and all that. My mom never did that, and I really appreciate that. I was never thrown anything in my face, whereas I know a lot of other kids, like my friends, they've been told, "Oh yeah, we've seen your mom at the bar." And I'm sure that didn't help their life at all.

. . . There are a lot of kids, like for instance, those gangs out there, whose moms are involved in drug dealing too, so they're one-hundred percent at fault for how their kids turn out. And the mothers are out there having twenty million boyfriends, when the girl or the boy goes out and gets pregnant or catches AIDS or something.

. . . There's these two women across the street. They don't work, they stay at home. I always say they rot. [She laughs.] They stay home and rot. They just sit out there in their lawn chairs. I mean their kids could be out running in the street and, ya know, what's the use? Their kids are out in the street and they don't go and get them.

For Eva, bad mothers are those who are too lazy or too preoccupied with drugs, alcohol, and boyfriends to properly supervise their kids.

Stephanie is an affluent mother who resides in a wealthy, gated community. (Her children are playing in the swimming pool as we talk and enjoy the magnificent view from her patio.) Her parents both worked in a law firm while she was growing up: her father as a professional, her mother as a clerical employee. Stephanie currently stays at home with her four children most of the time, although she is also involved in a vast number of organized volunteer activities. She tells me:

I try to always be with my friends that can relate to what I'm saying — not to the ones that have nannies and housekeepers and an eighteen-month-old and a four-year-old and all they can think about is going out and getting a job just so they have their own spending money. And yet you look at those children and you think, "Oh, they have everything." They can afford to go to good schools, they do neat things with their folks, but you see what I'm saying, it's the *look*, it's not really what's behind that.

. . . There's parents here that drop them off [at day care] at 6:30 in the morning and pick them up at 6:00 at night. And if you want to do that so you can drive around in a Volvo and take a vacation in Mexico, I think somebody really needs to step back and go, "What's important?"

. . . And here in this community, you're going to see that, because it's pretty affluent. Kids who are three years old and are telling their mothers they hate them, yet she doesn't stop to think, "Well, if I fired my nanny and stayed home, instead of running around to fashion shows, maybe I could make this better."

For Stephanie, bad mothers are those who evidently care more about maintaining the image of themselves and their children as members of the wealthy elite than about actually providing their kids with time and nurturance.

Stephanie and Eva's differing images of the "bad mother" reflect their distinct social worlds and the different cultural conceptions and normative standards connected to them. In Stephanie's world, it seems as if all women can afford to hire nannies and take trips to Mexico; she is therefore concerned with the "frivolous rich" who would ignore their children and focus their attention on fancy clothes, cars, and homes. For Eva, however, the world holds another set of dangers. Her concern is with the "promiscuous poor" who would ignore their children while they go out to get drunk, take drugs, and have sex. Stephanie and Eva are not unique. Many of the middle-class mothers I spoke with raised criticisms of mothers who left their kids at home with maids who "hardly speak English," who provided their children with too many Nintendo videos, and who packed their kids off to boarding school or summer camp and then "didn't even come pick them up — they sent their nanny to pick them up, because they're out to lunch." A good middle-class mother, I'm told, will spend time interacting with her children rather than attending fancy parties, will make sure her children's emotional needs are met before she concerns herself with plans for remodeling the kitchen, and will be there on time to pick up the kids each day. Many working-class and poor mothers, on the other hand, criticized mothers who took drugs, left their kids to play on dangerous streets alone, and spent their income so early in the month that they didn't have enough to feed the kids by the end of the month. Their baseline standard for a good mother was one who provided a hard-working role model, kept the kids clean and healthy, and bought shoes for the children before she bought things for herself.

In spite of the obvious disparity in reference groups and baseline standards, working-class and poor moms are far more likely to recognize the wealth, ideology, and practices of middle- and upper-middle-class mothers than the latter are to recognize and understand the life-styles of the poor and working classes. Almost no middle-class mothers mention those less financially fortunate than themselves when speaking of child rearing.[14] Working-class and poor mothers, on the other hand, repeatedly bring up images of wealthier families. Although they are unlikely to see such families in their own neighborhoods, the image of affluence (and the apparent happiness and comfort that attend it) is everywhere: in the news, on television, and in *Parenting* magazine as well as *Cosmopolitan*. This greater awareness means that most working-class and poor mothers hope that their own children will grow up to be part of such privileged families, even if they cannot imagine reaching such heights themselves.[15] And just as Eva would be pleased to hire the very same nannies that Stephanie scorns, imagining them as skilled nurturers and highly competent teachers far preferable to those at the military's subsidized day-care center where she now sends her daughter, most working-class and poor moms believe that nannies, maids, boarding schools, and summer camps would offer their kids much more than what they now receive. But such luxuries are so far beyond their budgets, so different from the practices they see in their neighborhoods, that they often seem nearly impossible to attain.

Wealthier mothers have the money and the access to transportation to send their children to tumbling classes, piano lessons, judo classes, swimming lessons, child psychologists, and, perhaps most crucially, to day-care centers, preschools, and private schools where the facilities are clean and bright, where the toys and games and instruction are carefully chosen, and where the teachers and caregivers are well trained. Laura, for instance, takes her ten-year-old daughter to dancing and etiquette classes, her nine-year-old son to soccer practice, and her five-year-old daughter to a therapist. As a homeroom mother, she also arranges school parties, sets up fund raisers, and provides gifts for her daughter's teacher. She has always hired someone to clean her home, and she currently has a live-in au pair; in the past she has had nannies. Her younger children attend an elite preschool; the older children go to private schools.

Lupe, unlike Laura, considers a trip to the grocery store a special outing for the kids; piano lessons would not even cross her mind. Even when free activities are available for the kids, there is always the problem of transportation. (Lupe does not have a car, and the public transportation system in her area is grossly inadequate.) And Lupe felt compelled to leave her last job when she discovered that the family caregiver she used was not only neglecting the children but physically abusing them as well:

> She was not feeding them when they were hungry, she was not giving them anything to drink when they were thirsty. . . . I found out, I mean, she abused my kids. I mean, right out hit them, bruised two of them once, and said, "Oh, they fell." And then to find out that she threatened to hit them again if they told on her!
>
> I'd say that the worst thing about this is that it was a family member — not my personal family, but a part of the family. [This abuse was] something that I never wanted my kids to experience, because I did. . . . It took everything inside me not to do damage or harm to the person who hurt my kids.

After this experience, Lupe felt that she had no option but to return to welfare; if she couldn't trust a family member, she argued, she couldn't trust anyone. Besides, that particular caregiver was the only one she could afford and the only one located on an available bus line.[16] Surely such financial difficulties and the problems that attend them interfere with the ability of working-class and poor mothers to provide for their children as they would like.

All mothers are eager to spare their children from a life of financial hardship. But their perceptions of the proper road to achieving this tend to differ according to their class background. One of the primary goals of working-class and poor mothers is to provide their children with what they understand as a high-quality education. Over and over I hear these refrains: "I'd like to see him get a really good education, be really smart"; "the main thing is education, so she doesn't have to struggle"; and "I just hope they just do school and education good." Not only are these mothers interested in seeing to it that their children get good grades in school, but they regularly attempt to prepare for this process early on. One mother speaks of how she and her husband had been "pinching pennies" to save for their son's college education ever since he was born. Another tells me she had read a book on the importance of educating children from the moment of conception, teaching them to value classical music and "how to read, and to recognize different languages, colors, sounds" while they are still in the womb; she played classical music and talked to her belly throughout her last two pregnancies and is convinced that this is the best piece of advice she's ever received. Another mother had heard that it was good to use flash cards with young children (telling them, "That's a frog, that's a barn, this is a car") when they were barely old enough to speak; although she hasn't had a chance to use these methods, she feels sure they're a very good idea. Yet another tells me:

> The best advice that I did get [was] from this one lady (only because I seen her daughter, the outcome). [It was] that she read to her daughters when they were real small, like Angela's age, one-and-a-half, two, three. And they grew up to be, you know, really smart and getting high grades. And also, making sure that they always listen to classical music.

The child's education, in terms of both formal schooling and the acquisition of what Bourdieu (1977, 1984) calls the "cultural capital" that comes with knowledge of such things as classical music, is a primary concern for many poor and working-class mothers. They see this as the most direct route for their children to achieve middle-class status.

More affluent mothers, on the other hand, almost never bring up the importance of the child's schooling. Although one would guess that education would be less of an issue for the very rich, whose children's future financial security is assured by inherited wealth, most middle-class mothers surely recognize that higher education is key to achieving or maintaining middle-class status. Numerous studies document the middle-class interest in preparing for and financing their children's schooling (e.g., Bourdieu 1977; Bourdieu and Passeron 1977; Carnoy and Levin 1985; Lareau 1987). But very few of these mothers explicitly stress formal education in the context of discussions about child rearing. One might argue that, for these mothers, a quality education for their children is not the focus of explicit commentary precisely because it is *assumed.*[17]

Middle-class mothers, therefore, place their emphasis elsewhere. Although all mothers seem to want their kids to grow up with a strong sense of self-worth, middle-class mothers are especially likely to stress the child's psychological development, particularly the promotion of self-esteem. Stephanie, for instance, proclaims that her major goal is to give her children "healthy self-esteem"; with that, she says, "they've probably got it made in the shade," whereas without it, "they're crippled, or limited." For mothers of all classes, promoting a sense of self-worth entails loving children and giving them a sense that they're more important than new cars and fancy clothes. But for middle-class and upper-middle-class moms, it also often means something more. Time and time again, the importance of giving the child "choices" came up as the basis for the development of such self-esteem. One professional-class mother told me that the most important piece of advice she had ever received was with reference to "the importance of giving your child some control for their sense of self and, you know, to give them choices." Another put it this way:

> I'd like them to have a really good sense of self; I'd like them to feel really comfortable in the fact that they are who they are, they're independent. I'd like them to see that there's a lot of choices you can make in your life.

These sentiments were echoed consistently:

> I give [my daughter] a lot more ability to have choices than I think I was given. I don't give her global control, but I give her a choice. Like, "here's three things." Sometimes it works, sometimes it doesn't. But I'm trying to give her a sense of herself. And I want to give her the ability to have some control.

The connections between offering choices, promoting self-esteem, and furthering a sense of independence are clear. For these mothers, self-esteem is related, implicitly or explicitly, to self-motivation, self-direction, self-reliance, and self-assertion. The importance of promoting these characteristics is, in turn, connected to the importance of preparing these kids to become successful members of the higher classes—initiating them into the experience of independent decision making that will theoretically serve them well as future entrepreneurs, corporate managers, and professionals (see especially Kohn 1969).

Related to mothers' attempts to spare their children from a life of hardship is the fact that working-class and poor mothers seem to be more likely than their middle- and upper-middle-class counterparts to believe that other people know more about child rearing than they do. Eva, for instance, thinks of those who write child-care books as experts possessing a knowledge that is superior to her own. She explains: "They've had a lot of training, and schooling. So I feel good about opening a book. You know, it's proven so." Other working-class and poor mothers may not be so certain that expert advice is proven truth, but they are more likely than middle-class moms to listen to radio and television programs that focus on child rearing and to see these, as well as the manuals, as an important form of self-education.[18] A number of poor and working-class mothers also consider their day-care providers as important sources of advice. Janet, for instance, considers her day-care provider as her *primary* source of advice:

> She's the one who lets me know how [my son is] doing, what she's teaching him. She always gives me ideas. I come to drop him off and she's playing videos on TV, children's videos, you know. And I always ask her, "Where do you get those?" Those are neat. But I never buy them because I know he's always there and he's got them. She always gives me ideas about him being sick, what to use. She knows all about different kinds of medicines and their side effects. It's amazing to me. I mean, I totally trust her. She lets me know. She taught him how to use a spoon. Things that I just don't have time to do now. . . . She's doing this kind of stuff with him, teaching him things, flash cards, that kind of thing.

By contrast, no professional-class mothers describe their children's paid caregivers as more competent and knowledgeable than themselves.[19] In the same terms, no middle-class mothers mentioned their admiration for working-class child-rearing methods. Yet many working-class and poor mothers think of the wealthier moms they know as role models. For instance: "I had this one lady friend, her kids are the best kids. They come from a very wealthy family and the kids are just normal kids. They're real well-mannered kids. I've got a lot of respect for her ways of doing stuff." Such mothers thus express their desire to learn about child rearing from those they see as more educated and more financially secure than themselves. And by doing so, such mothers indicate an implicit lack of confidence in their own child-rearing abilities as well as the pressure they feel toward more intensive (middle-class) methods.

A final difference in the child-rearing ideologies of these two groups of mothers, a difference that is connected to all the others, involves their attitudes about discipline. Although there is no class difference among the mothers I spoke with in terms of the number who say they spank their children, middle-class and upper-middle class mothers are much more likely to emphasize that they spank "occasionally," only spank "on the butt," reserve spanking for "special circumstances" ("when they've just run out in the street or something"), and are always careful to be "in control" when they spank their kids.[20] These same mothers are also slightly more likely than working-class and poor women to say they use time-out as a primary form of discipline. This method, in turn, is connected to the stronger tendency of middle-class mothers to focus on negotiating and reasoning with their children, whereas working-class and poor mothers are somewhat more likely to emphasize the importance of giving their children set rules. The middle-class mothers' focus on time-outs and negotiation is also connected to their stronger emphasis on giving the child independence-fostering choices, including choices regarding forms of punishment and reward.

These class distinctions with reference to discipline also come out in what these two groups of women understand as the difference between a "good child" and a "bad child." The majority of mothers tend to emphasize that "there really is no such thing as a bad child." Yet working-class and poor mothers are far more likely than their wealthier counterparts to say that a good child is one who is "obedient," who "minds adults," who "listens," and who is "compliant." More precisely, over half of the working-class and poor mothers I interviewed thought that obedience and compliance were valuable traits in children, while less than one-fifth of middle-class mothers mentioned these as important or desirable characteristics. One working-class mother, for instance, had seen Brazelton on television and was appalled by his remarks regarding a child whom she felt was "bratty" and misbehaved. Brazelton, she told me, had advised the child's mother to allow her son to continue in his current behavior since it was the child's "choice" of behavior that mattered. This working-class mother found such advice simply outrageous; "obedience," she said, is the mark of a good child. She continued:

> I believe in spanking. When [my daughter is] demanding, or when she talks back, when she says "I want," we use the number system. If you get to three, and she hasn't done what she's told, you have to spank her. Just one, two, or three times.

The stress on set rules and external discipline can be explained in part by the fact that providing choices and engaging in negotiation are luxuries of time and money that many working-class and poor mothers simply cannot afford.

But there is another reason for this method that was made explicit by the following working-class mom:

> Discipline, that's very important to me. Because if children can't respect their own mother and father, they're certainly not going to respect a boss, or an employer, or the law. And that's important.

Teaching their children to respect adults, listen to adults, and obey adults is for many working-class and poor mothers the best way they know to prepare the children for their futures. Given that these kids will ultimately have fewer opportunities than their wealthier counterparts to make choices and assert their individuality and independence, the strategies of some less financially fortunate mothers make a good deal of sense (see esp. Kohn 1969).

These differences with regard to discipline mean that the child-rearing methods favored by working-class and poor mothers are less labor-intensive than those of their middle- and upper-middle-class counterparts. An obedient and compliant child, after all, is less demanding than an assertive and independent one. Establishing a system of standardized and strictly enforced rules requires less time and individualized attention than carefully providing the child with a set of bounded choices and negotiating with the child to establish the rules for proper behavior and appropriate punishment.[21] The time and labor that working-class and poor mothers thus "save," however, is replaced with a whole range of broader financial and practical sacrifices that these mothers make on behalf of their children — sacrifices that many middle-class mothers would find hard to imagine.

Piano lessons are different from bus rides to the grocery store. And demanding compliance is different from negotiating choices. But these differences between upper- and lower-class mothers should not obscure their common recognition of the larger ideology of intensive child rearing and their shared commitment to good mothering.[22] When Stephanie and Eva talk about bad mothers, for instance, they are both talking about mothers who neglect their children — mothers who do not provide their children with sufficient nurture, sufficient time, and appropriate role models. When Lupe left her paid job and returned to welfare so that her children would not be abused in day care, she was surely making a sacrifice for her children that more than matched the time, money, and energy required to provide for swimming lessons and Little League participation. It is also not difficult see that the middle-class mothers' focus on the child's self-esteem is derived from the very same interest in seeing to the child's future welfare as the working-class and poor mothers' focus on providing for the child's education ("so they won't have to struggle"). Both groups of mothers focus on methods of discipline that they believe will assure their child's future happiness and success. Finally, when poor and working-class mothers look to those they think are more educated than themselves for suggestions on how to raise their children, they are simply struggling to be good mothers and often end up with much the same ideas about appropriate child rearing as middle-class mothers do. In short, class differences in mothering, while significant, do not pose a serious challenge to the dominance of the ideology of intensive mothering.

Mothers sort through the mail of available child-rearing ideas. This sorting process involves not only the explicit recommendations of friends, family, pediatricians, teachers, and the best-selling advisers but also the implicit guidelines for appropriate mothering that are disseminated by the wider culture. The ways that mothers catalog, rank, and interpret this information is, as I have argued, closely connected to their social position, cultural milieu, and practical circumstances. This diversity adds up to both individual and group differences in mothering. And these differences demonstrate that mothers are agents rather than automatons; they actively engage in producing and reproducing, shaping and reshaping, the ideology of appropriate motherhood.

Generally speaking, however, the ways mothers reshape this ideology do not erase the cultural contradictions of motherhood. All the mothers I spoke to feel pressure to live up to the image of a good mother, all of them recognize the central tenets of intensive mothering, and none would seek to transform that ideology in the name of a competitive pursuit of personal gain. For instance, one could argue that middle- and upper-middle-class mothers have the most to gain from downplaying their commitment to their children, since the outside world offers them interesting and prestigious work should they seek it, and since their financial resources make possible a life of relative comfort should they choose to stay at home. For working-class and poor women, on the other hand, mothering may be, relatively speaking, one of the more meaningful and socially valued tasks in which they might engage. Yet, both groups of women demonstrate an equal commitment to serious mothering. And, although the day-to-day practices of mothering may be less physically and financially draining for middle-class mothers, the child-rearing ideology of these women includes techniques that are actually more labor-intensive than those of their working-class counterparts. And those individual mothers whose past and present beliefs and circumstances have led them to reject portions of the ideology of intensive mothering, like Margaret and Mecca, continue to find it necessary to develop arguments that legitimate and explain their rejection, to feel the strain to place their children's needs above their own, and to point out the ways in which they do live up to the tenets of that dominant ideology. In short, mothers are faced with a massive amount of information and advice on appropriate child rearing, much of it recommends intensive mothering, and this fact fundamentally shapes the way mothers think about mothering.

5

Intensive Mothering
Women's Work on Behalf of the Sacred Child

Just as the differences among individual mothers should not mask the systematic differences among groups of women, so the class-based differences among mothers should not overshadow those ideas that most mothers hold in common. And those shared ideas, I will show, are grounded in the ideology of intensive mothering.

As I have argued, the ideology of intensive mothering and the extent to which mothers attempt to live up to it are responsible for the cultural contradictions of motherhood. The same society that disseminates an ideology urging mothers to give unselfishly of their time, money, and love on behalf of sacred children simultaneously valorizes a set of ideas that runs directly counter to it, one emphasizing impersonal relations between isolated individuals efficiently pursuing their personal profit. In other words, the cultural model of a rationalized market society coexists in tension with the cultural model of intensive motherhood. And this tension increasingly influences the lives of individual mothers as more and more of them enter the paid workforce and therefore participate directly in the world of the rationalized market. Yet, as I have shown, the history of child-rearing ideas and the words of today's child-rearing advisers seem to demonstrate that the more powerful and all-encompassing the rationalized market becomes, the more powerful becomes its ideological opposition in the logic of intensive mothering.

But the history of child-rearing ideas, the recommendations of best-selling child-rearing manuals, and the portraits of mothers I have provided thus far are not sufficient to demonstrate the persistence of this tension into the present day. Since we know that there are differences among mothers and that not all mothers heed the totality of the advice they receive, the extent to which the ideology of intensive mothering is internalized by mothers in general remains to be established.[1] That is the primary purpose of this chapter.

The evidence presented in this chapter does not constitute absolute proof that the ideology of intensive mothering is a shared one. But when combined with the evidence presented thus far, it makes a strong case for this position. The sample of mothers on which I draw, while not a national or systematically random sample, is made up of mothers who come from widely different backgrounds and who are now living in widely different social circumstances. Given this diversity, the consistency in their understandings of mothering is striking. These mothers provide a detailed elaboration of the ideology of intensive motherhood, and they do so with force, conviction, and even passion. Furthermore, the logic of appropriate child rearing they lay out closely matches the logic found in the millions of advice manuals that have been purchased by mothers across the nation. And both the advice in these manuals and the reasoning of mothers are stunningly consistent with the step-by-step historical emergence of the ideology of intensive child rearing.

In the following pages I attempt to tease out the logic of that ideology as contemporary mothers understand it.[2] As you listen to these mothers, it may seem at times that they are simply speaking in clichés, trite truisms, and all too well-worn phrases. But clichés and truisms should not be underestimated or discounted — they often highlight recurring cultural themes. Ultimately, our familiarity with many of the phrases used by these mothers is a measure of the deep and pervasive power of the ideology of intensive mothering and the extent to which all of us recognize at least portions of its logic.

The Responsibility of Individual Mothers

Christina is a working-class mother with two young children. In an arrangement that is an exception to the rule, her husband stays at home to care for the kids while Christina goes out to work at a full-time job. Yet even though she is the sole breadwinner, Christina is sure that the children are still primarily her responsibility.

Christina started working outside the home because her husband had quit his job in a fit of anger and had trouble finding another one. She was able to get a job that paid "a lot of money," so, as she puts it, "I really didn't have much of a choice; I didn't feel as if I had any other options." In fact, she admits, the time she spent as a stay-at-home mother nearly drove her "out of her mind"; she was quite happy to go back to work, to talk to people, and to use her brain. But she also emphasizes that she would have stayed home indefinitely if her husband hadn't left his job. She agrees with her husband that staying home to care for the kids is basically her obligation. She explains:

> If anyone cooks, I cook. And if anyone cleans, it's me, although I insist that the kids help me. So I still have all of the traditional roles, I just don't do a very good job at them 'cause I don't care. [She laughs.] I'm just doing what [my husband] expects.

Christina not only does all the cooking and cleaning but also visits the kids on her lunch break each day and takes responsibility for them in the evenings and on weekends. Although she clearly works a double shift, she tells me she is happy with this arrangement. It keeps her husband from feeling overburdened, it provides the family with medical benefits and some financial security, and it allows her to get out of the house. Nonetheless, she tells me, "The only reason I am working is *money*. Because, if that weren't so, I would have the obligation to stay home with my kids. That's just the way it is." Women's first obligation is to the children and the family, Christina believes; mothers should work for pay only if family finances absolutely require it.

Although Christina's situation is unusual and Christina herself maintains what seems to be, by most mothers' standards, an exaggerated sense of her own responsibility, her story points to the widely shared belief that women are primarily responsible for the care of home and children. In mothers' own accounts, they take primary responsibility for *every* child-rearing duty — including watching, feeding, disciplining, cleaning up after, and playing with children — in well over half the families in my sample. Mothers take primary responsibility for feeding and cleaning up after the children in four-fifths of these households. Those duties not performed primarily by the mother are generally reported either as "shared equally" with male partners[3] or as done by paid workers or other household members. There is not a single household in which fathers or male adults take responsibility for all child-rearing tasks, and men rarely take primary responsibility for any single child-rearing duty. Even nannies, housekeepers, au pairs, day-care providers, and others are more likely than male household members to be the main persons looking after the child. These findings become even more striking when it is noted that the mothers in my sample, on average, spend *four times* the hours men do as the primary caregivers. Specifically, the average number of hours that these mothers said they take primary responsibility for watching over the kids each weekday was 8.9. Their male partners, on the other hand, do the same for an average of 1.9 hours each day. One national study of married couples confirms this disparity: on average, mothers' caregiving accounts for 74 percent of the total hours spent in direct child care (excluding the housework and planning associated with child care), and fathers' caregiving accounts for the remaining 26 percent (Ishii-Kuntz and Coltraine 1992).[4]

Although nonparental caregivers are more likely than fathers to take responsibility for child rearing, few mothers consider such arrangements an acceptable solution. Older siblings, who in other times and places served as central alternate caregivers, are not considered viable, since most mothers feel older children should be at least fourteen before being entrusted with the care of younger children for any significant period. In addition, by the time these siblings are teenagers, most of them are at school much of the day and spend their remaining time (appropriately, their mothers say) in leisure activities, doing homework, or working for pay.[5] Adult relatives are sometimes acceptable substitute caregivers, but mothers do not always consider relatives competent caregivers, and also worry about asking them to do the job for free at the same time they fear they would transgress implicit rules for appropriate familial behavior if they paid them.

Nannies, au pairs, women who provide family day care, and employees of day-care centers are not considered wholly suitable substitutes for mothers either.[6] While in many cases such caregivers spend nearly as many hours with the children as mothers do, and many mothers think this is fine, almost all mothers also feel the need to compensate by ensuring that they themselves spend a good deal of "quality time" with their children (as Jacqueline and Rachel, for instance, testify). More important, as several mothers told me, paid caregivers can never *fully* substitute for mothers because they simply don't have the commitment to and love for the children that mothers have. As one mother put it,

> Yeah, I think I'd be the best one to take care of them. Even with their dad, I think I'm the best one. I think I'm the only one that would be able to give them a fair yes or no and be able to explain why yes and why no. As far as anybody else, *it's not their blood,* it's not theirs, their children, in order to take out the time to provide the yeses or the nos or the maybes or the playtime or the time playing when you're feeding them or choosing what they're going to wear to make them look nice, you know.
>
> I mean, you can pay somebody to do it, but to them it's a job, and it's like, "as long as they're clean." I know people that have taken care of kids and leave them in a corner watching TV all day. *They're not worried about the child, they're worried about the money.* So it's like, I think I'm the best one to take care of them. (Emphasis mine)

Blood and bonding, it seems, are thicker than money.

Mothers tell me that the only person other than the mother who *potentially* has the necessary commitment, love, and time for the children is the father. Yet not one of the mothers in my sample, including Christina, suggested that fathers should give up a paying job to stay home with the children. Most mothers *do,* on the other hand, argue that fathers should take more responsibility for caring for the kids than they currently do.[7] At the same time, however, most mothers also believe that there are problems with asking men to do more.

First, leaving the kids at home with their male partner, some women say, can be dangerous to the physical health and emotional well-being of the child. For instance:

> Little things happen when I leave [my daughter] with [my husband], and it's not really like he's such a good baby-sitter. What's the point of leaving her with him if he's not going to treat her right? . . . She said that "daddy tickled my stomach and when I hit him for tickling my stomach, he spanked me." Now that sounds like child abuse. I know that he would like to spank her, but he knows that as long as I'm around he's not going to spank her.

Unwarranted spankings and unsolicited touching are not the only things mothers worry about. Just as Cindy thought her husband was dangerous when he was taking "speed balls," another mother, fearing for her children, left her husband because "he was doing undesirable things, drugs and stuff." Yet another mother was forced to change her address in order to hide her children from their physically abusive father. She told me, "Better a bad father than no father at all just doesn't cut it with me."[8]

But, more often than not, the primary reason mothers hesitate to ask their partners to do much more of the child rearing is not so much that they consider these men dangerous but that they consider them incompetent.[9] A lot of men, it seems, can't handle the simplest required child-rearing tasks: "The way [my husband] takes care of [our son] is, he's like, I think he's *mindless,* to tell you the truth. He won't wipe his face off, he won't wash his face, he won't put his shoes on. I have to tell him to feed him or whatever." Sometimes, after a mother has asked a man to watch the kids, she discovers that his way of watching them is far from what she had in mind. For instance:

> Sometimes when I come home I can tell that [the kids have] been doing things that they weren't supposed to, like they've been in the bathroom, and things that they've gotten into, they've gotten hold of a pen and I see coloring on the chair, or somewhere. [Their father] wasn't watching them, maybe involved in a program or something like that. And that scares me because if he's not watching them right here, what if they go outside or on the street or, you know?

Men often seem to ignore the kids in this way, being too preoccupied with other things to pay enough attention:

> Well, I think men are different than women in how they take care of children. I think men tend to have their own schedule. He'll finish reading his paper, or he'll do, oh, he just doesn't respond as quickly as I respond, I find.

Other men, though they might do well enough at watching the kids and responding to them, are far less likely to clean up after the kids. This, in the long run, can make the mother's job even harder:

> Men. They're just different. I swear to you. Because you leave and you're gone for a day and it's like a *bombshell* hit. You pay for that too — you spend the next ten hours trying to get everything back together — because you have your way of doing it. That's not to say that it's the right way. What you want is you want them to do it *your* way. It's not gonna happen.

Connected to these problems is the complaint that even if male partners are willing to help, frequently they must be told precisely what to do. One mother, for instance, says that she needs to prepare an itemized list for her husband every time she leaves the house, spelling out just what has to be done. Another mother complains that men seem so blind to what needs to be done that it is often easier just to do the job oneself:

> There's so many things that I have to be doing that I wish that [my husband] could see without being told what I need. He hasn't been educated as a mother. . . . So I end up doing a lot of stuff myself rather than having to say, "Look, pick up." It's because he doesn't see it. And it's hard for women to understand that, because we were trained to see what other people's needs are. You're trained in taking care . . . so that's where the frustration is.

One of the explanations for men's incompetence, then, is that they simply aren't trained in "taking care" the way women are. And this lack of training is perhaps connected to mothers' observation that men are not exposed to the knowledge of appropriate child rearing that comes from reading books and talking to other mothers. For example:

> Men just don't show the same concern [with child rearing]. I don't know if it's that we [mothers] read more books, or we talk to more moms, [or that] we have more opportunity to talk at schools and stuff. Yeah, I think he's as concerned, I just don't think he's as on top of it.

Being "on top of it," according to mothers, requires more than knowing how to dress the kids and clean up after the kids. It means understanding the proper techniques for raising a child. In other words, at times it's not that men don't watch the children or suitably attend to the children's physical requirements but that they just don't use the right methods to foster the children's development. This, of course, is the case with the father who just reads his newspaper and fails to respond to the child's questions and concerns. And this sentiment is echoed by many mothers. For instance:

> [My husband will] just watch [the children] to make sure things don't go wrong. But he doesn't *interact*. When I'm gone and I'll come home, he'll be watching TV. I like to do stuff with them. And now [the kids], they know, they'll say [referring to the television], "That's not good for kids, Dad."

To men's incompetence, their lack of training in taking care, and their lack of knowledge regarding the best techniques, mothers add two additional characterizations. First, most men simply do not understand that raising children actually requires both a good deal of knowledge and a lot of work. And, second, many men do not recognize that acquiring this knowledge and engaging in this work could theoretically be considered the responsibility of *both* parents. This mother sums up these two points:

> I think [my husband] loves [our daughter], but I don't think he feels all that *responsible* for her, which sounds a little bizarre. I don't think he really feels like "How she turns out is up to me." I think he probably feels that she'll just *grow*. I don't think he feels like it's something that you really need to work at all that much. I guess he's interested, but he's not concerned. I think he figures that it's something that *I'm* doing, that it's my job and I'm doing that.

Whatever the reasons, mothers "know" that most men are simply less attentive to the needs of children than women are. And this means that asking a male partner to take more responsibility not only feels a bit like beating one's head against a wall but also that, even if the wall should give a little, it still *behaves* like a wall when it goes about its task.

Of course, it might be argued that mothers could learn a thing or two from the relaxed attitude of men toward child rearing. One mother actually suggested this:

> My husband was home on disability for a while . . . and he would leave [our daughter] in day care and go to the movies. I would *never* in my life think of doing that. It would just never have crossed my mind to do something like that. And I really thought that was a *horrible* thing to be doing. But when I think about it, I don't know what's so horrible about it. For mothers, it's true, you can never do enough for your kids.

At the same time that this mother implies that it might make sense for women to leave the kids with someone else occasionally and just go to the movies, she also suggests that the idea of putting the child aside in order to make more time for themselves seems to cross mothers' minds less frequently than it does fathers'. And when mothers do think such thoughts, they are far less likely to take them seriously.

This phenomenon is related to what Goodman (1990) has called the "guilt gap." No matter how much time fathers spend watching the children, they almost never spend as much time worrying about them as mothers do. Mothers in general are well aware of this gap:

> [My husband] doesn't do much of [the child rearing]. I worry about the children, he worries about work. . . . [And] I do it better than he does. I think most mothers would say that. He doesn't think as much about the consequences of what he does. He just does whatever he feels like at the moment.

Mothers worry about every consequence, while fathers, they claim, simply do what they feel like doing at the moment. Another mother reiterates:

> See, my kids are my world. I would not do anything without thinking of them first. I think a lot of men do, think more about themselves than what they're doing or leaving behind. . . . Not that it's the right thing to do. But, you know, once in a while, I'll feel like I want to just walk out and leave for a couple of hours. I got to find a baby-sitter. If [men] want to walk out, it's like, "I'll be back." They don't have to think about who's gonna take care of the kids.

This guilt gap is described with elegant simplicity, I think, by yet another mother: "I never feel free of my kids, where[as] I think that's very different from how the dad thinks of it. 'Cause when he goes, he's gone. And when he comes home, he's home." Fathers, in other words, can go to the movies and not worry about what they're leaving behind, because they know that mothers are in charge of the worrying. They simply go and enjoy the movie. Mothers, on the other hand, worry about whether it's okay to go to the movies and leave the kids at home, they worry about who will care for the children while they're at the movies, and frequently they worry about how well the kids are being cared for as they watch the movie.

In sum, though most mothers want their male partners to do more of the child rearing, they also worry that men don't know how to do it right, simply can't do it right, or are unwilling to do it right. These complaints point, in part, to mothers' sense of what the right kind of child rearing would look like. And in this mothers demonstrate that they accept many of the tenets of intensive parenting. The injustice, then, is that men apparently have not internalized the same logic.

At the same time that most mothers demonstrate an implicit resentment of the inequity in child-rearing abilities and responsibilities, many of these same mothers also seem to want to minimize or legitimate these problems. Even if they are otherwise dissatisfied with the fact that child rearing is not shared equally or undertaken with the same level of commitment and competence, other contingencies keep women from fully expressing this resentment or lead them to bury it under a list of reasons why they should be grateful for whatever help they do receive.[10] Listen, for instance, to this mother as she wends her way from an expression of resentment to an expression of gratitude:

> Sometimes [my husband is] more of a hindrance than a help. Basically because he's still a kid himself. He's spoiled, extremely spoiled. I don't think he could function, I honestly don't think he could function without me. He's not a very strong person. . . .
>
> [But] he does help me a lot, especially when I'm sick. You know, most men will say, "Get up off your ass, I don't care if you're sick, I'm hungry, feed me" [or] "the kids are crying, change them!" Any time I've honestly been sick, he's cleaned the house, he's taken care of the kids.[11]

Strategies for downplaying gender inequities in child rearing take a number of forms. Some mothers (especially stay-at-home mothers) will simply accept that child rearing is not something their male partners want to be involved in:

> It's not his thing. And we knew that going into parenthood. He was greatly ambivalent. He has much less patience, he gets tired. He's a lot less tolerant of noise and chaos. When he comes home from work he wants it quiet.

Other mothers who are willing to accept that it's simply "not his thing" sometimes conclude with, "After all, he's the breadwinner," or note, "He's so busy, when would he find the time?" Some mothers emphasize how their husbands provide them with emotional support, even if these men do not take much practical responsibility. Some insist that they should be happy that their husbands are at least understanding; recognizing that mothering takes time, such men don't complain about unwashed dishes and the like:

> Of course I wish [my husband would] help more. But he never complains if he's getting leftovers, and he never complains if I haven't made anything; he never complains about any of that. He's wonderful. I don't hear that the house is dirty. I don't hear that. I should be grateful about that.

But the largest proportion of legitimations of child-rearing inequities focus not on how men are incompetent or how they are bad fathers but on how they have a different *approach* to child rearing. As it turns out, the form this difference takes is rather consistent. The same woman who spoke of the bombshell that hit her home whenever her husband watched the kids later commented:

> Sometimes [my husband] does [child rearing] better [than I do]. Because *he's not bothered by the other things.* If lunch is all over the table, it doesn't matter

to him. If the toys are all over, he doesn't care. . . . I think he probably is able to enjoy that time much more than I because he's not obsessed with those other things that aren't that important. (Emphasis mine)

It is this same lack of obsessiveness that leaves men, I'm told, better equipped to play with the kids, while women do the other caretaking tasks:

[My husband] does it in a different way, but not bad. . . . I wouldn't know how to play with [my daughter], but I know how to take care of her when she's sick. So it sort of balances out. Sometimes I'm the taking care and he's the playing with.

Legitimations that focused on men's relaxed attitude, their playfulness, and their spontaneity were numerous. These two mothers provide further examples:

—There's some things that [my husband] does much better than I do, and there's some things that I do much better than he does. He's the one who introduces all the fun and spontaneity. In terms of taking the time to read books about how to do [child rearing] and, um, really thinking about it and those things, no. I mean he doesn't take the time.
—I think [my husband] probably does it better than I do. He plays chess with [our older son] for hours on end. But he is more relaxed about it, about his day, because I still feel the obligation, if I stay home all day, to make something to eat, to clean up, do the wash, whatever. He doesn't feel that way, so he's kind of free.

Connected to all this is the argument that since fathers generally don't spend as much time with the children as mothers do, they tend to take a more relaxed approach to child rearing:

I think [my husband] does more fun stuff, he's playful that way. . . . It's like anything, when you're with somebody constantly, you tend to get a little short with them or whatever. Since he doesn't spend as much time with them, he's fresher, he has a fresher outlook.[12]

This playfulness, this fresher outlook, of course, could well be tied to the same lax attitude that allows men to virtually ignore the kids when there are other, more interesting or desirable things to do. An observer might argue that fathers get to have all the fun while mothers are left with all the dirty work. But when mothers are focused on burying their resentment, these connections are not made.

There are probably a number of related reasons that women use such strategies. First, many mothers love their male partners and therefore do not want to paint them in a negative way. Second, since women generally have the sense that most husbands do not help out in child rearing, they are genuinely grateful when their *own* mates help out in some way. Further, in the context of a society that has limited women's access to prestige, mother's special competence in raising kids provides them with a position of honor within the household. Finally, one needs to recognize that some of these women may fear that their marriages will be threatened if they refuse to do the larger share of domestic chores. And most women are well aware that in cases of divorce it is usually mothers who end up with the primary financial responsibility for the kids. To maintain their sanity and their financial security, therefore, it is not surprising that many women search for ways to live with any resentment they feel regarding child-rearing inequities.[13]

Mothers know they do more of the child care, they know they do more of the worrying, and they know they are more competent than men when it comes to raising children. But many are not entirely sure why this is so. Many women speak as if this arrangement is simply natural or is "just the way things are." But it is hard to know whether this attitude means that women's predominant role in child rearing is genetic, traditional, or simply correct.[14] Some mothers seem to argue that much of this is based in male domination, but many also know that they feel a deep commitment to their children and that they do not experience this feeling as something men impose upon them. Is this commitment a matter of socialization or is it natural? The following mother, like others, expresses some uncertainty, switching from an argument regarding learned behavior to one based in biology:

> For most women you get all this modeling from watching your mother, you just pay attention to that more, for whatever reasons, because you're told to. And I also have to say that raising a girl and having her best friend be a boy and watching the two of them, I think there's something innate about the differences in their interests, because it's so dramatic. And the child rearing is not that different, that I can tell.

For many mothers it seems difficult to separate the nature from the nurture, perhaps in part because the process of socialization begins so early. But determining whether women's responsibility for parenting is a matter of domination, learned behavior, or genetics does not seem like such a crucial question in their daily lives. What's important is that it is consistent. They may not like it, but it's the way things are — mothers *do* take primary responsibility for raising the children, and for doing it right.

One final example of this sense of responsibility is to be found in mothers' responses to what was at the time of my interviews a prominent national news story about the serial killer Jeffrey Dahmer, who dismembered and ate the bodies of his young victims after he murdered them. The mothers I talked to regularly brought up this case, unsolicited. Some women used it to underline their worries about protecting their children in a violent and dangerous world. Just as often, however, their central concern was with the killer's mother, how she might be feeling, and what she might have done to prevent her son's crimes. One woman, Anne, echoing the sentiments of others, commented:

> You know, the fellow on the television who cut up all those people and everything. First of all I thought how his mother must be feeling to know that her son has done this. And then, a few thoughts later, I thought, what happened in his childhood? I didn't really blame her so much but I did think what could have possibly happened in his childhood to have turned this way? And if nothing happened, then are human beings really born with the capacity to do what he's doing?
>
> But [his mother] says she still loves him. I don't blame her, I'd probably still love [my daughter] if she did that too. But, my gosh, I start thinking, gee, maybe I should have put her to bed at eight o'clock every night [to keep her out of trouble].

Although Anne asks herself how Dahmer's mother feels, she doesn't ask, "How does his father feel?" or "How does his former day-care provider feel?" She assumes that the murderer's mother is the person most committed to this boy-now-man and most deeply tied to him emotionally. This assumed commitment and bond account for Anne's belief that his mother would feel at least somewhat responsible for Jeffrey's actions as an adult. And when Anne wonders what happened in Dahmer's childhood and whether she should put her daughter to bed earlier, she seems to suggest that mothers not only feel responsible but actually *are* at least partly responsible for the future actions of their children.[15]

In all this, mothers indicate that they understand very well this aspect of the ideology of intensive motherhood. Although fathers, paid caregivers, and others may help out, in the end it is mothers who are held responsible and who understand themselves as accountable not only for keeping the kids fed and housed but also for shaping the kinds of adults those children will become. And in keeping with this sense of responsibility are the methods mothers use to ensure the child's proper development.

Intensive Methods

No other question I asked of these mothers evoked as deep an emotional response as the question "How would you feel if you never had children?" None of my prior research prepared me for the intensity of feeling mothers expressed at the mere thought of not having children. Nearly one-quarter of the women I talked to actually cried when I asked them this question.[16] And the answers of nearly all mothers — "lonely," "empty," "missing something" — were stunningly consistent.[17]

Elaborating on their feelings of emptiness, of loneliness, of missing something, mothers point to a number of factors. Sometimes mothers associate these feelings with their desire to "make a mark on the earth" and to "create an extension of themselves and their love." More often, these feelings are said to be connected to the importance of creating a family. For instance:

> I've always wanted to be a mother and I don't think the thought has ever crossed my mind of not having children. And I think, if I didn't, something would be missing. I don't know, but I feel like that was such a big part of my life as a child, always watching my brothers and sisters and always a baby in the house. . . . Just that sense of family, it's very important to me.

Creating a family, it seems, means creating a set of relationships that are close, warm, loving, and meant to last. This in turn is associated, on the one hand, with what appears to be a longing to re-create one's own childhood as it was or should have been and, on the other, with an attempt to avoid the sense of isolation and loneliness that many mothers imagine they would experience if they grew older without having established a family.

For a number of mothers, having a child is not just a means of creating a family in general, it is specifically a way to have someone in particular to fully love and nurture. In this form of elaboration on the sense of emptiness, the something that is "missing" is the practice of "doing a lot of taking care of another person." In the words of another mother, "I just feel like I'm a nurturing person, so it's important to have someone to nurture."

Implied in the responses of these mothers is a sense that nurturing a child provides a different and perhaps superior form of gratification than does nurturing one's spouse. To understand this, one might look to the final form of elaboration mothers provide. Partly, they say, the sense of emptiness, loneliness, and missing something is their response to how they would feel if they were deprived of the unconditional love a child gives them in return for all that nurturing. As one mother puts it, "It's a lot of work, but it all pays back if they hug me or kiss me . . . if they just come up and kiss me, just out of the blue." Children provide a very special "undivided love," they tell me, with "no strings attached." This is a unique kind of closeness that comes with pregnancy, breast-feeding, and day-to-day care:

> [Raising children] brings us a sense of love we couldn't get from sex, or pleasures from, you know, going out, or doing something we like to do,

dancing, or watching a movie. Kids give us this inner pleasure that [we're] unable to get from anything, anyone.

In all these explanations for the depth of feeling associated with having and raising a child, then, *love* is the key. And it is clear that mothers experience this deeply. When they respond to the question "How would you feel if you never had a child?" their emotion is not so much a reflection on their decision to have children or on the way they felt before they had children but is instead a response to an image of being deprived of the children that they now have and their present experience of giving and receiving love. And this reciprocal love is a fundamental element of intensive mothering. Raising a child is therefore "naturally" (to use the term favored by Spock, Brazelton, and Leach) emotionally absorbing.

Not only is this love thought to be the basis of the necessary commitment to parenting, it is also, as Brazelton (1983b) advises, an absolutely "essential ingredient" for the proper rearing of a child. Mothers know this. They are well aware that children require loving attention, as Spock (1985: 3) suggests, "as much as they need vitamins and calories." As one mother put it, giving love is just "the basics":

> Just as long as you love them and you show patience and understanding, any problem will work out. And don't ask me where I learned that from, because I don't know. I think it's basically just the general idea, especially nowadays with psychiatrists and doctors and all these analysts and everybody. I think it's just the basics.

Another mother reiterates:

> I don't care if you're someone that lives on the street, if you have kids, if they have that one main, very important thing which is love, they don't care where they're at, they don't care where they live, just as long as they have you, they have that affection, that love.

Love is the basis of good child rearing, according to the logic of intensive motherhood, primarily because it is the basis of encouraging the child's happiness and child's goodness. One mother feels so strongly about this that she is willing to disagree with her own mother:

> [My son] was really attached to me and my mom's like, "Let him cry, put him down, he's got to learn not to be attached." Well, I didn't listen to her, I didn't want him to cry. That's cruel. . . . But now I've noticed, he is real secure. He seems a little more secure than my other kids were. And I think it's because we had that closeness.

The loving nurture that brings the child such emotional security extends beyond holding them when they are infants, as this mother brings out in her response to the question "How do children become good adults?":

> From coming from a home where they're loved no matter what, where they're accepted for who they are, where they're encouraged, nurtured, where it's okay to take risks, okay to try things, where it's okay to fail at things.

Just as the child gives nonjudgmental, noncontingent, absolutely accepting, unconditional love, a child deserves and requires this sort of love in return. The giving of this love, mothers tell me, can be very time-consuming:

> Sometimes I just hold [my daughter] all day. And I would think, "Boy, this is the most important thing I have to do today and it's really important and I'm not going to get to the post office and we're going to have pizza for dinner. This child really needs this and that's what I'm going to give her right now." And it was a big switch from coming from working [at a paid job] and feeling like I could achieve twenty-five things in a day and [instead] all I did was hold my baby that day. But I came to realize how important that was. I think children really have a right to that.

Constant nurture, if that is what the child needs, is therefore the child's right — even if it means the mother must temporarily put her own life on hold.

The importance of loving attention also comes up frequently, as I have noted, with reference to the problem of women's participation in the paid labor force and the attendant difficulty of finding a paid caregiver who will provide the child with appropriate nurture. Although paid caregivers may like children, one mother notes, they don't love children the way a mother does. Another adds: "*No* stranger can love your child the way you do." This fact creates a problem for women who want to, or have to, be apart from their children on a regular basis. One stay-at-home mother elaborates:

> I think that women's lib, for all its wonderful ideals and [the] progress that it has made, never really took into account the fact that a mother being gone from her child 50 hours a week is really, just destroys a lot of the bonding and the nurturing that needs to go on. I think it's been really detrimental to children. I think it's why there's so many divorces and so many problems. I think it's really rough on the kids — they're a lot more insecure [nowadays] about their place in the family, about their parents being there when they need them.

Fifty hours a week without maternal bonding is just bad for kids. And such sentiments are not confined to mothers who stay at home; paid working mothers share these worries. Regarding her concerns about day care, this paid professional woman comments:

> The main thing would be the workers and how much love and care they give the children. I don't care to have an itemized list of what my child eats during the day or what they played with and stuff. But I want to see the people who work there interact with the children in a certain kind of way. . . . I just don't think that you can pay somebody to do it. You can pay them to take care of basic necessities, but you can't pay them to care, and you can't pay 'em to love somebody.

Thus, one of the central problems with women's increasing participation in the labor force, according to the logic of intensive mothering as well as the logic of many mothers, is that it is simply impossible to *pay* someone enough to love your child. And that love is absolutely crucial.

The love that mothers feel for their children and the commitment that love engenders are crucial foundations for another basic tenet of intensive mothering: the child-centered nature of socially appropriate child rearing.

Child rearing is child-centered, first, in that the child is the center of attention and the child's needs come first:

> I pay a lot of attention to my daughter. I make it very clear to her that she's very important. If we're in the middle of something and the phone rings, I don't always answer the phone. I take time to be with her and to listen to her and to do what she wants to be doing.

For many mothers, other things must be put aside when the children need attention. This point is often brought out in mothers' descriptions of selfish behavior.[18] For instance:

> I think the reason people are given children is to realize how selfish you have been your whole life — you are just totally centered on yourself and what you want. And suddenly here's this helpless thing that needs you constantly. And I kind of think that's why you're given children, so you kinda think, okay, so my youth was spent for myself. Now, you're an adult, they come first. . . . Whatever they need, they come first.

In your youth, you are allowed to be selfish. But when you become a mother, you know that the children's needs come first.

Making the child's needs a priority is connected to the second way in which child rearing is child-centered. A good mother will, as Spock (1985: 200) puts it, "follow the baby's lead." Following the baby's lead, mothers argue, is (at least) a three-step process. First, it involves recognizing that children are people too:

> The idea is that your child is a person, totally deserving and capable of respect, giving and receiving, and that you talk to your child and you treat your child, [and] you explain to your child as you would any other person.

Not only do you need to respect your children as human beings, you also need to respect them as *individuals*. This means that a good mother will take the time to get to know the particular interests and desires of her own unique child (as one mother put it, "You learn your kid"). Above all, this process involves listening to the child. The following mother elaborates on the value of listening in her response to the question "What do you think is the most important piece of advice you have received on child rearing?":

> I think listening to your kids; not making assumptions about how they're feeling, what they're doing — really just taking the time to listen to them and let them talk and let them let you know what's going on. Kids need to learn to trust what they're thinking and feeling, and learn to identify what they're thinking and feeling. You [need to] take the time to sit down and help them to figure out what they need to be figuring out.

Listening to children in order to understand just who they are and what they want and need is regarded as crucial by most mothers. Even though they are small, dependent, and not always articulate about what they want, children deserve to be treated with this kind of respect: "Just because they're children doesn't mean we can bully them."

But respecting them, listening to them, and determining their interests and desires are not enough. As the third step in the process, the good mother responds to and acts upon what the child seems to be requesting. This means that the mother allows the child to control the process of child rearing in line with his or her needs and desires. As if taking a line right out of Spock's *Baby and Child Care,* one mother put it this way:

> I let them establish their own schedule. I respect the individuality of children and I respect children as people and I think they know who they are and they know what they need. Within reason, I let a child tell me when they're hungry and when they need to eat and when they don't and when they need to sleep and when they don't.

Although many mothers argue that their children are most comfortable if there are routines and, therefore, that some level of scheduling is required, mothers generally allow the children to establish those schedules. The child (implicitly or explicitly) tells the mother what activity she will engage in next. And the child also tells the mother what sort of material things he or she wants. Responding to the child's desires, then, includes buying the child what the child wants. Mothers tend to recognize that this is a relatively new development in raising children:

> Back then [when we were young], kids, they didn't get as much. We didn't have the money for that. But I think now, even when my husband and I don't have the money, it's like, "Okay, we'll work on it to get it." We work really hard to please him.

Just as this last mother implies that "working to please the child" is a relatively recent historical development, many other mothers state that placing the child's needs at the center of child rearing is different from the way things used to be. Listen to these three mothers:

> —I think parents now are giving more time, spending more time with their kids and wanting them to learn. Whereas before it was like, "Oh, leave that alone, you're too young for that."
> —Back then, kids were to be seen and not heard, that kind of thing. Now, it's like kids are heard and seen, they're people. And I think people recognize that.
> —I think people care more [now] about how kids feel, and the effect that they'll have. And back then I don't think they noticed it.

Another mother elaborates on her sense of the nature and basis of such changes:

> I think that in a way child rearing has become more focused on what's good for the child versus what's good for the parent. My mom would never sit down and really play with us. . . . But I think nowadays, whether it be that everyone's time is so scrunched, that everyone's kind of thinking more quality, and what's best for the child, what's quality time with them, it seems like it's more focused in on what's best for the child than on what's convenient or what works out best for the parent.

Another mother notes explicitly what the others imply—that this new focus on what the child wants and needs is a measure of progress:

> If you look back, people just had children so they could work on their farm. Now it's more like you're having children because you want to have children and you want to give life to that little person. And you're focusing on their well-being more than what they can do for you. This is better for kids.

In short, child-centered child rearing means doing what is best for your child rather than what is convenient for you as the parent; it means concentrating on what you can do for them rather than on what they can do for you. And this, many mothers tell me, is the way it *should* be.

The child-centered nature of socially appropriate child rearing is what makes it so labor-intensive. Of course, raising a child necessarily requires work; ministering to the physical and emotional needs of a small and dependent being takes time. But the ideology of intensive child rearing requires a good deal more of the mother than simply ensuring that the minimal requirements for affection and physical sustenance are met.[19] Just as mothers understand the development of child-centered, permissive methods as the creation of recent generations, so too do they recognize that child rearing is more labor-intensive than it once was. One mother implied the progressive nature of this change:

> Parenting classes have only come up recently. Years ago, you know what they called parenting classes? Teaching somebody how to change a diaper. *That's* what they called parenting! How to burp your child. That was being a good parent! If you could do those things you were considered a good parent. What happened to a child's emotional state of well-being? What happened to their mental well-being?

Mothers share much of the ideology that makes the process of raising a child labor-intensive. Working-class, poor, professional-class, and affluent mothers alike nearly all believe that child rearing is appropriately child-centered and emotionally absorbing. And, practically speaking, this common attitude means they understand that good child rearing requires the day-to-day labor of nurturing the child, listening to the child, attempting to decipher the child's needs and desires, struggling to meet the child's wishes, and placing the child's well-being ahead of their own convenience. All this is clearly time-consuming and labor-intensive. But, as noted in the previous chapter, it is middle- and upper-middle class mothers who are the most likely to take the labor-intensive tenet of intensive mothering to the extreme. In negotiating with the child, explaining to the child, reasoning with the child, apologizing to the child, and using methods meant to ensure internalized self-discipline, these mothers take the lead.[20]

Karen is a professional-class mom who takes the labor-intensive aspect of child rearing as far as any other mother. Karen is a well-paid, highly educated working woman who lives with her husband in an upper-middle-class suburb. She had left her job to stay at home when her first child was born and returned to work (albeit part-time) when her daughter began preschool. She has just had a second child (now four months old) and has cut back her paid work time even more, planning to work only ten hours a week until this child is old enough for preschool. The reason she has changed her paid work schedule so many times will perhaps become clear. Listen to Karen as she describes the methods of discipline she uses with her first child, now four years old:

> [We do] a lot of negotiating, kind of, trying to set some limits, but we don't say no to her. We try and do more of just working with her [rather] than the old "I'm the parent and what I say goes." We're not a hitting family. We try and use time out. We use various techniques depending upon the situation and depending upon the stages. Bottom line, we do not hit. We do not hit.
>
> I mean, these are the things that make your life very time-consuming and draining and emotionally, you're exhausted. And the older they get the better negotiator [they become]. And she's become a terrific negotiator.
>
> But a lot of times with her we use counting. You say, "I'm going to count to three and if this doesn't happen you're not going to get to watch a video." You have to stand by what you say. And then sometimes she gets hysterically crying because she can't watch a video. Then we'll say to her, "Well, what do you think would be a good punishment?" . . . She'll say, "I can't have dessert," or something like that. You know, try and work with her. And it is, sometimes it is exhausting, and a lot of times, by eight o'clock in the morning I'm exhausted.[21]

Karen uses a variety of techniques, all geared to raising her child as an individual who deserves to be treated with respect and whose intelligence, in the words of Leach (1986: 435) should not be "insulted." Not only does Karen never spank her child, she also avoids saying no to her. Instead, Karen reasons with her daughter, uses time-out, negotiates, and (even though she believes "you have to stand by what you say") allows her daughter to determine the appropriate form of punishment. Given this, it does not seem at all surprising that her four-year-old has become a "terrific negotiator." And, given that, it is not at all surprising that Karen often finds herself exhausted by eight o'clock in the morning.

Karen is not alone. Just as Spock, Brazelton, and Leach argue that one must avoid the type of discipline that involves demands for absolute obedience and the threat of physical punishment, many middle-class mothers especially use all manner of techniques to avoid spanking or saying no to their children. One method mentioned by a number of mothers is to focus on children's positive behavior and to reinforce that rather than punishing them for bad behavior:

> What I really work on with [my daughter] is instead of saying "You can't do this and you can't do that," is saying "This is the desired behavior in this situation." [Then I place a] sticker on the sticker chart and when they get so

many stickers then they get a reward. And that works very well with her if we're consistent about doing it (which we're not always, I'm sorry to say).[22]

But positive reinforcement alone is not enough. Elaborating on another common technique, the following mother tells me that when her son is "naughty," she thinks it is important to discuss the problem with him and ask him to repeat the behavior in the right way:

> If he's real naughty, I don't wait 'til later for us to talk about it. I go back to where he was and [say], "Let's do this all over again." So it's like restitution. [I ask him to] show me the right way. And that takes a lot of patience and a lot of time. But I think it's so much better. It makes everything take twice as long, but they just catch on better, and they realize that "I'm not going to get what I want until I do it the right way."

This type of discussion and example setting is closely connected to the most common form of avoiding physical punishment and the command of no: the explanation. Good mothers, I'm told, will "sit down and explain" the situation to their children: "I think if you sit down and explain. Explain. It has a lot to do with children. They need for you to talk to them and explain why . . . not just telling them no." This sort of explanation, of course, involves reasoning with the child. And this mother, even though she recognizes that young children are not yet able to understand reason, still thinks it is important to use it consistently:

> I talk to my children a lot. I try to explain things to them. It's hard, when they have no reason — they're not that developed. I always try to talk to them about things though, because I think eventually they'll evolve [to that capacity for reason].

In other words, even if the child cannot understand, this is no excuse for telling them to do something, as Leach (1986: 435) suggests, "without telling them why." The following mother sums up many of these labor-intensive techniques by providing her own ordered list of the methods she uses to avoid spanking or saying no to children:

> We start with negotiating, explaining it to her. Sometimes we attempt to distract her. We try everything and if she just goes into "Oh boy, this is a chance to be defiant," then we proceed to a time out.[23]

All this takes "a lot of time and a lot of patience." But, mothers tell me, it's worth it, because kids deserve it.

Although it would seem that mothers who stay at home with the children all day bear the greater burden of such intensive care, many paid working mothers feel the need to double their efforts at the end of each workday in order to compensate for the time they have spent away from home. Furthermore, these mothers are far more likely than their stay-at-home counterparts to struggle with the time-consuming requirements of choosing alternative caregiver arrangements and monitoring the quality of such care. Sending the child to a paid caregiver does little to ease the stress on mothers: as one woman put it, whenever she has trouble with her current day-care provider, she comes "completely unglued." Working-class and poor mothers are just as likely to experience this anxiety as are their wealthier counterparts.

First, the choice of the type of alternative care is a difficult one. Potentially, one has the option of asking relatives to care for the kids, taking the kids to family day care, using a commercial day-care center or, if one can afford it, bringing a nanny, an au pair, or a full-time housekeeper into the home. These decisions are complicated by widespread reports of child neglect and abuse in certain types of day care. Many mothers, for instance, cite a June 1991 installment of *Prime Time Live,* which exposed day-care centers in Louisiana that were understaffed, neglectful of the children and, in at least one case, guilty of physically abusing them. Such stories, coupled with the ubiquitous coverage of child molestation in day-care centers (particularly the McMartin case), are taken as evidence by many mothers that child abuse and neglect at day-care centers are prevalent and that one must be constantly on guard against them. Women have a hard time deciding what to do. Although it might seem that such worries would lead mothers to avoid commercial day-care centers altogether, the decision is more complicated. Some women use this evidence to explain why family day care is preferable; others argue that commercial centers are still better, because such facilities are more likely to have "a room open to view" and make it easy for one to "drop in any time." In addition, "just knowing that there are a lot of other parents coming in and out" does something to assure one that "there won't be anything bad going on."

Although the problems of child molestation, abuse, and neglect are a central concern, a number of other considerations enter into the choice of caregiver. The few women who can afford them tend to use nannies, housekeepers, or au pairs, since this choice gives mothers a chance to interact with and oversee the caregiver on a regular basis and ensures that the children are safe at home. (Those in this elite group can add a high-quality preschool as the children get older, "so they can interact with kids their own age.") But for most moms, the choice is among commercial day-care centers, relatives, and family day care. Nationally, only 3 percent of employed mothers use nannies, au pairs, or housekeepers as the primary alternative caregivers. Day-care centers are used by 28 percent, another 28 percent use their spouses, 20 percent use family day care, and 19 percent use a relative ("Who's Minding the Children?" 1993).

Every type of paid child care has its own advantages and disadvantages. Commercial day-care centers may be the "large institutional types," in which the children become "cattle" and the caregivers cannot always provide the "one-on-one interaction" that children need; on the other hand, mothers tell me that in such centers "you are more likely to find people who know a lot about child rearing and child development." Family day care provides a "homey" atmosphere and is less likely to be "too crowded," but it might be a problem because "it's somebody's crazy home," because the mother taking care of the kids could just be trying "to make some money on the side," or because the caregiver might be more concerned with the well-being of her own children than she is with yours. In some cases a relative is considered preferable, since "there's nothing like a grandmother for loving grandchildren — there's really no replacement" and "the one thing that nannies [and other such paid caregivers] don't have is the long-term commitment to your kid." But relatives are not always available, and when they are, one sometimes has to worry because they are "too old-fashioned" and therefore do not understand contemporary child-rearing techniques. The choice, to the extent that one actually has a choice, can be a very difficult one.[24]

Whatever choice a mother makes, there are always things to worry about. Mothers want their paid child-care arrangements to be conveniently located and affordable, but they also look for places where the child-to-caregiver ratio is low, where the facilities are "clean and organized," where the children are "not just watching TV," where their child will not "just be one of a bunch of kids that basically are baby-sat," where the "kids get attention," where there are "many toys to play with," where the children "do little activities," and where the caregivers provide the kids with "new experiences." And while many mothers want their children to be learning and properly stimulated, they also worry about places that overemphasize the children's intellectual development: "I think all the other stuff falls into place, the learning the ABCs and all that other stuff. They're going to learn all that stuff later on and I can't see pushing the academics and all that other stuff. Let them be a kid." This means that, in many cases, the child-care arrangement needs to strike that perfect balance: "I didn't want it to be overwhelming — too much activity, or too big, too many kids. I didn't want it to be boring, too small." Connected to all this, of course, is the issue of the proper attributes of the paid caregiver. Mothers look for someone who "feels comfortable and enjoys what she's doing," who is "upbeat," who "really likes kids," and who "won't try to quash the kid's spirit." And, of course, it is crucial that the caregiver be a loving nurturer. Some mothers will put aside all other considerations if they can find a truly loving child-care provider, but other mothers are also concerned that such caregivers be well trained. For instance, this woman, speaking of the day-care center she had chosen for her son, says, "I don't know that schooling necessarily makes you a better nurturer, but I know I also like the fact that the teachers had child-rearing classes and child-development classes." Making all these choices clearly requires a good deal of time as well as a great deal of emotional and cognitive energy.

To make such determinations, mothers regularly talk to their friends, visit a number of facilities, and interview prospective caregivers. Nonetheless, many continue to feel anxious. They worry, as this mother does, that "I can get an interview and I can get a feeling for what they're like, but I don't really *know* them." In order to know them better, most mothers continue to interact with the caregiver on a regular basis; some, following the suggestion of Leach, even spy on their caregivers. Furthermore, as Brazelton recommends, most mothers are careful to watch their kids for signs of unhappiness or discomfort with the day-care situation. As one mother noted, "I wanted her to look forward to going. So I use my kids as a barometer. If they don't like it, if they're apprehensive at all, then I wouldn't let 'em go." Thus, if the situation turns out to be unsuitable, the process of finding the appropriate paid caregiver arrangement begins anew. And this, not surprisingly, causes many mothers to "come unglued." In sum, ensuring that the requirements of good alternative care are maintained consistently not only produces a good deal of anxiety among mothers; it is also obviously a labor-intensive process.[25]

In fact, many mothers think that child rearing is about the hardest job there is. Three-quarters of the mothers in my sample believe that it is *more* demanding than the work of an average corporate executive or other professional. Not only does it require giving all one's love, being constantly attentive to another person's needs, trying to understand all their desires and, for many, consistently reasoning with a little person whose logic may differ from their own, it also requires that one be ready and willing to do this *twenty-four hours a day*:

> I think the hardest job in the world is being a mom. I really do. I will argue the matter with any corporate lawyer. See if they can do that twenty-four hours a day. This is a job that, if it were any other job, you would have to wear a beeper around your neck. You're on call constantly. Your life is not your own anymore after you have a child, because it's theirs.

Part of the reason that the methods of nurturing, listening, responding, explaining, negotiating, distracting, and searching for appropriate alternative care are so labor-intensive, so time-consuming, so energy-absorbing is, as I have noted, that parents (especially mothers) understand themselves as largely responsible for the way their children turn out:

We make good children. Parents make good children. . . . . All children are born equal. We make them. Society makes them, [but] their parents have a great deal to do with what they become. What we teach them, how we love them, what we can give to them as learning tools, we're totally in control of that. That's why, being a parent, you have to carry a lot of guilt, a lot of sleepless nights to worry about if you're doing the right thing.

The guilt, the sleepless nights, and the worry about doing it appropriately are common to many mothers. As it turns out, nearly all the issues that they worry about follow directly from the logic of intensive child rearing.

Two final elements must be added. First, appropriate child rearing, according to this model, is expert-guided. This may at first seem contradictory, since we know that mothers do not always trust the so-called experts, read child-rearing manuals selectively, interpret what they do read, and are nearly as likely to get child-rearing suggestions from day-care providers, friends, family and, above all, other mothers. Nonetheless, mothers *do* buy child-rearing manuals (as their best-selling status testifies), they *do* often consult these manuals, they *do* frequently make a point of watching television shows and listening to radio programs that feature child-rearing experts, they *do* take their children to pediatricians, and they *do* (albeit only occasionally) take their children to child psychologists. If the advice of these experts was not valued, mothers would do none of these things. In other words, even if they take what the experts say advisedly, they do not generally treat it as complete nonsense.

Furthermore, as the close match between the advice of the best-selling child-rearing advisers and the language of mothers demonstrates, the information passed about in conversation between a mother and her friends, relatives, day-care providers, and other mothers often mimics the talk of the experts. As I have suggested, however, this is not to say that the experts produce an ideology that is simply imposed on passive mothers. It is probably at least equally true that what the experts say is what mothers want to hear. Although a reciprocal process is therefore at work, it nonetheless remains true that child rearing is, to a large extent, expert-informed.

Finally, according to the ideology of intensive mothering, appropriate child rearing is expensive. First, for those who can afford them, there are the costs of the tumbling classes, the swimming and judo and piano and dancing lessons, the child psychologists, and the special child-centered outings and vacations. For many, there are also the costs of the child's education, from preschool through college. Then there is the expense of child-maintenance accessories — the toys, the books, and the designer fashions — all of which go well beyond the already high price of simply providing for the child's physical needs.[26] It is, in short, quite expensive to "follow the child's lead," to provide them with what they desire, and to purchase all the goods necessary to ensure what the experts understand as healthy development.

One must also take into account the lost wages involved. The majority of stay-at-home mothers in my sample left their previous jobs specifically because they felt it was in their children's best interests for them to do so. A large number of paid working mothers stayed at home or cut back their paid work hours during the time their children were infants. A few mothers have managed to dovetail their schedules with their husbands' (as Spock suggests), so that at least one parent is home with the child for the maximum time possible. Over half the professional-class, paid working mothers in my study have reduced the number of hours they devote to their careers in order to have more time with their children. All of this is costly. And when you add to this the cost of hiring someone to care for the child while the mother is away plus the cost of assuring that the child receives the best paid care possible, the high price of appropriate child rearing becomes clear.[27]

What all this adds up to, of course, is child-rearing methods that are child-centered, expert-guided, emotionally absorbing, labor-intensive, and financially expensive. And it is the individual mother who is ultimately held responsible for assuring that such methods are used. But this is not the end of the story. As the reader will remember, there is one final element in the present-day model of intensive mothering.

Sacred Children, Sacred Mothering

Just as the child-rearing manuals of Spock, Brazelton, and Leach suggest that children are to be valued for the innocence and purity that distinguish them from the corruption of adult life in this "disenchanted world," just as they argue that appropriate child rearing not only stands apart from but actually operates in opposition to the logic of the "ME generation," so too do mothers celebrate the inherent goodness of children, believe that their innocence must be protected, and proclaim that the task of child rearing is more important than the pursuit of personal gain. According to the logic of intensive mothering, children and child rearing should be treated as sacred, and both should be protected from the contaminating logic of our rationalized market society.

Mothers' belief that children are innocent and pure is brought out in a number of ways. First, it is apparent in the talk of the unconditional love that children give: that "unpremeditated, guileless kind of affection" that one cannot get from anyone else. The implication, of course, is that adults are often too calculating, too jaded, too concerned with what they might gain or lose from giving love to provide the pure kind of love children do. Additionally, there is the talk of children's wide-eyed wonder, their ability to experience the world with joy in a way that no adult can, since adults, it seems, are too cynical and too caught up in their day-to-day struggles. One mother expresses it this way:

> Kids are so full of joy and [so] spontaneous, and life is exciting to them. And as you get older, you get hardened, where you're just putting your nose to the grindstone and not really taking the time to enjoy yourself sometimes. Kids are innocent and fun.

Further, the belief in childhood innocence and purity comes out strikingly in mothers' conviction that there are no bad children. When asked, "What do you think of as a good child as opposed to a bad child?," nearly half of the mothers I interviewed pointed out that there simply is no such thing as a bad child. Speaking of her two-year-old son, one mother told me: "My friends always think, 'Well, you never tell him he's bad.' And I'm like, well, he's not. I never met a bad child, and I don't think I ever will. They're so young, how can they be bad?" Adults, on the other hand, can be bad. They can, as one mother put it, betray the innocent child's trust: "I just looked and I thought, here he is, totally innocent. He has to trust me, and I don't have to be nice. But they have to trust you, they don't have any other choice. It's people that betray that trust." And even if children *act* badly, this does little to damage their image as innocents. Their bad behavior, mothers tell me, is only a sign that adults have treated them inappropriately:

> The old saying . . . 'There's not a bad child' is true. A child is only bad if whoever raises that child raises them that way. We had a couple of children [visit] here, they're just little demons. They constantly hit other kids, they made it a point to steal their toys but, I mean, it wasn't *their* fault. To look at their parents, they were the worst, you know, they constantly cussed around them, they allowed them to see violent and explicit movies that you wouldn't look at yourself. I mean, it's not the kid's fault, they're only that way if they're in that kind of surrounding.

Childhood innocence, in other words, is inherent:

> I don't believe kids are born bad. There's things I watch on Oprah Winfrey and crap, [with the theme] "Are Kids Born Bad?" And they [the guests] say, "Yes, I think they're born bad. It's in their genes." *Pleeease*. Kids are *not* born bad. It's like, give me a break!

Even if the *Oprah Winfrey Show* might suggest otherwise, most mothers seem to believe that children are born innocent.

Mothers also believe that it is very important to protect and preserve the purity and innocence of childhood. This comes up, for instance, in their concern about sending their children to paid caregivers who "stress academics" over exploration: they don't want their children to be forced to grow up too fast. Children should be allowed to play: "They're only kids once and we've got our whole lives to be on the fast track and be pushing and pushing — let 'em play." In other words, children need to be spared from the competition and the responsibility that come with adult life. If they want to, they should be allowed to "just lie around and look at the clouds or whatever." And this is because life as an adult is "tough" and "long," whereas childhood is "fleeting." Mothers just "want the kids to enjoy being kids for as long as they can." So they protect them.

This protection includes guarding them from what is perceived as the dangerous and corrupt world outside the home. A number of mothers said they had asked themselves, "Why am I bringing this innocent baby into this nasty world?" Many answer the question the way this mother does: "When you have this child, you think you want the best thing for them, and you try to shield them from all of those terrible things as long as you possibly can." Just as Jacqueline thinks it is important to provide her children "a safe and secure but limited experience of the world that's enlarging at the right speed" and Cindy thinks children should be protected from all the "stuff" that goes on outside the home for as long as possible, other mothers also say: "You think, close their ears, shut their eyes, let them be innocent for a little while." In other words, it's not just that these mothers want to protect their children from physical harm and from the experience of hatred, violence, competition, and stress, but they also want to protect them from *knowledge* of this dog-eat-dog world.

Needless to say, these innocent children whose purity must be protected and whose childhood must be preserved are emphatically *not* productive laborers contributing to a family economy. With the exception of Mecca, who is nostalgic for her own childhood participation in the family economy back in Latin America, no mother mentions using children as laborers, and no mother, including Mecca, would consider it appropriate to put children to work so that parents might profit from such labor. In fact, no mother even discusses the possibility of her own financial gain from the future wage-earning capacity of her children. When a mother does talk about her hopes for her child's future success, she makes it clear that this has nothing to do with the child's monetary success and everything to do with his or her future happiness.

Although these beliefs may seem obvious because they are so widespread and deeply entrenched, from at least one point of view, they are odd. Considering the amount of time, energy, and money these mothers expend on their children, and considering that they live in a world where maximizing personal profit is understood as not only acceptable but desirable, why wouldn't they seek a tangible return on their investment? The answer is found in the logic of intensive mothering itself. According to that logic, children should be valued not for the material gains they might bring to their parents but for their goodness, innocence, and inherently loving nature — all of which mark their distance from the corrupt outside world. Children are not calculating, jaded, individualistic competitors; they are loving beings who can be trusted absolutely. And while child rearing is understood as "exhausting, hard work," a good mother would never treat the child as a troublesome inconvenience to be set aside when a more lucrative investment opportunity arises.

Thus, not only are children understood as distinct from participants in the larger corrupt world, but child rearing also stands in opposition to the self-interested, competitive pursuit of personal gain. Given that child rearing is primarily women's work, this means that motherhood, like childhood, has a special sacred status. Just as it is the child's innocence that makes childhood sacred, it is the mother's unselfish and nurturing qualities that make motherhood sacred. Giving of oneself and one's resources freely is the appropriate code of maternal behavior, and any concern for maximizing personal profit is condemned.

We have already seen a number of indications of this ideology. First, we might recall that the definition of a bad mother is one who drops off the kids at 6:30 A.M., picks them up at 6:00 P.M., and doesn't think twice about them in the interim, one who sends her kids to boarding school so that she can take "vacations in Mexico," one who leaves the kids at home so that she can attend fancy parties and fashion shows, or one who takes drugs, goes out to bars, and has "twenty million boyfriends." A bad mother, in other words, is a mother who neglects her kids for selfish reasons, because she is more concerned with her personal fulfillment, her leisure pursuits, her material possessions, and her status than she is with her children. All this is closely tied to the logic of sacred children and sacred mothering.

And, as we've heard before, the opposition between good child rearing and the pursuit of financial gain comes out in mothers' discussions of their difficulties in finding the proper alternative care arrangements. Not only is it important for the child to receive enough love and attention and to be exposed to the right experiences, but the caregiver has to recognize, as mothers do, that the well-being of children is more important than money. As one mother said, "You don't want a situation where the day-care provider is just taking in kids to make some money." Or, as another put it, "I don't want my little child to look like dollar signs in front of their eyes." Children are, and should be, outside of market valuation.

All this is connected to the idea that raising a child is one of the most important and meaningful things a person can do. Certainly child rearing is more important than leisure activities and the freedom to do as one pleases. This mother explains:

> I mean, you have no time to yourself really and you think about those days where you just went to a movie or you went and worked out . . . and you just didn't have to ask anybody. Your significant other could take care of themselves. And all of that changes when you all of the sudden have a family. But, the other stuff, like, you ask yourself, "How many movies can you go to?" and "How many times can you go out to dinner?" [Raising a child] gives you something in your life much more meaningful than having just that freedom.

Raising a child is also more important than most careers, precisely because careers are generally only a means to further self-fulfillment and material interests, as the following mother points out:

> You're dealing with a little person's life [whereas] . . . a career is something that's for *you* more. It's more for what you're doing for yourself kind of, and where you want to go. But I think for children, for child rearing, you need to think of it as, it's more for *their* life. . . . I mean, it's a whole other life that you're responsible for. That's why it's more important, because it's a person, it's a human being. Whereas a career is sort of, in a way, a material thing.

Many mothers feel that it is important to show their kids that they are more important than money or material things. For instance:

> Children really need to know that you're doing the best that you can and you're not choosing to be away from them for something material or for your own gain, at a young age. If they learn that you can choose something over them, I think it sends them a lot of really funny messages. I think it tells them that money and materialism is a lot more important than it really is. And there's not a lot of happiness there.

In fact, the very definition of good mothering includes the willingness to give up things so that your children can have things. And this is something that many mothers seem glad to do:

> When you talk to women who don't have children, there's a real barrier there. I think they have a hard time understanding the closeness that you have with your own child. They have a hard time understanding why I would *want* to give up something to see my kids have something, why I would want to give it

up, why I would want to go without something. They have a hard time understanding. But it's just a matter of priorities. . . .

It's just that love that you share, that caring feeling, that makes you want to give up something so that somebody else could have something. When you only have yourself to depend on, you can kind of set your life up exactly the way you want to because it's only you. Then when there's kids, there's their needs to think about.

In mothering, apparently, it really *is* better to give than to receive — at least with reference to material possessions and considerations of financial gain. But, mothers tell me, children actually give back in other ways that are much more important and more valuable.

One of the things children hold the promise of giving in return for all of a mother's sacrifices is long-term intimate ties. This promise of a lasting and loving relationship is implied in mothers' sense that they would be lonely, empty, and missing something if they were without children. As one mother commented: "It would be lonely. There wouldn't be anybody to take care of you when you were older. Nobody to come visit you. There would be no Mother's Day or Father's Day." It is precisely because mothers and children share that very special unconditional love that mothers tend to believe that their relationships with their children will last and that their children will be visiting them, caring for them, and celebrating their intimate ties together when they get older.[28] Mothers want to create this close, durable bond not only for themselves but for their children as well. This is where the importance of family comes in:

For me, I just feel like I want to have family around me. I want to have the children for my sake because I want to have a sense of being part of a whole family. And for their sake, I want them to have each other, on the theory that the more people you have to love you the better off you are.

The moral lesson here is that the person who is "rich" is not the person with money but the person who is kind, considerate, and generous and has formed close, long-lasting relationships. Although this may seem an overly sentimentalized vision, many mothers articulate this lesson with great sincerity. Much of what mothers say, in other words, contains an underlying condemnation of the self-interested pursuit of monetary gain and a celebration of the importance of caring for others. And this is a central tenet of the ideology of intensive mothering.

Mothers also often seem to imply that child rearing, more than many other practices, serves to teach, reiterate, and reinforce this moral lesson. The following mother, for example, points out that having children has taught her to be less self-centered:

> I certainly can say that having children has taught me more than anything else I've ever done. Because they're a part of you, having them let you in on this wonderful thing. I think I've grown up. I think I'm more patient and realistic. I think I'm *much* less self-centered.

Just as children give back the same unconditional love they receive, at the same time that they may leave us with fewer individual freedoms and private possessions, they also teach us about the joy that comes from sharing. As this mother puts it:

> When [my daughter] was born I had this sudden extreme appreciation for my mother. [She laughs.] I was calling her on the phone all the time. Until we have children, we're allowed to be very selfish. Not in a bad way, but, your life is yours and you do what you choose to do with it, and you think about what you want to think about. Now you have to share. But it makes certain things one enjoys even more enjoyable—'cause an ice cream tastes twice as good when you know you only get a half of it because you have to share it with somebody else.

By teaching us not to be selfish, raising children provides training in human relationships of mutual obligation in a way that few other relationships in modern societies can. And this, in part, is why the relationship between mother and child is such an intensive one.

While much of the ideology of intensive mothering may operate in opposition to the logic of the outside world, it does contain its own systematic logic. And once you are *inside* the logic of the ideology of intensive mothering, the connections among all its elements begin to make a good deal of sense. The willingness to nurture the child, to listen to the child, to decipher the child's needs, to respond to the child's desires, to respect the child, to consult the experts for suggestions on what the child may require, to search long and hard for the appropriate alternative caregivers to watch the child should the parent be unavailable—in short, the willingness to expend a great deal of physical, emotional, cognitive, and financial resources on the child—follows directly from the requirement of placing the child at the center of one's life and putting the child's needs above one's own. Centering one's time and energy on the child hardly seems surprising given two of the other central elements in the logic of intensive child rearing. First, there is the fact that the child is understood as innocent, loving, and pure, and therefore deserving of protection from the corrupt and cruel outside world. Second, there is the emotional intensity of mothers' feelings for their children that flows from the love they experience as they nurture that innocent (and dependent) child. Both of these tenets are understood as based in nature. Thus, one's "natural" love for the "inherently" sacred child necessarily leads one to engage in child-centered, expert-guided, emotionally absorbing, labor-intensive, and financially expensive child rearing.

This set of assumptions gives us a model of intensive *parenting*. Why, then, does the individual mother take primary responsibility? First, according to this logic, family members in general are best suited for child care because their contact with the child coupled with their personal stake in the child's future make them the most loving and the most likely to have the required commitment. Given today's isolated nuclear family, parents have the closest relationship with the child. And of the two parents, mothers are the better suited for intensive child rearing not only because women get pregnant and lactate but also because, as mothers explain, men are "emotional midgets" with "one-track minds" who only think "man-thoughts" and can only understand bread-winning (and dinosaurs). Women, on the other hand, can keep track of all the details, are good at juggling many tasks at once and, above all, are inherently good nurturers.

But, as we know, it is possible to see the world differently if one starts with a different set of assumptions. *Outside* of this logic, for instance, one could conceivably take the attitude that many mothers attribute to men: namely, the assumption that children "simply grow" and that there's not much one has to do to assure that this process goes smoothly. Taking a similarly distanced stance, one might be led to wonder: if the love that parents, especially mothers, feel for their children is natural, then how do we explain the fact that, historically and cross-culturally, child rearing has not always been child-centered? We also need to ask ourselves: If children are inherently innocent, pure, and in need of protection, why have they been at various times and places considered sinful, dangerous, and impure, and, far from being sequestered, sent quickly out to work? Finally, many have convincingly argued that there is nothing the least bit inherent about the different characteristics and competencies of men and women. Surely we could (theoretically) dispense with the logic of intensive mothering in a context where the economic system demands a wholly different way of thinking and behaving, where there are many indicators that the political system values children little (e.g., Coontz 1992; Kamerman 1995; Keniston 1977), and where many mothers' work schedules leave them emotionally, cognitively, and physically drained by the end of the day.

Yet, as I have demonstrated in this chapter, the overwhelming majority of women to whom I spoke clearly recognize the ideology of intensive mothering, understand its logic, use its language, and are committed to living up to its tenets. They believe they are primarily responsible (whether they like it or not), they see the child as innocent, pure, and beyond market pricing, they put the child's needs first (in word if not always in deed), and they invest much of their time, labor, emotion, intellect, and money in their children. *Their* answer to the question of why they make this tremendous investment is contained in the logic of intensive mothering itself. For them, the joy of sharing, the love they feel, and the love that children promise to return are sufficient reward.

6

The Mommy Wars
Ambivalence, Ideological Work, and the
Cultural Contradictions of Motherhood

I have argued that all mothers ultimately share a recognition of the ideology of intensive mothering. At the same time, all mothers live in a society where child rearing is generally devalued and the primary emphasis is placed on profit, efficiency, and "getting ahead." If you are a mother, both logics operate in your daily life.

But the story is even more complicated. Mothers in the United States participate directly in the labor market on a regular basis; the rest remain at least somewhat distant from that world as they spend most of their days in the home. One might therefore expect paid working mothers to be more committed to the ideology of competitively maximizing personal profit and stay-at-home mothers to be more committed to the ideology of intensive mothering. As it turns out, however, this is not precisely the way it works.

Modern-day mothers are facing two socially constructed cultural images of what a good mother looks like. Neither, however, includes the vision of a cold, calculating businesswoman — that title is reserved for childless career women. If you are a good mother, you *must* be an intensive one. The only "choice" involved is whether you *add* the role of paid working woman. The options, then, are as follows. On the one side there is the portrait of the "traditional mother" who stays at home with the kids and dedicates her energy to the happiness of her family. This mother cheerfully studies the latest issue of *Family Circle,* places flowers in every room, and has dinner waiting when her husband comes home. This mother, when she's not cleaning, cooking, sewing, shopping, doing the laundry, or comforting her mate, is focused on attending to the children and ensuring their proper development. On the other side is the image of the successful "supermom." Effortlessly juggling home and work, this mother can push a stroller with one hand and carry a briefcase in the other. She is always properly coiffed, her nylons have no runs, her suits are freshly pressed, and her home has seen the white tornado. Her children are immaculate and well mannered but not passive, with a strong spirit and high self-esteem.[1]

Although both the traditional mom and the supermom are generally considered socially acceptable, their coexistence represents a serious cultural ambivalence about how mothers should behave. This ambivalence comes out in the widely available indictments of the failings of both groups of women. Note, for instance, the way Mecca, a welfare mother, describes these two choices and their culturally provided critiques:

> The way my family was brought up was, like, you marry a man, he's the head of the house, he's the provider, and you're the wife, you're the provider in the house. Now these days it's not that way. Now the people that stay home are classified, quote, "lazy people," we don't "like" to work.
>
> I've seen a lot of things on TV about working mothers and nonworking mothers. People who stay home attack the other mothers 'cause they're, like, bad mothers because they left the kids behind and go to work. And the other ones aren't working because we're lazy. But it's not lazy. It's the lifestyle in the 1990s it's, like, too much. It's a demanding world for mothers with kids.

The picture Mecca has seen on television, a picture of these two images attacking each other with ideological swords, is not an uncommon one.

It is this cultural ambivalence and the so-called choice between these paths that is the basis for what Darnton (1990) has dubbed the "mommy wars."[2] Both stay-at-home and paid working mothers, it is argued, are angry and defensive; neither group respects the other. Both make use of available cultural indictments to condemn the opposing group. Supermoms, according to this portrait, regularly describe stay-at-home mothers as lazy and boring, while traditional moms regularly accuse employed mothers of selfishly neglecting their children.

My interviews suggest, however, that this portrait of the mommy wars is both exaggerated and superficial. In fact, the majority of mothers I spoke with expressed respect for one another's need or right to choose whether to go out to work or stay at home with the kids. And, as I have argued, they also share a whole set of similar concerns regarding appropriate child rearing. These mothers have not formally enlisted in this war. Yet the rhetoric of the mommy wars draws them in as it persists in mainstream American culture, a culture that is unwilling, for various significant reasons, to unequivocally embrace either vision of motherhood, just as it remains unwilling to embrace wholeheartedly the childless career woman.[3] Thus, the charges of being lazy and bored, on the one hand, or selfish and money-grubbing, on the other, are made available for use by individual mothers and others should the need arise.

What this creates is a no-win situation for women of child-bearing years. If a woman voluntarily remains childless, some will say that she is cold, heartless, and unfulfilled as a woman. If she is a mother who works too hard at her job or career, some will accuse her of neglecting the kids. If she does not work hard enough, some will surely place her on the "mommy track" and her career advancement will be permanently slowed by the claim that her commitment to her children interferes with her workplace efficiency (Schwartz 1989). And if she stays at home with her children, some will call her unproductive and useless. A woman, in other words, can never fully do it right.

At the same time that these cultural images portray all women as somehow less than adequate, they also lead many mothers to *feel* somehow less than adequate in their daily lives. The stay-at-home mother is supposed to be happy and fulfilled, but how can she be when she hears so often that she is mindless and bored? The supermom is supposed to be able to juggle her two roles without missing a beat, but how can she do either job as well as she is expected if she is told she must dedicate her all in both directions? In these circumstances, it is not surprising that many supermoms feel guilty about their inability to carry out both roles to their fullest, while many traditional moms feel isolated and invisible to the larger world.

Given this scenario, both stay-at-home and employed mothers end up spending a good deal of time attempting to make sense of their current positions. Paid working mothers, for instance, are likely to argue that there are lots of good reasons for mothers to work in the paid labor force; stay-at-home mothers are likely to argue that there are lots of good reasons for mothers to stay at home with their children. These arguments are best understood not as (mere) rationalizations or (absolute) truths but rather as socially necessary "ideological work." Berger (1981a) uses this notion to describe the way that all people make use of available ideologies in their "attempt to cope with the relationship between the ideas they bring to a social context and the practical pressures of day-to-day living in it" (15). People, in other words, select among the cultural logics at their disposal in order to develop some correspondence between what they believe and what they actually do.[4] For mothers, just like others, ideological work is simply a means of maintaining their sanity.

The ideological work of mothers, as I will show, follows neither a simple nor a straightforward course. First, as I have pointed out, both groups face two contradictory cultural images of appropriate mothering. Their ideological work, then, includes a recognition and response to both portraits. This duality is evident in the fact that the logic the traditional mother uses to affirm her position matches the logic that the supermom uses to express ambivalence about her situation, and the logic that the employed mother uses to affirm her position is the same logic that the stay-at-home mother uses to express ambivalence about hers. Their strategies, in other words, are mirror images, but they are also incomplete — both groups are left with some ambivalence. Thus, although the two culturally provided images of mothering help mothers to make sense of their own positions, they simultaneously sap the strength of mothers by making them feel inadequate in one way or the other. It is in coping with these feelings of inadequacy that their respective ideological strategies take an interesting turn. Rather than taking divergent paths, as one might expect, *both* groups attempt to resolve their feelings of inadequacy by returning to the logic of the ideology of intensive mothering.

The Frumpy Housewife and the Push toward the Outside World

Some employed mothers say that they go out to work for pay because they need the income.[5] But the overwhelming majority also say that they *want* to work outside the home. First, there's the problem of staying inside all day: "I decided once I started working that I need that. I need to work. Because I'll become like this big huge hermit frumpy person if I stay home." Turning into a "big huge hermit frumpy person" is connected to the feeling of being confined to the home. Many women have had that experience at one time or another and do not want to repeat it:

> When I did stay home with him, up until the time when he was ten months old, I wouldn't go out of the house for three days at a time. Ya know, I get to where I don't want to get dressed, I don't care if I take a shower. It's like, what for? I'm not going anywhere.

Not getting dressed and not going anywhere are also tied to the problem of not having a chance to interact with other adults:

> I remember thinking, "I don't even get out of my robe. And I've gotta stay home and breast-feed and the only adult I hear is on *Good Morning America* — and he's not even live!" And that was just for a couple of months. I don't even know what it would be like for a couple of years. I think it would be really difficult.

Interacting with adults, for many paid working mothers, means getting a break from the world of children and having an opportunity to use their minds:

> When I first started looking for a job, I thought we needed a second income. But then when I started working it was like, this is great! I do have a mind that's not *Sesame Street!* And I just love talking with people. It's just fun, and it's a break. It's tough, but I enjoyed it; it was a break from being with the kids.

If you don't get a break from the kids, if you don't get out of the house, if you don't interact with adults, and if you don't have a chance to use your mind beyond the *Sesame Street* level, you might end up lacking the motivation to do much at all. This argument is implied by many mothers:

> If I was stuck at home all day, and I did do that 'cause I was waiting for day care, I stayed home for four months, and I went crazy, I couldn't stand it. I mean not because I didn't want to spend any time with her, but because we'd just sit here and she'd just cry all day and I couldn't get anything done. I was at the end of the day exhausted, and feeling like shit.

Of course, it is exhausting to spend the day meeting the demands of children. But there's also a not too deeply buried sense in all these arguments that getting outside the home and using one's mind fulfill a longing to be part of the larger world and to be recognized by it. One mother made this point explicitly:

> [When you're working outside the home] you're doing something. You're using your mind a little bit differently than just trying to figure out how to make your day work with your kid. It's just challenging in a different way. So there's part of me that wants to be, like, *recognized*. I think maybe that's what work does, it gives you a little bit of a sense of recognition, that you don't feel like you get [when you stay home].

Most employed mothers, then, say that if they stay at home they'll go stir-crazy, they'll get bored, the demands of the kids will drive them nuts, they won't have an opportunity to use their brains or interact with other adults, they'll feel like they're going nowhere, and they'll lose their sense of identity in the larger world. And, for many of these mothers, all these points are connected:

> Well, I think [working outside is] positive, because I feel good about being able to do the things that I went to school for, and keep up with that, and use my brain. As they grow older, [the children are] going to get into things that they want to get into, they're going to be out with their friends and stuff, and I don't want to be in a situation where my whole life has been wrapped around the kids. That's it. Just some outside interests so that I'm not so wrapped up in

how shiny my floor is. [She laughs.] Just to kind of be out and be stimulated. Gosh, I don't want this to get taken wrong, but I think I'd be a little bit bored. And the other thing I think of is, I kind of need a break, and when you're staying at home it's constant. It's a lot harder when you don't have family close by, [because] you don't get a break.

In short, paid working mothers feel a strong pull toward the outside world. They hear the world accusing stay-at-home moms of being mindless and unproductive and of lacking an identity apart from their kids, and they experience this as at least partially true.

Stay-at-home mothers also worry that the world will perceive them as lazy and bored and watching television all day as children scream in their ears and tug at their sleeves. And sometimes this is the way they feel about themselves. In other words, the same image that provides working mothers with the reasons they should go out to work accounts for the ambivalence that stay-at-home mothers feel about staying at home.

A few stay-at-home mothers seem to feel absolutely secure in their position, but most do not.[6] Many believe that they will seek paid work at some point, and almost all are made uncomfortable by the sense that the outside world does not value what they do. In all cases, their expressions of ambivalence about staying at home mimic the concerns of employed mothers. For instance, some women who stay at home also worry about becoming frumpy: "I'm not this heavy. I'm, like, twenty-seven pounds overweight. It sounds very vain of me, in my situation. It's like, I'm not used to being home all the time, I'm home twenty-four hours. I don't have that balance in my life anymore." And some stay-at-home mothers feel as if they are physically confined inside the home. This mother, for example, seems tired of meeting the children's demands and feels that she is losing her sense of self:

> There's a hard thing of being at home all the time. You have a lot of stress, because you're constantly in the house. I think having a job can relieve some of that stress and to make it a lot more enjoyable, to want to come home all the time. . . . My outings are [limited]. I'm excited when I have to go grocery shopping. Everything I pick is what they eat, everything they like, or what they should eat. Me, I'm just *there*. I'm there for them. I feel that I'm here for them.

Both of these stay-at-home mothers, like over one-third of the stay-at-home mothers in my sample, plan to go out to work as soon as they can find paid employment that offers sufficient rewards to compensate (both financially and ideologically) for sending the kids to day care. Most of the remaining mothers are committed to staying at home with the children through what they understand as formative years. The following mother shares that commitment, while also echoing many paid working mothers in her hopes that one day she will have a chance to be around adults and further her own growth:

> Well, we could do more, we'd have more money, but that's really not the biggest reason I'd go back to work. I want to do things for myself, too. I want to go back and get my master's [degree] or something. I need to grow, and be around adults, too. I don't know when, but I think in the next two years I'll go back to work. The formative years — their personality is going to develop until they're about five. It's pretty much set by then. So I think it's pretty critical that you're around them during those times.

One mother stated explicitly that she can hardly wait until the kids are through their formative years:

> At least talking to grown-ups is a little more fulfilling than ordering the kids around all day. My life right now is just all theirs. Sometimes it's a depressing thought because I think, "Where am I? I want my life back." . . . I mean, they are totally selfish. It's like an ice cream. They just gobble that down and say, "Let me have the cinnamon roll now."
> . . . [But] I had them, and I want them to be good people. So I've dedicated myself to them right now. Later on I get my life back. They won't always be these little sponges. I don't want any deficiency — well, nobody can cover all the loopholes — but I want to be comfortable in myself to know that I did everything that I could. It's the least I can do to do the best I can by them.

Mothers, she seems to be saying, are like confections that the kids just gobble down — and then they ask for more.

Thus, many stay-at-home moms experience the exhaustion of meeting the demands of children all day long, just as employed mothers fear they might. And many stay-at-home mothers also experience a loss of self. Part of the reason they feel like they are losing their identity is that they know the outside world does not recognize a mother's work as valuable. This woman, committed to staying at home until her youngest is at least three years old, explains:

> You go through a period where you feel like you've lost all your marbles. Boy, you're not as smart as you used to be, and as sharp as you used to be, and not as respected as you used to be. And those things are really hard to swallow. But that's something I've discussed with other mothers who are willing to stay home with their kids, and we've formed a support group where we've said, "Boy, those people just don't know what they're talking about." We're like a support group for each other, which you have to have if you've decided to stay at home, because you have so many people almost pushing you to work, or

asking "Why don't you work?" You're not somehow as good as anybody else 'cause you're staying at home; what you're doing isn't important. We have a lot of that in this society.

Another mother, this one determined to stay at home with her kids over the long haul, provides a concrete example of the subtle and not-so-subtle ways in which society pushes mothers to participate in the paid labor force, and of the discomfort such mothers experience as a result:

As a matter of fact, somebody said to me (I guess it was a principal from one of the schools) . . . "Well, what do you *do*? Do you have a *job*?" And it was just very funny to me that he was so uncomfortable trying to ask me what it was in our society that I did. I guess that they just assume that if you're a mom at home that it means nothing. I don't know, I just don't consider it that way. But it's kind of funny, worrying about what you're gonna say at a dinner party about what you do.

And it's not just that these mothers worry about being able to impress school principals and people at cocktail parties, of course. The following mother worries about being "interesting" to other women who do not have children:

I find myself, now that I'm not working, not to have as much in common [with other women who don't have children]. We don't talk that much because I don't have that much to talk about. Like I feel I'm not an interesting person anymore.

In short, the world presents, and mothers experience, the image of the lazy, mindless, dull housewife — and no mother wants to be included in that image.

The Time-Crunched Career Woman and the Pull toward Home

Stay-at-home mothers use a number of strategies to support their position and combat the image of the frumpy housewife. Many moms who are committed to staying at home with their kids often become part of formal or informal support groups, providing them an opportunity to interact with other mothers who have made the same commitment. Others, if they can afford the cost of transportation and child care, engage in a variety of outside activities — as volunteers for churches, temples, and community groups, for instance, or in regular leisure activities and exercise programs. They then have a chance to communicate with other adults and to experience themselves as part of a larger social world (though one in which children generally occupy a central role).

But the primary way that stay-at-home mothers cope with their ambivalence is through ideological work. Like paid working mothers, they make a list of all the good reasons they do what they do. In this case, that list includes confirming their commitment to good mothering, emphasizing the importance of putting their children's needs ahead of their own, and telling stories about the problems that families, and especially children, experience when mothers go out to work for pay.

Many stay-at-home mothers argue that kids require guidance and should have those cookies cooling on the kitchen counter when they come home from school:

> The kids are the ones that suffer. The kids need guidance and stuff. And with two parents working, sometimes there isn't even a parent home when they come home from school. And that's one thing that got me too. I want to be home and I want to have cookies on the stove when they come home from school. Now we eat meals together all the time. It's more of a homey atmosphere. It's more of a *home* atmosphere.

Providing this homey atmosphere is difficult to do if one works elsewhere all day. And providing some period of so-called quality time in the evening, these mothers tell me, is not an adequate substitute. One mother elaborated on this point in response to a question about how she would feel if she was working outside the home:

> Oh, guilty as anything. I know what I'm like after dinner, and I'm not at my best. And neither are my kids. And if that's all the time I had with them, it wouldn't be, quote, "quality time." I think it's a bunch of b.s. about quality time.

And quality time, even if it *is* of high quality, cannot make up for children's lack of a quantity of time with their mothers. This argument is often voiced in connection with the problem of paid caregiver arrangements. Most mothers, whether they work for pay or not, are concerned about the quality of day care, but stay-at-home mothers often use this concern to explain their commitment to staying at home. This mother, for example, argues that children who are shuffled off to a series of day-care providers simply will not get the love they need:

> I mean, if I'm going to have children I want to *raise* them. I feel really strongly about that. Really strongly. I wish more people did that. Myself, I think it's very underestimated the role the mother plays with the child. I really do. From zero to three [years], it's like their whole self-image. [Yet, working mothers will say,] "Well, okay, I've got a caretaker now," "Well, that nanny didn't work out." So by the time the children are three years old they've had four or

five people who have supposedly said "I'll love you forever," and they're gone. I think that's really tough on the kids.[7]

Since paid caregivers lack that deep and long-lasting love, I'm told, they won't ever be as committed to ministering to the child's needs as a mom will:

> I don't think anybody can give to children what a mother can give to her own children. I think there's a level of willingness to put up with hard days, crying days, cranky days, whining days, that most mothers are going to be able to tolerate just a little bit more than a caretaker would. I think there's more of a commitment of what a mother wants to give her children in terms of love, support, values, etcetera. A caretaker isn't going to feel quite the same way.

Stay-at-home mothers imply that all these problems of kids who lack guidance, love, and support are connected to the problem of mothers who put their own interests ahead of the interests of their children. A few stay-at-home mothers will explicitly argue, as this one does, that employed mothers are allowing material and power interests to take priority over the well-being of their kids:

> People are too interested in power, they just aren't interested in what happens to their kids. You know, "Fine, put them in day care." And I just feel sad. If you're so interested in money or a career or whatever, then why have kids? Why bring them into it?

Putting such interests ahead of one's children is not only somehow immoral; it also produces children with real problems. The following mother, echoing many stories about "bad mothers" that we have heard before, had this to say about her sister:

> My sister works full-time — she's a lawyer. And her kids are the most obnoxious, whiny kids. I can't stand it. They just hang on her. She thinks she's doing okay by them because they're in an expensive private school and they have expensive music lessons and they have expensive clothes and expensive toys and expensive cars and an expensive house. I don't know. Time will tell, I guess. But I can't believe they're not going to have some insecurities. The thing that gets me is, they don't *need* it. I mean, he's a lawyer too. Basically, it's like, "Well, I like you guys, but I don't really want to be there all day with you, and I don't want to have to do the dirty work."

These are serious indictments indeed.

It is just these sorts of concerns that leave paid working mothers feeling inadequate and ambivalent about *their* position. Many of them wonder at times if their lives or the lives of their children might actually be better if they stayed at home with the kids. Above all, many of them feel guilty and wonder, "Am I doing it right?" or "Have I done all I can do?" These are the mothers who, we're told, have it all. It is impossible to have it all, however, when "all" includes two contradictory sets of requirements. To begin to get a deeper sense of how these supermoms do not always feel so super, two examples might be helpful.

Angela is a working-class mother who had expected to stay home with her son through his formative years. But after nine months she found herself bored, lonely, and eager to interact with other adults. She therefore went out and got a full-time job as a cashier. She begins by expressing her concern that she is not living up to the homemaking suggestions she reads in *Parenting* magazine, worrying that she may not be doing it right:

> I get *Parenting* magazine and I read it. I do what is comfortable for me and what I can do. I'm not very creative. Where they have all these cooking ideas, and who has time to do that, except for a mother who stays home all day? Most of this is for a mother who has five, six hours to spend with her child doing this kind of thing. I don't have time for that.
>
> So then that's when I go back to day care. And I know that she's doing this kind of stuff with him, teaching him things. You know, a lot of the stuff that they have is on schooling kinds of things, flash cards, that kind of thing. Just things that I don't do. That makes me feel bad. Then I think, "I should be doing this" and "Am I doing the right thing?" I know I have a lot of love for him.

Although she loves her son and believes that this is probably "the most important thing," she also feels guilty that she may not be spending a sufficient amount of time with him, simply because she gets so tired:

> I think sometimes that I feel like I don't spend enough time with him and that's my biggest [concern]. And when I am with him, sometimes I'm not really up to being with him. Even though I am with him, sometimes I want him to go away because I've been working all day and I'm exhausted. And I feel sometimes I'll stick him in bed early because I just don't want to deal with him that day. And I feel really guilty because I don't spend enough time with him as it is. When I do have the chance to spend time with him, I don't want to spend time with him, because I'm so tired and I just want to be with myself and by myself.

Even though Angela likes her paid work and does not want to give it up, the problems of providing both a quantity of time and the idealized image of quality time with her child, just like the challenge of applying the creative cooking and child-rearing ideas she finds in *Parenting* magazine, haunt her and leave her feeling both inadequate and guilty.

Linda is a professional-class mother with a well-paying and challenging job that gives her a lot of satisfaction. She spent months searching for the right preschool for her son and is relieved that he is now in a place where the caregivers share her values. Still, she worries and wonders if life might be better if she had made different choices:

> I have a friend. She's a very good mom. She seems very patient, and I never heard her raise her voice. And she's also not working. She gets to stay home with her children, which is another thing I admire. I guess I sort of envy that too. There never seems to be a time where we can just spend, like, playing a lot. I think that's what really bothers me, that I don't feel like I have the time to just sit down and, in a relaxing way, play with him. I can do it, but then I'm thinking "Okay, well I can do this for five minutes." So that's always in the back of my mind. Time, time, time. So I guess that's the biggest thing.
>
> And just like your question, "How many hours a day is he at preschool and how many hours do you spend per day as the primary caregiver?" just made me think, "Oh my gosh!" I mean they're watching him grow up more than I am. They're with him more than I am. And that makes me feel guilty in a way, and it makes me feel sad in a way. I mean I can just see him, slipping, just growing up before me. Maybe it's that quality-time stuff. I don't spend a lot of time, and I don't know if the time I do spend with him is quality.
>
> [But] if I just stay at home, I'll kind of lose, I don't know if I want to say my sense of identity, but I guess I'll lose my career identity. I'm afraid of that I guess. . . . My friend who stays at home, she had a career before she had her children, but I forget what it was. So that whole part of her, I can't even identify it now.

On the one hand, Linda envies and admires stay-at-home moms and worries about not spending enough quality time with her son, or enough play time. She is also upset that her day-care provider spends more hours with her son each day than she can. On the other hand, Linda worries that if she did stay at home she'd lose her identity as a professional and a member of the larger society. "Time, time, time," she says, there's never enough time to do it all — or at least to do it all "right."

The issue of time is a primary source of paid working mothers' ambivalence about their double shift. Attempting to juggle two commitments at once is, of course, very difficult and stressful. This mother's sense of how time pressures make her feel that she is always moving too fast would be recognizable to the majority of paid working mothers:

> I can see when I get together with my sister [who doesn't have a paid job] . . . that she's so easygoing with the kids, and she takes her time, and when I'm with her, I realize how stressed out I am sometimes trying to get things done.

And I notice how much faster I move when I shop. . . . She's so relaxed, and I think I kind of envy that.

The problem of moving too fast when shopping is connected to the problem of moving too fast when raising children. Many paid working mothers envy those who can do such things at a more relaxed pace.

For a few employed mothers (two out of twenty in my sample) the problems of quality and quantity time outweigh the rewards of paid work, and they intend to leave their jobs as soon as they can afford to do so. This woman is one example:

> I believe there's a more cohesive family unit with maybe the mother staying at home. Because a woman tends to be a buffer, mediator, you name it. She pulls the family together. But if she's working outside the home, sometimes there's not that opportunity anymore for her to pull everyone together. She's just as tired as the husband would be and, I don't know, maybe the children are feeling like they've been not necessarily abandoned but, well, I'm sure they accept it, especially if that's the only life they've seen. But my daughter has seen a change, even when I was only on maternity leave. I've seen a change in her and she seemed to just enjoy it and appreciate us as a family more than when I was working. So now she keeps telling me, "Mom, I miss you."

When this mother hears her daughter say "I miss you," she feels a tremendous pull toward staying at home. And when she talks about the way a family needs a mother to bring its members together, she is pointing to an idealized image of the family that, like quality and quantity time, weighs heavily in the minds of many mothers.

The following paid working mother also wishes she could stay at home with the kids and wishes she could be just like the television mom of the 1950s who bakes cookies every afternoon. But she knows she has to continue working for financial reasons:

> Yes. I want to be Donna Reed, definitely. Or maybe Beaver Cleaver's mother, Jane Wyatt. Anybody in an apron and a pretty hairdo and a beautiful house. Yes. Getting out of the television set and making the most of reality is really what I have to do. Because I'll always have to work.

But the majority of paid working mothers, as I have stated, not only feel they need to work for financial reasons but also *want* to work, as Angela and Linda do. Nonetheless, their concerns about the effects of the double shift on their children match the concerns of those employed moms who wish they could stay at home as well as mimicking those of mothers who actually do stay at home. This mother, for instance, loves her paid work and does not want to give it up, but she does feel guilty, wondering if she's depriving her kids of the love and stimulation they need, particularly since she does not earn enough to justify the time she spends away:

> Honestly, I don't make that much money. So that in itself brings a little bit of guilt, 'cause I know I work even though we don't have to. So there's some guilt associated. If kids are coming home to an empty house every day, they're not getting the intellectual stimulation [and] they're not getting the love and nurturing that other mothers are able to give their kids. So I think in the long run they're missing out on a lot of the love and the nurturing and the caring.

And this mother does not want it to seem that she is putting her child second, but she feels pressure to live up to the image of a supermom:

> I felt really torn between what I wanted to do. Like a gut-wrenching decision. Like, what's more important? Of course your kids are important, but, you know, there's so many outside pressures for women to work. Every ad you see in magazines or on television shows this working woman who's coming home with a briefcase and the kids are all dressed and clean. It's such a lie. I don't know of anybody who lives like that.
>
> There's just a lot of pressure that you're not a fulfilled woman if you're not working outside of the home. But yet, it's just a real hard choice.

This feeling of being torn by a gut-wrenching decision comes up frequently:

> I'm constantly torn between what I feel I should be doing in my work and spending more time with them. . . . I think I would spend more time with them if I could. Sometimes I think it would be great not to work and be a mom and do that, and then I think, "well?"
>
> I think it's hard. Because I think you do need to have contact with your kid. You can't just see him in the morning and put him to bed at night because you work all day long. I think that's a real problem. You need to give your child guidance. You can't leave it to the schools. You can't leave it to churches. You need to be there. So, in some ways I'm really torn.

The overriding issue for this mother is guidance; seeing the children in the morning and putting them to bed at night is just not enough.

This problem, of course, is related to the problem of leaving kids with a paid caregiver all day. Paid working mothers do not like the idea of hearing their children cry when they leave them at day care any more than any other mother does. They are, as we have seen, just as concerned that their children will not get enough love, enough nurturing, enough of the right values, enough of the proper education, and enough of the right kind of discipline if they spend most of their time with a paid caregiver. To this list of concerns, paid working mothers add their feeling that when the kids are with a paid caregiver all day, it feels as if someone else is being the mother. One woman (who stayed at home until her son was two years old) elaborates:

> Well, I think it's really sad that kids have to be at day care forty hours a week. Because basically the person who's taking care of them is your day-care person. They're pretty much being the mother. It's really sad that this other person is raising your child, and it's basically like having this other person *adopting* your child. It's *awful* that we have to do that. I just think it's a crime basically. I wish we didn't have to do it. I wish everybody could stay home with their kids and have some kind of outlet. . . .
>
> And I think having a career is really important, but I think when it comes time to have children, you can take that time off and spend it with your kid. Because you can't go backwards, and time does fly with them. It's so sad. . . . I hear people say, "Oh, my day-care lady said that so-and-so walked today or used a spoon or something." I mean it's just so devastating to hear that you didn't get to see that.

Leaving one's child with a paid caregiver for hours on end is therefore a potential problem not only because that "other mother" may not be a good mother but also because the real mother misses out on the joys that come from just being with the child and having a chance to watch him or her grow. This is a heartrending issue for many mothers who work outside the home.

Once again, the arguments used by stay-at-home mothers to affirm their commitment to staying home are mimicked by the arguments paid working mothers use to express their ambivalence about the time they spend away from their children. And again, though the reasoning of these women is grounded in their experiences, it is also drawn from a widely available cultural rhetoric regarding the proper behavior of mothers.

The Curious Coincidence of Paid Work and the Ideology of Intensive Mothering

Both paid working moms and stay-at-home moms, then, do the ideological work of making their respective lists of the reasons they should work for pay and the reasons they should stay at home. Yet both groups also continue to experience and express some ambivalence about their current positions, feeling pushed and pulled in two directions. One would assume that they would cope with their ambivalence by simply returning to their list of good reasons for doing what they do. And stay-at-home mothers do just that: they respond to the push toward work in the paid labor force by arguing that their kids need them to be at home. But, as I will demonstrate, working mothers do *not* use the mirror strategy. The vast majority of these women do not respond to the pull toward staying at home by arguing that kids are a pain in the neck and that paid work is more enjoyable. Instead, they respond by creating a new list of all the reasons that they are good mothers even though they work outside the home. In other words, the ideological work meant to resolve mothers' ambivalence generally points in the direction of intensive mothering.

Most paid working mothers cope with their ambivalence by arguing that their participation in the labor force is ultimately good for their kids. They make this point in a number of ways. For instance, one mother thinks that the example she provides may help to teach her kids the work ethic. Another says that with the "outside constraints" imposed by her work schedule, she's "more organized and effective" as a mom.[8] Yet another mother suggests that her second child takes just as much time and energy away from her first child as her career does:

> I think the only negative effect [of my employment] is just [that] generally when I'm overstressed I don't do as well as a mother. But work is only one of the things that gets me overstressed. In fact it probably stresses me less than some other things. I think I do feel guilty about working 'cause it takes time away from [my oldest daughter]. But it struck me that it's acceptable to have a second child that takes just as much time away from the other child. *That* I'm not supposed to feel guilty about. But in some ways this [pointing to the infant she is holding] takes my time away from her more than my work does. Because this is constant.

More often, however, paid working mothers share a set of more standard explanations for why their labor-force participation is actually what's best for their kids. First, just as Rachel feels that her income provides for her daughter's toys, clothing, outings, and education, and just as Jacqueline argues, "I have weeks when I don't spend enough time with them and they suffer, but those are also the weeks I bring home the biggest paychecks," many mothers point out that their paid work provides the financial resources necessary for the well-being of their children:

> How am I supposed to send her to college without saving up? And also the money that I make from working helps pay for her toys, things that she needs, clothes. I never have to say, "Oh, I'm on a budget, I can't go buy this pair of shoes." I want the best for her.

Some mothers express a related concern—namely, what would happen to the family if they did not have paying jobs and their husbands should die or divorce them? One women expressed it this way:

Well, my dad was a fireman, so I guess there was a little bit of fear, well, if anything happened to him, how are we gonna go on? And I always kind of wished that [my mother] had something to fall back on. I think that has a lot to do with why I continue to work after the kids. I've always just felt the need to have something to hold on to.

The second standard argument given by employed mothers is that paid caregiver arrangements can help to further children's development. With respect to other people's kids, I'm told, these arrangements can keep them from being smothered by their mothers or can temporarily remove them from bad family situations. With reference to their own children, mothers emphasize that good day care provides kids with the opportunity to interact with adults, gives them access to "new experiences" and "different activities," "encourages their independence," and allows them to play with other kids — which is very important, especially now that neighborhoods no longer provide the sort of community life they once did:

They do say that kids in preschool these days are growing up a little more neurotic, but I don't think that my daughter would have had a better life. In fact I think her life would have been a thousand times worse if I was a low-income mother who stayed home and she only got to play with the kids at the park. Because I think that preschool is really good for them. Maybe not a holding tank, but a nice preschool where they play nice games with them and they have the opportunity to play with the same kids over and over again. I think that's really good for them. Back in the 1950s, everybody stayed home and there were kids all over the block to play with. It's not that way now. The neighborhoods are deserted during the week.

Third, several mothers tell me that the quality of the time they spend with their kids actually seems to increase when they have a chance to be away from them for a part of the day. Listen to these mothers:

— When I'm with them too long I tend to lose my patience and start yelling at them. This way we both get out. And we're glad to see each other when we come home.
— If women were only allowed to work maybe ten to fifteen hours a week, they would appreciate their kids more and they'd have more quality time with them, rather than having to always just scold them.
— I think I have even less patience [when I stay home with the children], because it's like, "Oh, is this all there is?" . . . Whereas when I go to work and come home, I'm glad to see him. You know, you hear people say that they're better parents when they work because they spend more quality time, all those clichés, or whatever. For me that happens to be true.
— And now when I come home from work (although I wish I could get off

earlier from work), I think I'm a better mom. There you go! Because when I come home from work, I don't have *all* day, just being with the kids. It's just that when I'm working I feel like I'm competent, I'm a person!

Getting this break from the kids, a break that reinforces your feeling of competence and therefore results in more rewarding time with your children, is closely connected to the final way paid working mothers commonly attempt to resolve their ambivalence. Their children's happiness, they explain, is dependent upon their *own* happiness as mothers. One hears this again and again: "Happy moms make happy children"; "If I'm happy in my work then I think I can be a better mom"; and "I have to be happy with myself in order to make the children happy." One mother explains it this way:

> In some ways working is good. It's definitely got its positive side, because I get a break. I mean, now what I'm doing [working part-time] is perfect. I go to work. I have time to myself. I get to go to the bathroom when I need to go to the bathroom. I come home and I'm very happy to see my kids again. What's good for the mother and makes the mother happy is definitely good for the kids.

In all these explanations for why their participation in the paid labor force is actually good for their kids, these mothers want to make it clear that they still consider children their primary interest. They are definitely not placing a higher value on material success or power, they say. Nor are they putting their own interests above the interests of their children. They want the children to get all they need. But part of what children need, they argue, is financial security, the material goods required for proper development, some time away from their mothers, more quality time when they are with their mothers, and mothers who are happy in what they do. In all of these statements, paid working mothers clearly recognize the ideology of intensive mothering and testify that they are committed to fulfilling its requirements.

To underline the significance of this point, let me remind the reader that these paid working mothers use methods of child rearing that are just as child-centered, expert-guided, emotionally absorbing, labor-intensive, and financially expensive as their stay-at-home counterparts; they hold the child just as sacred, and they are just as likely to consider themselves as primarily responsible for the present and future well-being of their children. These are also the very same mothers who put a tremendous amount of time and energy into finding appropriate paid caregiver arrangements. Yet for all that they do to meet the needs of their children, they still express some ambivalence about working outside the home. And they still resolve this ambivalence by returning to the logic of intensive mothering and reminding the observer that ultimately they are most interested in what is best for their kids. This is striking.

Continuing Contradictions

All this ideological work is a measure of the power of the pushes and pulls experienced by American mothers today. A woman can be a stay-at-home mother and claim to follow tradition, but not without paying the price of being treated as an outsider in the larger public world of the market. Or a woman can be a paid worker who participates in that larger world, but she must then pay the price of an impossible double shift. In both cases, women are enjoined to maintain the logic of intensive mothering. These contradictory pressures mimic the contradictory logics operating in this society, and almost all mothers experience them. The complex strategies mothers use to cope with these contradictory logics highlight the emotional, cognitive, and physical toll they take on contemporary mothers.

As I have argued, these strategies also highlight something more. The ways mothers explain their decisions to stay at home or work in the paid labor force, like the pushes and pulls they feel, run in opposite directions. Yet the ways they attempt to resolve the ambivalence they experience as a result of those decisions run in the *same* direction. Stay-at-home mothers, as I have shown, reaffirm their commitment to good mothering, and employed mothers maintain that they are good mothers even though they work. Paid working mothers do not, for instance, claim that child rearing is a relatively meaningless task, that personal profit is their primary goal, and that children are more efficiently raised in child-care centers. If you are a mother, in other words, although both the logic of the workplace and the logic of mothering operate in your life, the logic of intensive mothering has a *stronger* claim.

This phenomenon is particularly curious. The fact that there is no way for either type of mother to get it right would seem all the more reason to give up the logic of intensive mothering, especially since both groups of mothers recognize that paid employment confers more status than motherhood in the larger world. Yet images of freshly baked cookies and *Leave It to Beaver* seem to haunt mothers more often than the housewives' "problem that has no name" (Friedan 1963), and far more often than the image of a corporate manager with a big office, a large staff, and lots of perks. Although these mothers do not want to be defined as "mere" housewives and do want to achieve recognition in the outside world, most would also like to be there when the kids come home from school. Mothers surely try to balance their own desires against the requirements of appropriate child rearing, but in the world of mothering, it is socially unacceptable for them (in word if not in deed) to place their own needs *above* the needs of their children. A good mother certainly would never simply put her child aside for her own convenience. And placing material wealth or power on a higher plane than the well-being of children is strictly forbidden. It is clear that the two groups come together in holding these values as primary, despite the social devaluation of mothering and despite the glorification of wealth and power.

The portrait of the mommy wars, then, is overdrawn. Although the ideological strategies these groups use to explain their choice of home or paid work include an implicit critique of those "on the other side," this is almost always qualified, and both groups, at least at times, discuss their envy or admiration for the others. More important, as should now be abundantly clear, both groups ultimately share the same set of beliefs and the same set of concerns. Over half the women in my sample explicitly state that the choice between home and paid work depends on the individual woman, her interests, desires, and circumstances. Nearly all the rest argue that home is more important than paid work because children are simply more important than careers or the pursuit of financial gain. The paid working women in my sample were actually twice as likely as their stay-at-home counterparts to respond that home and children are more important and rewarding than paid work.[9] Ideologically speaking, at least, home and children actually seem to become more important to a mother the more time she spends away from them.

There *are* significant differences among mothers — ranging from individual differences to more systematic differences of class, race, and employment. But in the present context, what is most significant is the commitment to the ideology of intensive mothering that women share in spite of their differences. In this, the cultural contradictions of motherhood persist.

The case of paid working mothers is particularly important in this regard, since these are the very mothers who, arguably, have the most to gain from redefining motherhood in such a way as to lighten their load on the second shift. As we have seen, however, this is not exactly what they do. It is true, as Gerson (1985) argues, that there are ways in which paid working mothers do redefine motherhood and lighten their load — for instance, by sending their kids to day care, spending less time with them than their stay-at-home counterparts, legitimating their paid labor-force participation, and engaging in any number of practical strategies to make child-rearing tasks less energy- and time-consuming.[10] But, as I have argued, this does not mean that these mothers have given up the ideology of intensive mothering. Rather, it means that, whether or not they actually do, they feel they *should* spend a good deal of time looking for appropriate paid caregivers, trying to make up for the lack of quantity time by focusing their energy on providing quality time, and remaining attentive to the central tenets of the ideology of intensive child rearing. It also means that many are left feeling pressed for time, a little guilty, a bit inadequate, and somewhat ambivalent about their position. These stresses and the strain toward compensatory strategies should actually be taken as a measure of the persistent strength of the ideology of intensive mothering.

To deepen the sense of paradox further, one final point should be repeated. There are reasons to expect middle-class mothers to be in the vanguard of transforming ideas about child rearing away from an intensive model. First, middle-class women were historically in the vanguard of transforming child-rearing ideologies. Second, while many poor and working-class women have had to carry a double shift of wage labor and domestic chores for generations, middle-class mothers have had little practice, historically speaking, in juggling paid work and home and therefore might be eager to avoid it. Finally, one could argue that employed mothers in the middle class have more to gain from reconstructing ideas about appropriate child rearing than any other group — not only because their higher salaries mean that more money is at stake but also because intensive mothering potentially interferes with their career trajectories in a more damaging way than is true of less high-status occupations. But, as I have suggested, middle-class women are, in some respects, those who go about the task of child rearing with the greatest intensity.

When women's increasing participation in the labor force, the cultural ambivalence regarding paid working and stay-at-home mothers, the particular intensity of middle-class mothering, and the demanding character of the cultural model of appropriate child rearing are taken together, it becomes clear that the cultural contradictions of motherhood have been deepened rather than resolved. The history of child-rearing ideas demonstrates that the more powerful the logic of the rationalized market became, so too did its ideological opposition in the logic of intensive mothering. The words of contemporary mothers demonstrate that this trend persists in the day-to-day lives of women.

7

Love, Self-Interest, Power, and Opposition
Untangling the Roots of Intensive Mothering

Rachel, who lives in both the public and private spheres, exemplifies the depth of the cultural contradictions of contemporary motherhood. As a woman, she has been taught that her primary responsibility is to maintain the logic that dominates family and intimate life, a logic requiring a moral commitment to unremunerated relationships grounded in affection and mutual obligations. As a mother, she knows that this includes taking individual responsibility for the maintenance of intensive methods on behalf of her innocent and "priceless" child. But as a paid working woman, she regularly experiences the logic that dominates the world of formal economic and political life, a logic emphasizing the individualistic, calculating, competitive pursuit of personal gain. And as a career woman, she has made a commitment to long-term, uninterrupted participation in that world. Given this commitment, the demands of intensive mothering seem to do nothing but drain away her time, interfere with her pursuit of financial rewards, diminish her status, and leave her feeling exhausted and inadequate by the end of her daily double shift. Yet Rachel does not give up on one commitment for the other but steadfastly juggles both. And, as I have shown, Rachel is not unique.

The fact that Rachel maintains these two commitments is a measure of the persistent strength of both the ethos of a rationalized market society and the ideology of intensive mothering. But, as I have argued, theoretically speaking there are a number of reasons to believe that the logic of the market should be winning out and the ideology of intensive mothering fading away. The scope of the market, after all, has long overshadowed the scope of intimate, personal ties. And just as Weber, Marx, and Tönnies suggested that the ethos of impersonal, self-interested, competitive relations would eventually penetrate all spheres of life, so too have contemporary scholars more recently argued that this ethos is increasingly invading what once appeared as the last institutionalized holdout — the family. Capitalism is now imploding, the state regulates ever-more aspects of what were once private family matters, all human behavior is increasingly pictured as that of *homo economicus,* the "motive of gain becomes a justification for action" (Polanyi 1944: 30) in the family as elsewhere, and family members compete among themselves for power and financial resources (see, e.g., Bellah et al. 1991; Bentson 1984; Habermas 1989, 1987; Hartmann 1981a; Rapp et al. 1979; Sahlins 1976). The wall between the public and private spheres, always inadequately maintained, now has many cracks. When this is coupled with women's apparent refusal to remain on their assigned side and their decision to instead seek out recognition and remuneration in the public sphere, one would expect this fragile barrier to completely crumble and the ideology of intensive mothering to be crushed under its weight.

In a larger social context that not only devalues intensive mothering but actually serves to undermine it, why hasn't this ideology been reconstructed to one more in line with the logic of instrumental rationality, profit maximization, and the practical needs of paid working mothers? Current scholarship on women and the family, though complex and diverse, can be synthesized, classified, and interpreted to yield three possible answers.

1) For some, this is the question of a cynical, uncaring academic who fails to recognize that intensive child rearing is actually based in the reality of children's needs — the growing historical recognition of which is a measure of progress in knowledge following from ongoing, and natural, parental love.

2) For other scholars, this is the question of an overly sentimental and gullible woman who ignores the fact that the ideology of intensive child rearing is actually disappearing, particularly among well-compensated working women who are now busy maximizing their self-interested gain.

3) Alternately, it has been argued that this question and the two answers provided above miss the point completely. Intensive mothering is neither a choice made by women nor a symbol of love and progress in society; rather, it is an indication of the power of men, whites, the upper classes, capitalists, and state leaders to impose a particular form of family life on those less powerful than themselves.

These analyses at first seem mutually exclusive. Each of them is too one-sided, and none of them, if taken alone, is sufficient. But I argue that portions of these arguments, if developed in certain directions, can help to highlight not only certain aspects of what mothers are doing but also different facets of the cultural contradictions in which mothers are enmeshed. To understand the depth of those contradictions more fully, however, one further analysis must be added. The ideology of intensive mothering must also be understood as one form of a larger cultural opposition to the ideology of rationalized market societies. Mothers, in other words, are engaged in an explicit and systematic rejection of the logic of individualistic, competitive, and impersonal relations. This final analysis, emphasizing opposition, underlines and embraces the tensions that mothers experience, just as it embraces the tension between arguments about love and self-interest and arguments about those who have power over mothers and the ways mothers themselves are powerful. When these four analyses are taken together, it becomes clear that the beliefs of today's mothers and the cultural contradictions of motherhood point to a persistent, wide-spread, and irreducible cultural ambivalence about a social world based on the motive of individual gain, the impersonality of bureaucratic and market relations, and the calculating behavior of *homo economicus*.

Parental Love and Progress in Knowledge

One way to understand the development and persistence of the ideology of intensive child rearing is to focus, as many scholars do, on the love that parents express for their children. The logic of the argument (implicitly or explicitly) runs as follows. Parents naturally love their children. Because of this, they want to give their children all that they need. Parents therefore seek out knowledge that will help them to understand children's needs. And the more that they come to learn about the depth and complexity of children's needs, the more the job of child rearing becomes an emotionally, cognitively, and physically taxing job. There are no cultural contradictions, then, because intensive parenting follows naturally, and therefore immutably, from the complexity of children's needs and the depth of parental love.

Historically speaking, Shorter (1977) uses a version of this argument to explain what he understands as the spontaneous blooming of parental love and appropriate child rearing that emerged when modernization finally "freed" individuals from traditional constraints on expressions of their love. Sears (1975) extends this analysis, arguing that the empathic child rearing thereby developed naturally led to an ever-greater number of child-development experts, philanthropic and research institutes, and scientific studies dedicated to knowledge about childhood—all of which, in turn, led to ever-better treatment of the young (see also Cleverly and Phillips 1986). DeMause (1974) expands on this logic, asserting that parental love and empathy can explain the history of child rearing universally, across time and cultures. Love, he tells us, leads all parents to regress to the age of their children, to reflect on how they felt when they were that age, and to use those reflections to raise their children as they themselves would have wanted to be raised. These instinctual insights, over generations, mean that parents naturally gain more and more knowledge of children's needs and therefore become increasingly able to treat children as they deserve to be treated. This set of analyses purports to explain why nurturing the child's development of conscience replaces the rod, why a focus on the child's special goodness replaces attention to the child's uncoordinated and animalistic qualities, and why a concern for the child's healthy psychological development replaces the use of children as productive laborers. The history of child rearing, in these terms, is a history of positive evolution following naturally from parental love.

This argument is implicitly or explicitly accepted by many others. First, there are the maternal-attachment theorists—from Erik Erikson and John Bowlby to Selma Fraiberg—who argue that intensive maternal love is crucial to meet the complex needs of children (see Dally 1982; Eyer 1992; Margolis 1984). Second, there is a whole range of thinkers who are less certain that mothers are the only appropriate caregivers but are nonetheless sure that today's child-rearing methods are grounded in parental love and are absolutely necessary to the well-being of children (e.g., Held 1983, 1990; Hewlett 1987, 1991; Ruddick 1982). Finally, there is a much larger group of scholars who simply take for granted the natural quality of parental love, the truth of scientific theories of childhood development, and the historical superiority of today's methods of raising children. Although all three groups may suggest that various changes in child-rearing practices are necessary, parental love and children's needs are treated as universal absolutes that are both sacred and untouchable.

This is also the argument that is most powerful among contemporary mothers. Without question, mothers experience their own child-rearing beliefs and practices as a measure of their love for their children. Further confirming this analysis, they seek information on children's needs, they attempt to meet those needs through their child-rearing practices, they believe that there is continuing progress in knowledge regarding child rearing, and they regularly reflect on their own childhoods, attempting to repeat what they felt was right and to avoid the mistakes their parents (especially their mothers) made in raising them.[1] For these women, there is no need to analyze the roots of such beliefs and behaviors — raising children simply *is* an intensive task, and a loving mother necessarily wants to do it right.

There are, however, some problems with this argument. Although parents may have experienced an emotional response to children akin to love for many centuries or even for all time, the specific meaning of this love, and the ideas and practices that follow from it, are socially constructed and vary according to social context. The shortcomings of this argument's universalizing tendencies become most apparent when cross-cultural variations in forms of love and child rearing are taken into account. In attempting to explain historical variation, this analysis does so by inappropriately applying modern concepts retrospectively. The central problem here is that this perspective tends to be naive about the different circumstances, differential power relations, and distinct interests involved in any given construction of appropriate parental love and appropriate child-rearing practices. For instance, the emphasis on natural and progressive advances in knowledge about children ignores the evidence that new methods of child rearing as they arose historically were not necessarily perceived as progress by all concerned. Further, the implicit belief in the absolute superiority of present-day Western methods would certainly not meet with agreement in other cultures, which, by the measures here used, would appear backward and deficient in their understanding and treatment of children. One could also debate the claim that centuries of parental love and expert guidance have guaranteed that the lives of American children today are better or that children are happier, more liberated, more justly treated, or more fully prepared for their lives as adults than children were in the past or are in other cultures.

But perhaps the most glaring gap in the logic of this argument is that the nurturant love that is understood as the natural basis for all this progress in child rearing is almost always, in actual practice, the nurturant love of *mothers*. Claims that this love is parental ignore its gendered nature. And attempts to argue that women have a natural aptitude for mothering similarly neglect the circumstances, power relations, and interests that have made women primarily responsible for mothering and that have led so many to actually believe that women's mothering abilities are somehow natural, essential, or inevitable.[2]

Nonetheless, this argument should not be dismissed altogether. Most parents (especially mothers) seem to love their children, and there certainly is a tremendous amount of information available on the perceived needs of those children. We also know that the emotion we call love is a very powerful one that can induce people to go to great lengths on behalf of the beloved. Further, this argument does seem to capture the reality of a general historical tendency toward greater emotional investment in children among parents in the modern West. It also effectively underlines the reasoning used by mothers themselves to explain their commitment to intensive mothering. But there are questions left unanswered. What is lacking, above all, is an understanding of the cultural logic that transforms love into an ideology of intensive mothering, and that does so in a wider social context that appears extremely hostile to it.

Self-Interest: Mothers as Rational Bookkeepers

All that mothers say about child rearing seems to deny an analysis that would portray them as individuals engaged in the self-interested pursuit of gain. They state emphatically that appropriate child rearing involves sacrifice and that the needs of children should and do take priority over any interest they might have in power or material gain. The sole benefit they seek by raising a child, they argue, is the reward of love.

But according to some scholars, mothers are simply utilitarians in disguise. In a world where all people carefully weigh the costs and benefits of every move they make in an attempt to maximize their personal advantage, mothers, these scholars say, are not unique. And this form of analysis is extremely powerful in our society. In fact, many people believe it to be a matter of common sense that individuals will act in their self-interest, assuming that this is simply human nature. If we follow this logic, we would expect that mothers do not sacrifice anything more than what they expect to receive in return.[3]

Extending this argument, scholars imply that all historical and cross-cultural forms of mothering are purely a function of self-interested calculations of status, wealth, and power. When an investment in child rearing offers a profitable return, mothers (and parents) will expend the time, effort, and money necessary for the task. But, historically speaking, as children's economic value as present or future family workers declines, mothers will necessarily be expected to invest less in child rearing. Among mothers today, some may still find certain aspects of intensive mothering useful in their status-seeking efforts, but most mothers, especially paid working mothers, will logically strive to simplify child rearing after carefully weighing its costs and benefits. In all respects, mothers are calculating "rational actors."[4] There are no cultural contradictions, since all people at all times seek to maximize their personal gain. And this is equally true of mothers at home with their children as it is of businessmen at work in corporate America.

For contemporary mothers, the central cost-benefit analysis revolves around the question of whether to stay at home or go out to work for pay. With reference to married women who stay at home with their children, the answer would seem clear. They do it because they cannot find work that pays well enough or provides enough status to compensate for the effort they would have to expend on the second shift. If these women do not have husbands or some other source of support, they simply weigh the benefits of the type of work available against the costs of welfare. When women do stay at home to care for their children, they make claims to engage in intensive techniques because this position helps justify their lack of income. But, according to the logic of self-interest, these women still attempt to organize the task of child rearing in the most efficient and cost-effective manner possible.[5]

Once women have a chance to gain more status, power, or material success outside the home, they will choose to remain childless or they will have fewer children. If they take the latter route, these scholars imply, they will simply expend less of themselves on raising those children. As far as possible they will ignore child-rearing experts who advise them to be full-time mothers and urge them to treat child rearing as a time-consuming and emotionally, mentally, and monetarily expensive task. They will develop rationalizations to justify their time away from the kids — including an emphasis on quality time and on the importance of children's interaction with a variety of adults. They will cut back on the amount of housework they do. And if possible they will hire housekeepers and gardeners, use disposable or commercially laundered diapers, and either serve their children prepared foods or take them to fast-food restaurants. Above all, they will increasingly make use of paid caregivers and enlist the help of their husbands.

In this scenario, all mothers are efficiency-maximizing self-seekers, and intensive mothers are a dying breed. As more and more women seek and gain status and material rewards in the paid labor force, the logic of intensive mothering will simply fade away.[6]

Although mothers do not understand their mothering in this way, it is also quite clear to the outside observer that there are many ways in which they do pursue their self-interest. They look for ways to efficiently manage their time and their resources. They cut back on housework and they seek out commercial substitutes for cooking and cleaning if they can afford them. Employed women especially make use of paid caregivers and ask their husbands for more help.

Additionally, there seems to be no question that much of what women say indicates a concern to valorize their position as mothers and thereby enhance their social status. They speak of the knowledge of child development required in order to do their job right, hold a strict set of standards for appropriate child care, compare themselves to women they consider bad mothers, insist that intensive techniques are essential to good child rearing, and imply that their job as mothers is a highly complex one requiring the analytical, interpretive, and independent decision-making capacities of a professional. They also attempt to assure their children's future status. Working-class and poor mothers emphasize the schooling they think their children will need to get ahead, and middle-class mothers emphasize the self-discipline and independent decision-making skills they believe necessary to middle-class status. In a connected way, mothers seem to understand their children's success as a reflection and enhancement of their own. When middle-class mothers take their children to dance classes, piano lessons, and museums, for instance, they accomplish two tasks at once — grooming the children for their future class position by providing them with the appropriate cultural capital and demonstrating their own class status relative to mothers who cannot afford such luxuries or do not recognize them as an essential element of good child rearing.[7]

One can make sense of women's historical attempts to valorize mothering using this same form of analysis. Early claims to nurturing, moral motherhood, for instance, can be interpreted as part of a self-interested strategy devised by white, middle-class mothers of the late eighteenth century who were attempting to cast themselves as critically important at a time when their diminishing potential for making economic contributions to the (then-urban rather than farming) household made their marriage-market position precarious. Along the same lines, middle-class mothers of the late nineteenth century who undertook to train working-class and poor homemakers in proper child-rearing techniques effectively managed to emphasize their own special skills as mothers and to create a place for themselves in the social-work profession. Mothers at the turn of this century surely seem to have been seeking status when they set out to establish their identity as "scientific managers" in the home at a time when such expertise in computing efficiency was considered highly valuable.[8] By the same logic, the more intensive the techniques of appropriate child rearing become, the more mothers can claim that their job is a demanding and complex enterprise requiring high levels of knowledge and skill.

Much of this analysis, in other words, rings true. But there are two central problems. First, this argument tends to apply the term *interests* so broadly as to make it meaningless. Second, this argument cannot explain paid working mothers' persistent commitment to intensive mothering.

By simply assuming the instrumentally rational calculation of self-interested advantage, this line of analysis does not explain why individuals are sometimes interested in money, sometimes status, sometimes power, sometimes long-term gain, sometimes short-term gain, and sometimes even less predictable advantages like emotional sustenance, a sense of community, the maintenance of certain ethical standards, and the achievement of economic and social justice. If taken to its logical conclusion, this argument would not recognize the difference between putting your eight-year-old to work as a prostitute and sending her to private school: in both cases, one would be maximizing selfish interests by maximizing the child's earning capacities. But one choice is surely considered more socially acceptable than the other. The problem here is that the totality of the impact of historically constructed cultural, economic, and political systems is simply subsumed under the rubric of "interests." What is lacking is an understanding that all interests are socially shaped — that they are not individual interests nor are they straightforward, obvious, or given in nature. To explain why self-interested people understand some things as more valuable than others, we need to examine the wider system of social beliefs and circumstances in which they are enmeshed. This holds true with reference to questions of why women would believe that efficiency and material gain are their central goals just as it holds true with reference to why some methods of child rearing are deemed more appropriate and more worthy than others.

More important, but following from the same theoretical difficulties, is the fact that though these scholars assume that the more women enter the paid labor force and the more they have access to relatively well-paid and high-status jobs, the less intensive child rearing becomes, history and contemporary mothers seem to indicate just the opposite. Certainly many mothers want the public recognition, personal fulfillment, and material rewards that can attend participation in the paid labor force (as those in my sample make clear), but they do not simply set aside the perceived needs of their children or the logic of intensive mothering in order to pursue such interests.

Although many paid working women do choose to remain childless or to have fewer children, it is hard to know whether they do so simply to maximize their efficiency and personal gain or whether their sense of the time and energy required for good child rearing makes them feel ill equipped to do the job properly. Among the mothers in my sample, it is clear that employed women, just like stay-at-home mothers, spend a great deal of time worrying about their kids and using child-rearing techniques that are far from efficiency-maximizing and cost-effective. Even though mothers do ask fathers to help out, the methods fathers use are considered appropriate *only* if they are intensive. Mothers do send their kids to day care, but they also expend much time and energy (and, if they can afford it, a good deal of material resources) to assure that their children get the best in child-care services — and even then many still worry about the time they spend away. While many mothers do emphasize quality time, one might also point out the sense of guilt regarding unfulfilled obligations that this notion implies and the sense of emotional commitment and moral obligation that is hidden just beneath its surface. Finally, it would take significant financial rewards to compensate for the time, money, and energy that these mothers expend on their children, yet most do not expect these children to be sending home commensurate monthly payments in their later years. All this is true despite the awareness of paid-working mothers that the ethos of the market values their paychecks, their productivity, and their achievements in the workforce far more than it values their maintenance of the methods of intensive motherhood. And those women with the most well-paid, high-status jobs, as I have shown, actually use methods that are slightly more labor-intensive than those of women who have less to gain in the paid labor force.

None of these these phenomena can be neatly explained by a simple argument about the calculation of self-interest. There is, in addition, the problem that this analysis seems to dismiss mothers' own arguments about their love for their children. Nowhere is it suggested that love is a utility that mothers would want to maximize.[9] Furthermore, in and of itself, this argument does not explain why it is mothers rather than parents who engage in intensive child rearing. Nonetheless, mothers in general do attempt to manage their time and resources efficiently and to maximize their prestige as good mothers, and middle-class mothers in particular do attempt to mark their class status through their child-rearing techniques. In these terms, this argument has the virtue of illuminating the ways in which women are reasonable, active self-seekers rather than simply passive, overly emotional caregivers. But this is not the same as saying that mothers are self-interested in the sense of putting their own gain ahead of the well-being of others. Rather, we can imagine mothers, like all people, as attempting to maximize their "social assets," and thereby their cultural prestige.[10] To make sense of this struggle requires a thorough analysis of social circumstances and a recognition that interests are socially defined and often far from selfish. And, one still has to wonder, in a society where the most status seems to go to successful businesspeople, why would women seek status from good mothering?

The Differential Interests at Stake

One person's self-interested gain might be another person's loss — it all depends on whose ox is being gored. To predict the likelihood of winning or losing in this battle of oxen, one needs to determine who has the strongest oxen in the first place. In other words, while all people may in fact be self-interested, some people are in a better position than others to ensure that their interests are met. From this point of view, it is a mistake to focus on the profit-maximizing efforts of mothers themselves, since they are, after all, a relatively powerless group. Those who really benefit from the ideology of intensive mothering, as many scholars imply, are those who wield the most power economically, culturally, and politically — namely, men, whites, the upper classes, capitalist owners, and state leaders.

First, an ideological emphasis on particular family forms and models of child rearing may be implicated in attempts to maintain political stability and state power (e.g., Donzelot 1979; Gordon 1988; Platt 1977; Stone 1977; Zaretsky 1982). The state has long attempted to regulate family matters and, ever since the Progressive Era, has been key in legislating and enforcing certain family forms. Welfare policies, tax laws, compulsory schooling, juvenile courts, and child labor laws, for example, have all contributed to the establishment of a particular form of parenting. To the extent that government officials have an interest in controlling potentially volatile populations and in sparing the coffers from the potential of new and multiple public demands, the internal logic of intensive mothering may be quite useful. A mother's ongoing dedication to educating the young in particular social norms helps to ensure the creation of law-abiding, tax-paying citizens, and the particularly time-consuming process of training children in self-discipline and individual responsibility makes a significant contribution toward sparing the state from future pressures to widen its welfare roles or raise the minimum wage or subsidize housing, child-care, or medical expenses. As Donzelot (1979) argues, social workers, public schools, the courts, and law-enforcement officers all contribute to training mothers and children at the same time that they serve government interests in "policing the family."[11] To the extent that this process runs smoothly, mothers will consider it their duty to send the kids to school, keep them off the streets, teach them obedience, and ensure that they grow up to be individuals who are, simultaneously, compliant in the face of authority and independent, individuals who consider themselves solely responsible for their own welfare.

Many scholars have also argued that capitalists are well served by women's commitment to child rearing (e.g., Acker 1988; Bentson 1984; Ehrenreich 1989; Ehrenreich and English 1978; Hartmann 1981a; Kessler-Harris 1982; Matthaei 1982; Slater 1976; Weiner 1985; Zaretsky 1976; Zuckerman 1975). First, claiming that women's primary responsibility is to keep the home and raise the children helps convince women that they can be paid lower wages, since their earnings are only secondary to those of their husbands. Further, treating women as responsible for childcare means that the job of grooming young workers for the future is accomplished at a minimal cost to those who will employ them. The prolonged protection of childhood innocence that is contained in the logic of intensive mothering is useful to employers, since it includes the possibility of extensive schooling and thereby helps to create a flexible and well-trained labor force at a relatively low cost. The logic of meeting all the child's needs and desires means that mothers are encouraged to buy all those baby accessories, fancy toys, and children's designer fashions. And, again, child-rearing techniques meant to instill self-discipline and a sense of personal responsibility are especially important in that they not only help in the development of self-motivated managers but also help create workers who will blame only themselves when they lose their jobs or find their wages inadequate. In addition, the permissive, child-centered nature of intensive mothering helps to create little consumers. Trained in having all their desires met, these children grow up hungry to buy every new commodity that capitalism produces.

Further, a major line of analysis implies that the ideology of intensive mothering serves men (e.g., Delphy 1984; Hartmann 1981a, 1981b; Kessler-Harris 1982; Mainardi 1970; Margolis 1984; Matthaei 1982; Polatnick 1983; Ulrich 1982; Weiner 1985). As has been true since the days of the Puritans, the present-day model of appropriate child rearing frees men from having to do the grunt work of looking after the dirty, demanding, dependent beings that are their progeny. And the fact that women's responsibility for child rearing is part of a larger system that makes women responsible for all household chores means that men are often supplied with personal maids, chefs, and laundresses. More important perhaps, this system helps to ensure that men are spared from women's competition in the labor market. Those women who stay at home to care for children leave many openings for men, and even when women do work for pay, their identification with domesticity means that they tend to be segregated in those poorly paid occupations dubbed "women's work." Furthermore, the newer, more intensive version of mothering means that employed women work so hard at home and feel so responsible for the kids and so guilty about the hours they spend away that they do not have the time or the energy to compete with men for the more lucrative positions in the higher rungs of the career ladder. Finally, the ideology of intensive mothering serves men in that women's commitment to this socially devalued task helps to maintain their subordinate position in society as a whole.

Child-rearing ideologies have also helped to maintain the privileged position of those who are native-born, those who are white, and those who are members of the middle and upper classes. Historically, ideas of appropriate child rearing were an integral part of the middle-class claim to superiority over the languishing, frivolous rich and the gaudy, untutored poor. Native-born whites of the dominant classes today have surely benefited from the fact that they are the ones most likely to have the cultural and economic resources as well as the time to define and engage in the form of mothering that is considered proper. Recent immigrants and members of lower-income and nonwhite communities in the United States, on the other hand, are consistently placed at a practical, economic, and status disadvantage in these terms. Members of such groups may also thereby lower their children's chances for economic gain, since their child-rearing methods are, for instance, less likely to be valued and rewarded by the school system and less likely to provide the cultural capital necessary for a well-paying job. For much the same reasons, middle- and upper-class whites are not only liable to maintain the economic benefits connected to their class and race but also are likely to gain the advantage of a certain social legitimacy for their economically and culturally privileged position.[12]

The words of mothers offer little explicit help in confirming or denying this line of thought. In my small sample, Latinas and African-American women clearly recognize racial oppression, but these are the only groups that seem to argue that the injustice and oppression in their lives are systematic and straightforward. Although many working-class and poor women recognize inequality in the class system and a few rail against the very rich, most seem to accept the system as a relatively fair one in which nearly everyone has an equal opportunity to get ahead. Poor mothers are often dissatisfied with government bureaucracy, given that they suffer the weight of the welfare system, yet they also seem to be resigned that this is the price they must pay in order to receive assistance — after all, they imply, as individuals who control their own lives, they are ultimately responsible for their fate. Some paid working mothers are dissatisfied with the way their bosses treat them, with their inflexible schedules, with the size of their paychecks, or with the high cost of children's toys and shoes, but none seem to feel that their child-rearing practices are controlled by the state and capitalism. On the other hand, since almost half of these women define themselves as feminists and nearly all express some resentment of men's incompetence or men's unwillingness to help domestically, one would suspect that they understand men as oppressors of a sort. But this attitude is actually a bit more complicated. When I asked these mothers, "Who do you think has it better, men or women?" many argue that a life of nurturing and child rearing is far preferable to a life of fighting wars and being primarily responsible for the financial support of the family.[13] Even male domination, in this sense, is not necessarily experienced as obvious or unambiguous. Above all, not one of the mothers I talked to understood her child-rearing efforts as an unjust burden or as a task imposed on her by others more powerful than herself.

These facts, however, do little to dent this argument. The power and the privileging of men, whites, the upper classes, the market, and the centralized state operate as interconnected systems whose logics are necessarily hidden — since people might (and sometimes do) revolt if they recognize these systems as unjust. Ideological coercion, in this sense, is much more efficient and effective than physical coercion. These forms of ideological coercion are not so much the result of a self-conscious conspiracy but, rather, are developed over time through a process of trial and error. Arguments about "equal opportunity" and "individual responsibility" for one's social position, in these terms, are simply ideological mechanisms meant to disguise systematic injustice. So too is the ideology of intensive mothering. It operates to convince women that they want (or at least should want) to commit themselves to a task that, in fact, ultimately serves those with the power to manipulate and control ideas.[14] The ideology of intensive child rearing, then, is both the result of and a form of *disguising* domination.

With this in mind, there are many indications that mothers are serving the interests of the powerful. The child-rearing techniques of lower-class, non-white, and immigrant women are treated as inferior, and, partly because of this, their children are less likely to get ahead (e.g., Bourdieu 1977, 1984; Collins 1971b; Lareau 1987). Women in general do far more than their fair share of child rearing and housework, and there is much evidence that they spare men from heavier competition in the labor force. Mothers do attempt to raise their children as obedient citizens who will neither revolt against nor become dependent upon the state. And they are certainly producing workers for the future at a relatively low cost at the same time that they seem to be (perhaps unwittingly) training their kids to be heavy consumers of commercial goods.

This is, without a doubt, the most powerful argument for explaining why it is women rather than men who are held primarily responsible for child rearing.[15] It also provides a broader social context for understanding arguments about the love or self-interest of mothers. The explicit emphasis on nurturant and intensive maternal love is interpreted in relation to the social circumstances in which it arose and developed and is understood as part of an ideology initiated, elaborated, and maintained by the more powerful groups in society. By emphasizing the social reality of unequal gender relations, this analysis also allows one to recognize that women's "self-interested" attempts to gain status have long focused on ideologies valorizing motherhood precisely because this has been one of the few avenues for achieving status left open to women. In the same terms, the extent to which white, middle-class women have been successful in making their notions of appropriate child rearing salient has had much to do with their relative privilege. And, if one is trying to make sense of why paid work, efficiency, and the competition for monetary success are the primary goals that self-interested people would seek to maximize, then a recognition that a rationalized market society is the context in which they operate offers a good deal of clarification.

There are, however, problems and ambiguities in this explanation as well. The interests of men, capitalists, the state, the upper classes, and native-born whites, it could be argued, do not *necessarily* lead them to press for intensive child rearing. Arguably, the form of ideological coercion that would make the most sense is one that convinced women to dedicate themselves to efficiency above all — both in the maintenance of the household and in the pursuit of the best-paid work available to them. Children would then be sent elsewhere to be raised by others. Some men, after all, might want sexy wives cooking hearty meals instead of ones busy with diapers and covered with infant spittle — and at times they have been known to make this clear (e.g., Rubin 1983). Women could also serve men quite well if they spent more of their time bringing home a larger portion of the family income. Capitalism could thus obtain full access to the energies of women in their prime productive years. It could also gain more customers by expanding the service industry in commercialized child care and boarding schools. And, theoretically at least, the child-care centers and boarding schools thus created could do a much more cost-effective job of preparing children for life in the market system — training them for future geographic mobility, helping them to develop the proper perspective on efficiency and the pursuit of profit, and preparing them more effectively for their respective futures as workers or managers by ranking and sorting them early on in accordance with their capabilities.[16] These "schools" for children could also serve the state well, allowing it to widen its net of regulation and control. White, middle-class women could then name themselves as the most efficient superwomen of all, and their privileged economic position would serve as the glue to make that label stick.

In other words, the ideology of intensive motherhood is clearly not the only way for the powerful to ensure that their interests are met. And beyond this, one still needs to ask, if power actually does allow people to create and manipulate ideologies at will, why would those whose privilege relies on a society dominated by the logic of profit-oriented, competitive, and individualistic relations develop an ideology whose overall logic runs in contradiction to that system? This remains something of a mystery.

Mothers' Work of Condemning Selfishness and Preserving Innocence

The image of an appropriate mother is one of an unselfish nurturer. And the ideology of the sacred child is one that measures a child's innocence and purity by the child's distance from the corrupt outside world. Both of these are central elements of the larger cultural model of intensive mothering, and both are implicated in the cultural contradictions of motherhood. This is no accident.

Just as the ideologies of equal opportunity and individual responsibility are not merely manipulative ploys meant to serve those in power but are also important, socially convincing ideologies for certain specifiable and significant reasons, so too are the ideologies of the sacred child and unselfish mothering important, socially convincing ideologies for certain specifiable and significant reasons. Although the cultural model of intensive mothering may, like the ideologies of equal opportunity and individual responsibility, partially serve to disguise certain forms of self-seeking and domination, its persistence is also a crucial indicator of something more.

When late eighteenth- and early nineteenth-century urban middle-class women set out to elaborate the significance of mothering, the ideology they used to engage in this "self-interested" strategy was one based on a critique of the logic of self-interest. The historical moment at which they made this argument was one when the population, more clearly than ever before, was feeling the power of industrialization. Yet the form of child rearing these women recommended was one that emphasized the distance of mothers and children from the logic of a rationalized market society. In many ways, this trend has only grown stronger over time. The more widely the rationalized market has spread its net, the more the child, the child's innocence, the child's needs, and the child's life have become a central focus of family life. This is far too systematic to be treated as mere coincidence.

That this trend is rooted in a form of implicit opposition to the logic of the marketplace is implied in the work of many scholars.[17] But this argument is illustrated most powerfully by the reasoning of mothers themselves. First, as I have argued, the language of profit-maximizing strategies, efficiency, contracts, and competition that is heard in so many other areas of life is lacking in mothers' discussions of child rearing. Mothers have a distrust of crass, commercial day-care arrangements. They say that the child's success is to be measured not in terms of money earned but in terms of the happiness the child achieves and the sharing, caring qualities she or he develops. And they certainly don't discuss how soon they will set the child to work. Mothering is emphatically not a profit-making enterprise.

Furthermore, according to mothers, children are emphatically not the individualistic, calculating competitors one encounters in the marketplace. There is no such thing as a bad child. Children are innocent and pure, untainted by the cynicism, aggression, and degradation of adult life. The seeming innocence and uncorrupted nature of children is what enables them to offer the unconditional love that mothers find so valuable. This is the love that promises to be the grounding for the kind of long-term intimate ties of warmth, understanding, and support that are so difficult to sustain in the larger world.

But perhaps the strongest indication of the opposition between the logic of intensive mothering and the logic of a self-interested, competitive, rationalized market society is mothers' persistent preoccupation with the theme of the good mother's lack of "selfishness." In their elaborations on this theme, they point clearly to the dichotomy between nurturing, moral mothers and the cold, calculating, amoral world. For instance, they tell me, people who are cold and uncaring put their own needs and convenience ahead of their child's need for love and closeness. This is clearly wrong:

> Someone else told me, this was from a doctor, they had a baby with colic and the wife was just going berserk all day with this baby at home, screaming all the time. So when he came home from work, he'd put the baby in the car seat, and put it in the closet and close the door because, he said, "there wasn't anything you could do for it anyway, so you might as well not have to listen to it cry." I mean, I could not believe it—he was serious! I just was stunned. Again, I think it's just *selfishness*.

We might all agree that placing one's colicky infant in a closet is abusive, but it is also merely an exaggerated example of what selfish people appear to do all too often. Bad mothers leave their children without the nurturing and guidance they need just so they can go to parties, take vacations, go out to bars, or make more money than they really need. Appropriate motherhood, on the other hand, involves sacrifice, as this mother points out: "For me, I sacrifice all the time. I figure it would be greedy for me just to live my life and, you know, be making money, and just be greedy and just live for myself. I wanted someone else to enjoy some of the stuff that I could give to them."

The notion of selfishness is often tied to making money and to materialism in this way. Another mother makes this point with reference to the importance of reassuring children that their mother's paid work is for the good of the family and not a matter of personal gratification:

Make sure you're reassuring the kids that what Mommy's doing [when she goes out to work for pay] *is not for herself*, but for all of them. The kids might think, "Oh, my mommy's only doing it for herself. She just wants to get good things for her, nothing for us." You should work to get money not for material things but for family togetherness. It's not . . . separate ways. It has to be together or nothing. That's the way I think. (Emphasis mine)

Materialism and money making for selfish reasons, according to this analysis, are in opposition to the logic of togetherness. Of the two, togetherness is clearly treated as more important. Reiterating this point, another mother argues that material possessions may be here today and gone tomorrow, but the relationship one establishes with one's child is much more lasting and much more valuable:

When I went to this high school reunion, a lot of the girls that don't have kids were the people that really bored me. Because they were into their designer sunglasses and they're really into their cars and that sort of thing. That's really what's important to them. One of them got a bigger engagement ring than another girl and the other one, she didn't like hers anymore. And it's like, who cares? It amazed me to think that that's really what's important to some people. . . . Nobody can take away your relationship and your love. They can steal your car and your stupid ring. [My son is] not a possession, but I just never loved anybody like this. [She cries.]

According to this mother, childless women, by focusing their attention on themselves and their material possessions, are missing something that is far more important.

In line with this logic is Rachel's condemnation of people like her boss:

There are people like my boss who have no conception at all of what it means to have children. . . . My child was sick, I would never have thought of leaving [her] side, I needed to be with her every second. . . . And [these people] they have no conception, they just don't understand. And I don't know what it is, selfishness or what. I feel like, yeah, they're missing something.

For Rachel, you may recall, people like her boss represent the cold, competitive business world that values financial profit above all else. And Rachel, like the mother quoted above, implies that such people are missing the close, warm, intimate relationship of nurturing and sharing that child rearing brings.

Mothers, as I have suggested, also argue that children actually help to teach us not to be selfish, by instructing us on the importance of nurturing and of giving: "I think we all have a tendency to get really selfish, and children come along, and you can't be selfish because they demand so much nurturing. It helps *you* to give more to them." Giving more to children is not just a lesson in austerity; the sacrifice that child rearing involves also reminds us of the joy of sharing: "because an ice-cream tastes twice as good when you know you only get half of it because you got to share it with somebody else." It is by bringing us this joy, another mother told me, that children help to reinforce "the theory that the more people you have to love, the better off you are."

According to the logic of intensive motherhood, it is through this same emphasis on loving, caring, and sharing that mothering can help to make the world a better place. The logic the following mother implies, for instance, is that children teach you to be loving and unselfish, you give love to them in return, and they grow up to be good and caring people:

> I feel like that Folger's commercial — that's the best commercial in the whole world, the one that's when you get up in the morning and you have a cup of coffee and those few minutes to think, and you're looking at your children playing on the floor and loving them and you realize that what could be better in life than being the person that takes care of somebody else's life. There's nothing more to life than just that. . . . This is the ultimate to leave behind when you go . . . people that are going to carry on your beliefs and be strong and good and loving people. And to know that you had something to do with that, that they're going to make the world a better place, one way or another.

Another mother reiterates this point in her response to the question "What qualities would you like to see in your son when he grows up?":

> [I'd like him to] be a person that's generous and kind to other people. It's sort of a ripple effect. There's a feeling of goodness that goes out. I think that's really important. Because I think there's so many problems, there's so much horror in the world, that those people that are helping in just the sense of being a good friend, being a good dad, being a good husband, that's all part of it. And that will affect their kids, and it just goes on and on.

Through this ripple effect, the more that mothers can mold kind and generous people, the more that those children will mold kind and generous children of their own, and the fewer problems and the less horror there will be in the world.

In all this, mothers argue that their work as mothers is quite different from the pursuit of self-interested gain — particularly the pursuit of material gain. They indicate that their primary interest in raising children is in the creation and sustenance of long-term ties of sharing and caring. They make it clear that this emphasis on sharing and caring not only benefits themselves and their children but also promises to make the world a better place. And they demonstrate that mothering implies a rejection of the logic of the rationalized marketplace.

This argument, of course, has its problems as well. First, one could interpret mothers' emphasis on unselfishness in a different way than I have here. Perhaps mothers are simply parroting the notion first made popular during the early nineteenth-century cult of domesticity — and by so doing are attempting to valorize their position by making use of one of the few claims to righteousness available to them as mothers. Perhaps this is an expression of their resentment. That is, one might argue that these mothers are actually unhappy about all the sacrifices they have made to raise children and that they envy the relatively spontaneous, less stressful, less physically and emotionally taxing life of the childless woman. Since it is too late for them to have that life, they try to glorify the tedious work of mothering at they same time that they try to degrade those who have what they secretly desire. And surely, for some women, portions of these interpretations may be valid.

But perhaps more important, it is dangerous to emphasize women's unselfish nurturing, as many feminist scholars have made clear, since this is the very same analysis used to portray women as passive caregivers — thereby supporting the views of those who would like to see women remain primarily responsible for raising the kids, disguising the ways that women actively and assertively pursue their own interests, and marking women as unsuited to positions of independence and authority in the public realm (see esp. Epstein 1988; Pollit 1992; Stacey 1986). This same argument is also dangerous in that it can be used to imply that nurturing and altruism are appropriately accomplished solely in the family, by women, and therefore need not apply to the political and economic realms or to the lives of men.

Although the gendered elements of this argument are dangerous, it is, like arguments about love, the argument of mothers themselves and should not be silenced or dismissed. When mothers stress this logic, their focus on unselfishness is not a passive selflessness but an active rejection of market logic. In this, as is also true of their arguments about love, mothers point to crucial and often hidden aspects of our culture. To put it another way, if the transition from arguments about self-interest to those regarding unequal power relations reminds us to ask who has the strongest oxen, this analysis reminds us to ask what cultural beliefs lead people to have an interest in oxen to begin with. The cultural logic operating here offers an alternative account of what might count as status, power, or self-interest. In this sense, the ideology of intensive mothering persists not only in spite of the fact that it runs counter to the logic of impersonality, competition, and personal profit but precisely because it does.

Cultural Ambivalence

These four arguments coexist in tension. Although we might like to believe that both intensive child rearing and self-interested calculations of personal advantage are human nature, the empirical inadequacies and logical inconsistencies of such an analysis are apparent. And though we might attempt to explain the tension between arguments about self-interest and arguments about unselfish nurturing by claiming that the powerful have forced women to engage in intensive mothering even though these women would certainly prefer to be studying their profit-and-loss statements at the end of each business day, this analysis not only contains its own inconsistencies but also completely disregards mothers' deep commitment to a fully elaborated model of unselfish caregiving. What is lacking in each case is an understanding of the complex cultural logics that guide human thought and action. Human nature is culturally shaped; interests are culturally defined. In these terms, while an argument about cultural opposition may also suffer from certain forms of one-sidedness and narrow-mindedness, it does successfully highlight the opposing cultural logics in which mothers' behavior and beliefs are embedded. And, taken together, these four analyses make it apparent that the very same cultural tensions that haunt mothers haunt scholars and others as well.

These tensions can be seen in the conflicts between people like Rachel and her boss, between the demands of work life and the demands of family life, between the pushes for women to place their children at the center of their lives and the pulls these women experience to seek recognition in the public world. These same tensions are also expressed in the way people often treat their coworkers as both competitors and intimates, give money to a charity because doing so both provides a tax break and is thought to be a worthy cause, consider their bosses as unwelcome authority figures as well as friends, and drive polluting cars to work each day at the same time they carefully recycle their aluminum cans when they come home. All these contradictions mark a fundamental cultural ambivalence about a society based solely on the pursuit of self-interested gain. Motherhood, in this sense, is one central field upon which a much larger struggle is waged.

My argument about mothers' opposition to a rationalized market society does not supersede or nullify arguments about unequal power relations or self-interested calculations of profit. Mothers are, in part, rational bookkeepers endeavoring to maximize their social assets and to organize their lives in efficient ways. Mothers are also social subordinates whose mothering, in part, serves the interests of those more powerful than themselves. But it would require a long theoretical stretch to simply explain away the ideology of intensive mothering as merely a cunning ploy devised to cover up the advantages that mothers seek or as solely a manipulative strategy meant to serve the powerful. Mothers operate in part according to a logic opposing that of self-interested gain — not because this is a necessity, not because they are irrational or selfless, and not because they are forced to, but because they are actively participating in a rejection of that logic. If women were simply calculating "rational actors" operating according to the logic that dominates in the marketplace, they could easily dispense with the ideology of intensive motherhood. And if they did so, there would be no cultural contradictions and motherhood would not hold the symbolic power that it does in our culture.

This way of opposing the logic of rationalized market societies is not necessarily a self-conscious opposition, it is not the opposition of isolated individuals, and, as I have noted, it is surely not the only form of such opposition. As Polanyi (1944) points out, if the self-regulating market alone determined the fate of the earth and its inhabitants, the earth would be polluted beyond recognition and the broken bodies of laborers would be strewn like garbage across the land. To stem this tide, Polanyi argues, people have engaged in a countermovement, a form of opposition to market logic that includes, for instance, the establishment of labor unions, worker-safety provisions, social security programs, welfare systems, environmental protection agencies, and national parks. People have not necessarily seen their work in establishing such programs and provisions as opposition to market logic, and their efforts are certainly not the work of isolated individuals. On a different level, the same is true of the form of opposition implicit in the ideology of intensive mothering. When women engage in this opposition, they generally do not make a self-conscious decision to oppose the system that values competitive individualism and material advantage. And although they do not engage in collective action per se, they are also not acting as isolated individuals. They act as members of a culture that maintains two contradictory ideologies, and their actions take place in the context of a social hierarchy that gives women primary responsibility for creating and maintaining nurturing ties.

The mothering relationship is not the only human relationship that holds symbolic power as a form of opposition. The ideologies of socially appropriate romantic love, friendship, and family ties, in particular, all treat considerations of financial profit, status seeking, and efficiency as taboo.[18] Of course, the same tensions that exist in the mothering relationship are present in love, friendship, and family relations. We know, for instance, that many people fall in love and establish friendships out of convenience, in attempts to heighten their own status or material gains, and as a way to exercise forms of power. And we know that people's level of commitment to family members is sometimes grounded in these same concerns. Although such practices point to significant realities, the cultural ideals that guide these relationships remain equally significant. The ideology guiding the relationship between mothers and children is, I would argue, particularly powerful in this regard, precisely because it is understood as more distant and more protected from market relationships than any other.

If mothering is one of the central practices meant to provide a crucial counterpoint to the corruption, impersonality, and individualistic competition of the larger society, the place that ordinary people in their everyday lives find hope for this sort of counterpoint has increasingly narrowed. Early in the history of this nation, citizens were understood as struggling to achieve some form of the common good, and mothers saw their role as instilling the values of virtuous citizenship in their children. Home, women, and mothers were imagined as a source of purity and goodness: home was sweet, women were pious, passionless, and pure, and mothers were unselfish, nurturing, and moral. But over time the image of a morally pure home was increasingly scarred as households were invaded by the logic of technical efficiency, juvenile courts and social workers, public schools, TV dinners and manufactured clothing, and visions of a competition for resources among family members. Claims to the virtue and moral righteousness of women were further tainted by a hesitancy to claim any single definition of morality as an absolute or shared one. More and more, at least some women seemed far from pious, passionless, and pure. In the present era the virtue of citizens has become a distant echo, as evidenced in widespread disenchantment with a political process perceived as competitive and corrupt. One of the few sources left for making the world a better place seems to be grounded in the ethic of maternal love and unselfishness and in children's apparent innocence, purity, and goodness.

Adding to this trend is the fact that as the implosion of self-interest and competition proceeds, ties of friendship, love, and family have come to seem increasingly tenuous. The more one begins to wonder if friends might be moving on to a better job or simply using those around them for their own gain, then the more one might expect the concern to establish lasting ties of mutual obligation and commitment to be centered on the family. The more divorce becomes the norm, the more unreliable and unstable relationships with adult family members seem, and the more that popular psychology advises people to pick and choose which adult family members they will remain close to, then the more one would expect people to seek out other friendships. But the more unreliable both friendships and adult family relationships become, the more one's attention comes to be focused on relations between mother and child. One mother implied this in her response to the question "How do you think you'd feel if you never had children?":

I'd be really lonely. Because a husband, well, you can have two, three, four husbands, you know. Big deal. But your children are something that's a part of you. It's not the same with them. Because your husband will get up and leave one day and you can get another one. That's why.

And that's why, at least in part, the more the larger world becomes impersonal, competitive, and individualistic and the more the logic of that world invades the world of intimate relationships, the more intensive child rearing becomes.

It is as if there has been a long-term shrinkage in the possibilities for sustainable human ties. Ariès (1962) alludes to this process when he argues that the historical separation of private, family life from public, community, and work life brought about a decline in the wider social interaction of previous eras, when the full round of life was lived in public. As a consequence, he writes,

> the family has advanced in proportion as sociability has retreated. It is as if the modern family had sought to take the place of old social relationships (as these gradually defaulted), in order to preserve mankind from an unbearable moral solitude. (406)

What I am implying here is that, over time, the family has increasingly suffered from both the strain of attempting to take the place of wider social ties and from the implosion of the logic of the marketplace. As family relationships and other intimate relationships gradually default, even further strain is placed on the mothering relationship. This relationship comes to stand as a central symbol of the sustainable human ties, free of competition and selfish individualism, that are meant to preserve us, in Ariès's terms, from an unbearable moral solitude. This is a very tall order indeed.

As I have argued, the contemporary attempt at a solution to the cultural contradictions of motherhood is to ideologically separate the world of motherhood from the larger social world and thereby to make women responsible for unselfish nurturing while men are responsible for self-interested profit maximization. This, of course, is simply a new version of an older solution that initially included not only the ideological separation of public and private life but also the barring of "proper" (that is, white, middle-class) married women from participation in the paid labor force and the exclusion of all women from positions of public authority. Not only is this solution more difficult to maintain than ever before, it also retains the two central problems that were evident from its inception. First, it tends to absolve the public world from responsibility for the values of unselfish care, commitment to the good of others, and willingness to carry out such obligations without direct or material remuneration. Second, it contributes to the continued power and privilege of men by creating a social role for women that marks them, in cultural terms, as ill-prepared and unsuitable participants in the public world and leaves many, in concrete terms, too exhausted to successfully compete for positions of higher authority and prestige in that world.

In the long run, all this deepens the problem of what Hochschild (1989) has called the "stalled revolution." When the Industrial Revolution sent men out of the home to work for wages, Hochschild argues, there was a connected ideological revolution that encouraged women to stay at home and tend hearth and child. Now that women are leaving the home to work for wages, she asks, why hasn't there been a corresponding revolution to ease their burden? Hochschild suggests that the appropriate ideological revolution would encourage men to share in household chores and encourage corporations and the state to provide subsidized child care, job sharing, flex time, and parental leave.

As I have suggested, however, the ideological revolution that would actually correspond to the logic of its predecessor in the Industrial Revolution would be one that convinced a group of social subordinates to do the dirty work, just as male wage workers and businessmen once convinced women to take the lower-status position of staying at home. This is a solution that is already being carried out on a relatively small scale among the middle and upper classes. They look to the poor — particularly nonwhites or undocumented immigrants — to watch their children, clean their homes, and do their laundry. But this revolution, of course, leaves the majority of women behind. And it is a revolution that has not met with widespread cultural support.

Straying somewhat from the logic of that first revolution, on the other hand, we could come up with even more efficient and profit-maximizing solutions, as I have suggested. For instance, we could imagine twenty-four-hour day-care centers run by the state and staffed by (otherwise unproductive) older children and retirees. Or we could alter our perceptions of children's needs and minimize the efforts we put into raising them — by simply setting them out like seedlings and watching them grow. Although I have implied that there are portions of the ideology of intensive mothering that might be usefully altered in such a way as to ease the pressure on contemporary mothers, I have also argued that its logic contains a crucial form of cultural opposition that we should be hesitant to dismantle. There are, in other words, a number of good reasons to consider extreme versions of these solutions socially unacceptable, and the majority of mothers would certainly find them so.

To transform child rearing into shared work among social equals would require a revolution quite different from its predecessor. But to the extent that we value at least portions of the ideology of intensive mothering, such a revolution is surely in order. Under current circumstances, our best hope for easing women's burden remains increased public power for women, higher public status for those involved in caregiving, and greater paternal participation in child rearing. All of these solutions are interrelated. The more public power women gain, the more they can demand that men take greater responsibility for child rearing and the more child rearing (and all it symbolizes) will likely come to be publicly valued. Given the greater share of public power among men currently, the more fathers participate in raising children, the more they will demand that child rearing be publicly valued. And as child rearing increases in public status, the more likely it is that men will participate in it. Finally, the more that men participate in child rearing and the more it is socially valued, the more likely it becomes that attempts to convince business leaders and legislators to provide subsidized child care, job sharing, flex time, and parental leave will meet with success.

The struggle, tensions, and contradictions will probably persist for some time to come, however. After all, even if we achieve these ends, the tensions between the values of parenthood and the values of the marketplace will not disappear. Such social revisions will simply mean that *both* men and women will experience in their daily lives the contradictions in modern society that now plague women primarily; both men and women will have to juggle the two commitments, and both will have to switch gears every day when they come home from their paying jobs. With this newfound sharing of responsibility, however, the cultural contradictions of parenthood will perhaps become more open to public view and be confronted more equally, by all.[19]

The ideology of intensive mothering is not simply about children, or mothers, or even the family. It is instead an ideology that speaks to a more prevalent set of social and moral concerns. But the opposition to rationalized market societies implicit in this ideology is fragile and precarious, as I have shown. More important, this ideology has never been an entirely satisfactory solution to the problems of modernity. The cultural model of intensive mothering, after all, suggests that all the troubles of the world can be solved by the individual efforts of superhuman women. Clearly, this places a tremendous and undue burden on women, and one that becomes increasingly difficult to maintain as the ethos of rationalized market society invades the home and as more and more mothers enter that competitive and impersonal world when they go out to work for pay. But the continued importance of the opposition underlying this burden is clearly indicated in the way that it persists with such tenacity in the face of adversity.

To the extent that the valorization of nurturing mothers and innocent children is meant to protect us all from the full impact of a dog-eat-dog world, the opposition is crucial. At the same time, however, this ideology helps to reproduce the existing gender hierarchy and to contribute, with little social or financial compensation for the mothers who sustain its tenets, to the maintenance of capitalism and the centralized state. The fact that the preservation of this ideology is seen as private "women's work," means that men and public leaders can rest assured that women will hold up this half of the cultural world without aid or assistance. It is also important to recognize that this ideology tends to shroud family relations in a sentimentalized cloak, thereby hiding the reality of family violence and potentially conflicting interests of family members while also masking the subordination of women. If my analysis is correct, however, to overcome such problems entirely would require overcoming not only the gender hierarchy but also the tensions in modern society highlighted by the persistence of the ideology of intensive mothering.

Appendix A: Interview Questions

The following is the interview schedule I used with my thirty-eight respondents. Sometimes I changed the order of these questions, sometimes I used slight variations in phrasing the questions, and sometimes I asked follow-up questions. All of the interviews, however, followed basically the same scheme.

A. Introductory Questions

What are the names of your children?

What are their ages?

What is your husband's name?

When you got pregnant (with your youngest), was it the result of a conscious decision to have a child at that time?

What were your main reasons for having a child?

How do you think you would feel if you had never had children?

When it comes to feeding, bathing, nap times and playtimes, do you try to establish a set schedule or do you let your child set his or her own schedule?

What methods do you use to discipline your child/ren?

Do you think you [would/do] treat your male/female children differently?

Note: I am indebted to the work of Kathleen Gerson (1985) and Arlie Hochschild (1989) in the formulation of a number of these questions.

B. Child-Rearing Advice

Regarding your main source of child-rearing ideas (as noted on questionnaire), is this your most trusted source?

Is there anything about the advice you've received that you don't like?

Are there certain people you think of as experts on child rearing?

Does your mother give you advice on child rearing?

What is the most important piece of advice you have received about child rearing?

C. Ideas about Child Rearing

How would you describe a good child as opposed to a bad child?

How do you think they become good or bad children?

When your child grows up, what kind of qualities would you like to see in him or her?

Do you think of yourself as a good and competent mother?

Do you think people hold mothers responsible for how their children turn out?

Do you think this is fair?

D. Parents' Child-Rearing Ideas and Practices

How did you feel about your mother [working/not working] outside the home? Did you like it or dislike it?

Do you think your mother's child-rearing ideas and practices were different from your father's? In what ways?

Were they different from yours? In what ways?

What do you think your mother considered the most important thing to teach you?

E. Paid Work and Child Rearing

How do you think your [working/not working] has affected your ability to be a mother?

What are the main reasons you [are/are not] working right now?

Imagine that you were [working outside the home/staying at home] right now. How would you feel about that?

Do you believe that taking care of the home and raising children is generally more important and rewarding for a woman than having a job outside the home?

How important do you think it is that home life be different from work and life outside?

Do you think the home is or should be a sort of haven?

F. Adult Males in the Household (if present)

On the questionnaire you noted that your [adult male] helps out with child care. You say you [do/do not] want him to participate more. Why?

Do you think he does it as well as you?

Do you think he is as concerned with your child's development as you are?

G. Day Care

I see you [do/do not] send your child/ren to day care. What are your main worries about day care, if any?

With reference to your preference for type of child-care services, why do you think you would prefer [type noted on questionnaire]?

E. General

How do you think child-rearing ideas have changed since your mother's day?

Do you think these changes are measures of progress?

How do you think the fact that so many women are working outside the home these days has affected children?

In a perfect world, how would the task of child rearing be organized? That is, who would do it and where would it be done?

This is a hard question. When you think of the commitment you make, the responsibility you take on, and the sacrifices required of you in raising a child, do you think of yourself as doing it for something more than just yourself and your child?

Does being a mother help you to feel close to other women?

In general, who do you think has it better, men or women?

Appendix B: Survey Questionnaire

Each of the respondents in my study completed one of these surveys several days before the time of the interview.

> *I. These first questions are general ones about yourself and the people in your household.*

1. Is there an adult male (or males) in your household?
   yes _____ no _____
   A. If yes, what is his (their) relationship to you (e.g., husband, boyfriend, father)?
   B. What is his (their) age(s)?
2. Please indicate the age and sex of each of the children living in your household. If they are your stepchildren or adopted, check the space provided.
   age: _____ sex (M or F): _____ stepchild? _____ adopted? _____
   age: _____ sex (M or F): _____ stepchild? _____ adopted? _____
   age: _____ sex (M or F): _____ stepchild? _____ adopted? _____
   age: _____ sex (M or F): _____ stepchild? _____ adopted? _____
   age: _____ sex (M or F): _____ stepchild? _____ adopted? _____

Note: As with the interview schedule, I found the work of Kathleen Gerson (1985) particularly helpful in preparing this questionnaire.

3. Please indicate the age and relation to you of anyone else who lives in your household.

   age: _____ relation to you: _____

   age: _____ relation to you: _____

   age: _____ relation to you: _____

4. Do you work outside the home?

   yes _____ no _____

      A. If yes, what kind of work do you do?

      B. In what type of industry?

      C. How many hours do you work in an average week?

      D. How many years have you been working at this job?

5. What was the highest grade you attended in school?

6. If you are married, how many years have you been married to your current husband?

      A. Is this your first husband?

         yes _____ no _____

7. If you are currently unmarried, have you ever been married before?

   yes _____ no _____

8. If there is an adult male in your household (e.g., husband, father of your children, boyfriend), does he work?

   yes _____ no _____ no adult male in household _____

      A. If yes, what kind of work does he do?

      B. In what type of industry?

      C. How many hours does he work in an average week?

      D. How many years has he been working at this job?

      E. What was the highest grade he attended in school?

II. The following are questions regarding your ideas about children and child rearing.

9. Are you currently planning to have any more children?

   yes _____ no _____

      A. If yes, how many more children do you want to have?

10. Do you think of child rearing as a demanding and rigorous task?

    yes _____ no _____ not sure _____

11. Do you think that a mother must have a great deal of knowledge on child rearing in order to do it well?

    yes _____ no _____

12. Compared to the paid work of an average corporate executive or other professional, would you say that child rearing is more or less demanding and rigorous? (Choose one.)

    1 _____ child rearing more demanding

    2 _____ child rearing less demanding

13. Do you consider child rearing *primarily* a physical, moral, psychological, or intellectual task for you? (Check one.)

    1 _____ physical   3 _____ moral

    2 _____ psychological 4 _____ intellectual

14. If you had to choose, which would you say is more important for the child?

    1 _____ nurturing

    2 _____ a good education

15. How would you describe the basis of your child/ren's personality characteristics and intellectual abilities for the most part? (Check one.)

    1 _____ there from birth

    2 _____ a result of experience

    3 _____ equally inherited and based on experience

16. If you had to choose, which one of the following would you say is generally *most* important in determining how a child will do later in life? (Check one.)

    1 _____ early childhood experiences

    2 _____ late childhood experiences

17. When your child reaches high school age, which would you consider more important for him or her?

    1 _____ popularity among peers

    2 _____ academic success

18. In your opinion, which best describes the activity of mothering?

    1 _____ a natural, instinctual, commonsense-based task

    2 _____ something that needs to be learned

19. If you had to take a stand, would you say that children need both a mother and a father to be successful and well-adjusted?

    yes _____ no _____

III. The following questions are about your child-rearing practices.

20. Did you breast-feed your (2–4-year-old) child?

    yes _____ no _____

    A. If yes, for how many months?

21. Please estimate the number of times you took your (2–4-year-old) child to the doctor (for regular and emergency visits) in her/his first year.

22. Do *you* read to your (2–4-year-old) child?

    yes _____ no _____

    A. If yes, about how often?

23. Do you take your child/ren on outings that are solely for their leisure or education?

    yes _____ no _____

    A. If yes, about how often?

    B. Please name the most frequent outings.

24. About how many hours of television does your child watch per day?
25. Does your family eat dinner together?
    yes _____ no _____
    A. If yes, about how many times per week?
26. If you have older children, do they ever take full responsibility for the care of your younger children?
    yes _____ no _____
27. Speaking generally, at what age do you think a child is ready to take full responsibility for the care of a 2-year-old child (for a 6-hour period)?
28. Do you plan to give your child/ren religious instruction?
    _____ yes _____ no
29. Where do you plan to send your (2–4-year-old) child to school? (Check one.)
    1 _____ public school   4 _____ home school
    2 _____ private religious school   5 _____ other
    3 _____ other private school

IV. The following are questions regarding your sources of advice on child rearing.

30. Which of those listed below do you consider your sources of child-rearing ideas? (Check as many as you use as sources of advice.)
    1 _____ books   6 _____ other relatives
    2 _____ magazines   7 _____ doctor
    3 _____ television   8 _____ day-care worker
    4 _____ friends   9 _____ other
    5 _____ your mother
    B. If you had to choose just one, which of those sources would you consider your *primary* source of child-rearing ideas? (Check one.)
    1 _____ books   6 _____ other relatives
    2 _____ magazines   7 _____ doctor
    3 _____ television   8 _____ day-care worker
    4 _____ friends   9 _____ other
    5 _____ your mother
31. Approximately how many books on child rearing have you read?
    A. If you remember the titles or authors, please list.
32. Approximately how many magazines on child rearing have you read?
    A. If you remember the names of these magazines, please list.
    B. Of the books and magazines you have read, which *one* would you describe as most influential, helpful, or important to you?
    C. Which *one* would you describe as least influential, helpful, or important?
33. What books or magazines on child rearing do you own, if any?

34. If you own any books or magazines, who (of the following) bought *most* of them? (Check one.)

1 _____ self   4 _____ other friend
2 _____ husband   5 _____ a relative
3 _____ boyfriend   6 _____ other

35. Who recommended *most* of them? (Check one.)

1 _____ friends   3 _____ family
2 _____ professionals   4 _____ just picked them up

36. How do you usually use the books on child rearing?

1 _____ read from cover to cover
2 _____ pick out relevant portions

How do you usually use the magazines?

1 _____ read from cover to cover
2 _____ pick out relevant portions

37. The following is a list of topics most often covered in popular child-rearing manuals. Please check once if you have *read* on that topic, and check twice if you've found it an especially *useful* or important source of information.

	read	useful	
1	_____	_____	illness
2	_____	_____	feeding/bathing/sleeping
3	_____	_____	toilet training
4	_____	_____	posture/walking
5	_____	_____	general scheduling
6	_____	_____	talking
7	_____	_____	verbal/visual stimulation
8	_____	_____	child's schooling
9	_____	_____	intellectual stages
10	_____	_____	emotional stages
11	_____	_____	nurture/affection
12	_____	_____	crying
13	_____	_____	play
14	_____	_____	bodily contact
15	_____	_____	nervousness of child
16	_____	_____	comforters/pacifiers
17	_____	_____	spoiling
18	_____	_____	discipline
19	_____	_____	mother's depression
20	_____	_____	divorce
21	_____	_____	day care
22	_____	_____	working mothers
23	_____	_____	father's participation
24	_____	_____	other

38. This is the same list. Now I would like you to mark the space beside the topic if you have *talked to someone* (friend, family, professional) about this topic and check twice if you have found the advice especially *useful* or important.

	talked	useful	
1	_____	_____	illness
2	_____	_____	feeding/bathing/sleeping
3	_____	_____	toilet training
4	_____	_____	posture/walking
5	_____	_____	general scheduling
6	_____	_____	talking
7	_____	_____	verbal/visual stimulation
8	_____	_____	child's schooling
9	_____	_____	intellectual stages
10	_____	_____	emotional stages
11	_____	_____	nurture/affection
12	_____	_____	crying
13	_____	_____	play
14	_____	_____	bodily contact
15	_____	_____	nervousness of child
16	_____	_____	comforters/pacifiers
17	_____	_____	spoiling
18	_____	_____	discipline
19	_____	_____	mother's depression
20	_____	_____	divorce
21	_____	_____	day care
22	_____	_____	working mothers
23	_____	_____	father's participation
24	_____	_____	other

Who was the person you *most commonly* talked to about the above-marked topics? (Check one.)

1 _____ female friend   6 _____ doctor
2 _____ male friend   7 _____ social worker
3 _____ adult male in household   8 _____ day-care worker
4 _____ your mother   9 _____ other
5 _____ other relative

39. Has the advice you have received on child rearing from friends, family, professionals, books, and/or magazines led you to believe that child rearing is more or less difficult and demanding than you thought it was before you received the advice?

1 _____ more demanding
2 _____ less demanding

40. About how often do you talk to someone about your child/ren (on any topic)?

    1 _____ daily   4 _____ rarely

    2 _____ weekly   5 _____ never

    3 _____ once a month

> V. *These questions have to do with work outside the home.*

41. If you have never been employed, have you ever thought you would like to get a job?

    yes _____ no _____ have been employed _____

42. Do you expect to start or continue working outside the home in the next five years?

    yes _____ no _____ don't know _____

43. Speaking personally, which is the better decision regarding career and child rearing?

    1 _____ combine career and child rearing

    2 _____ focus primarily on either child rearing or career

(If you have never been employed, skip to *Section VI*. If you are currently working outside the home, answer the three questions in *Group A*. If you used to work outside the home, skip to *Group B* within this section.)

Group A

44. On the whole, how would you describe your job?

    1 _____ very interesting

    2 _____ okay

    3 _____ boring

45. Would you prefer working fewer hours at your job?

    yes _____

    no _____

46. If you could arrange things just the way you wanted, which would you prefer to be doing now?

    1 _____ staying inside the home

    2 _____ working in the paid labor force

Group B

47. When you worked, how did you find your job on the whole?

    1 _____ very interesting

    2 _____ okay

    3 _____ boring

48. If you could arrange things just the way you wanted, which would you prefer to be doing right now?

    1 _____ staying inside the home

    2 _____ working in the paid labor force

    If you'd like to work in the paid labor force, what kind of job would you like?

VI. *The following questions are about day care.*

49. Have you ever taken your child/ren to day care?
yes _____ no _____
A. If no, do you plan to?
yes _____ no _____
B. If yes, how old was your child when you first took her or him to day care?
C. Is your 2–4-year-old in day care now?
yes _____ no _____
D. About how many hours per week does she or he spend in day care? _____
E. What type of day care is it?
1 _____ private day care in someone's home
2 _____ a commercial day-care center?
3 _____ a day-care center at work
4 _____ a cooperative parent-participation day-care center
F. If you could arrange things just as you would like, would you prefer to have your child spend less or more time in day care?
1 _____ less time
2 _____ more time

50. Generally (or personally, if applicable), how do you view the use of day care?
1 _____ a necessity for a mother's work schedule
2 _____ a service that allows a mother the time needed for herself
3 _____ an activity for the child's enrichment

51. If you needed day care and had the choice of the following places for your child (without financial, transportation, or time restrictions), which would you choose? (Check one.)
1 _____ a relative within your own home
2 _____ a professional day-care worker in your own home
3 _____ a friend in her or his own home
4 _____ a professional day-care worker in her or his home
5 _____ a commercial day-care center
6 _____ a state-run day-care center
7 _____ other

52. Whom would you prefer to hire as a caretaker for your children?
1 _____ a man
2 _____ a woman
3 _____ no preference

VII. *The following questions are about how you and the members of your household share child care and housework.*

53. On the average weekday, how many hours during the day would you estimate you spend as the *primary* caretaker of your child/ren? (Do not count the time when your child is asleep at night.) _____

54. On the average weekday, how many hours during the day would you estimate that your husband or the primary adult male member of your household spends as the *primary* caretaker of your child/ren? (Do not count the time when your child is asleep at night.) _____

    A. Would you want him to spend more time as the primary caretaker?
       yes _____ no _____

55. Who *usually* does the following household and child-care tasks? ("Primary male" means your husband, boyfriend, or other adult male in your household. Choose one response in each category.)

    cleaning house: self _____ primary male _____
                                        shared equally _____ other _____

    yard work: self _____ primary male _____
                                        shared equally _____ other _____

    cooking meals: self _____ primary male _____
                                        shared equally _____ other _____

    shopping for food: self _____ primary male _____
                                        shared equally _____ other _____

    cleaning up after meals: self _____ primary male _____
                                        shared equally _____ other _____

    taking out the garbage: self _____ primary male _____
                                        shared equally _____ other _____

    doing the laundry: self _____ primary male _____
                                        shared equally _____ other _____

    paying bills: self _____ primary male _____
                                        shared equally _____ other _____

    watching the child: self _____ primary male _____
                                        shared equally _____ other _____

    feeding the child: self _____ primary male _____
                                        shared equally _____ other _____

    playing with the child: self _____ primary male _____
                                        shared equally _____ other _____

    cleaning up after the child: self _____ primary male _____
                                        shared equally _____ other _____

    disciplining the child: self _____ primary male _____
                                        shared equally _____ other _____

    If you marked "other" in one or more of the above categories, who is the "other" that does most of the tasks marked? _____

VIII. These are questions about your parents and your family of origin.

56. How many brothers and sisters do you have?
    sisters _____
    brothers _____

57. Did your father work outside the home when you were growing up?
    yes _____ no _____
    A. If yes, what kind of work did he do?
    B. In what type of industry?
    C. About how many years did he hold that job?
58. How do you think he felt about his job?
    1 _____ liked his work
    2 _____ would have preferred something else
59. What was the highest grade your father completed in school?
60. What was the highest grade your mother completed in school?
61. Did your mother work outside the home when you were growing up?
    yes _____ no _____
    A. If yes, what kind of work did she do?
    B. In what type of industry?
    C. About how many years did she hold that job?
    D. How do you think she felt about her job outside the home?
       1 _____ liked it
       2 _____ would have preferred something else
62. If your mother had had the choice, which situation do you think she would have preferred?
    1 _____ staying inside the home
    2 _____ working at a job outside the home
63. About how much time did your father spend with you compared to your mother?
    1 _____ more than mother   3 _____ much less
    2 _____ less   4 _____ about the same
64. From which of the following sources do you think your mother got advice on child rearing? (Check as many as you think she used as sources of advice.)
    1 _____ books   5 _____ her mother
    2 _____ magazines   6 _____ other relatives
    3 _____ television   7 _____ doctor
    4 _____ friends   8 _____ day-care worker
65. Of those, which do you think she considered her *primary* source of child-rearing ideas? (Check one.)
    1 _____ books   5 _____ her mother
    2 _____ magazines   6 _____ other relatives
    3 _____ television   7 _____ doctor
    4 _____ friends   8 _____ day-care worker
66. About how many hours *per week* would you estimate she used child-care services? _____

67. If your mother got help with child care, from whom did that child care come *most regularly?* (Check one.)

    1 _____ friends   5 _____ child-care center
    2 _____ her mother   6 _____ in-home nanny or housekeeper
    3 _____ older children   7 _____ no one
    4 _____ other relatives   8 _____ don't know

68. Do you think your mother treated (or would have treated) her male children differently from her female children?

    yes _____ no _____ don't know _____

IX. The following (final) questions concern your general background.

69. Are *most* of your close friends also mothers?

    yes _____ no _____

    A. Do you find that more of your friends are mothers now that you are a mother yourself?

       yes _____ no _____

70. Which of the following best describes your opinion about abortion?

    1 _____ should be based on the woman's choice
    2 _____ should be legal only under certain circumstances
    3 _____ should always be illegal

71. Do you consider yourself a feminist?

    yes _____ no _____

72. Generally speaking, which of the following best describes your political affiliation?

    1 _____ strong Democrat   4 _____ not very strong Republican
    2 _____ not very strong Democrat
    3 _____ strong Republican   5 _____ an independent

73. Which best describes your political beliefs?

    1 _____ radical   4 _____ conservative
    2 _____ liberal   5 _____ very conservative
    3 _____ middle-of-the-road   6 _____ don't think about it much

74. Were you raised in a particular religion?

    yes _____ no _____

    A. If yes, which one?

75. Do you consider yourself a member of a religious group today?

    yes _____ no _____

    A. If yes, which one?

    B. Are you an active member of a church or temple?

       yes _____ no _____

76. Which of the following *best* describes your ethnic heritage?

    1 _____ African-American   4 _____ Hispanic
    2 _____ American Indian   5 _____ white
    3 _____ Asian-American   6 _____ other

77. Please mark the figure that is your best guess of your total family income each year before taxes. Include all family income, including wages, salaries, interest, dividends, etc.

    1 _____ under $10,000   6 _____ $50,000–$59,000

    2 _____ $10,000–$19,000   7 _____ $60,000–$69,000

    3 _____ $20,000–$29,000   8 _____ $70,000–$79,000

    4 _____ $30,000–$39,000   9 _____ $80,000–$89,000

    5 _____ $40,000–$49,000   10 _____ over $89,000

    Do you know one or two other mothers of 2-, 3-, or 4-year-olds who might be willing to complete this survey?

    yes _____ no _____

    If yes, please give me their names and addresses.

    Do you think your own mother would be willing to complete a similar survey?

    yes _____ no _____

    If yes, please give me her name and address.

    Would you like to know the results of this survey?

    yes _____ no _____

Thank you very much.

Notes

CHAPTER 1: WHY CAN'T A MOTHER BE MORE LIKE A BUSINESSMAN?

1. This story is from one of thirty-eight depth interviews I conducted with mothers of two- to four-year-old children. For a discussion of my methodology, see the preface.

2. The "rational actor" model implies a curious but nonetheless prevalent definition of rationality. Superficially, the logic operates this way: all individuals behave in such a way as to maximize their self-interests in a system of scarce resources. This means that they will systematically calculate their "comparative advantage" and choose the path that offers the greatest rewards at the lowest expense. The logical implication is that a rational person will treat other people in a purely instrumental fashion — as mere resources or obstacles in the universal struggle to maximize personal gain. If individuals don't act this way, it is implied, they are simply stupid or irrational. See Elster (1989) on the importance of rational action in social life; Becker (1981) for an analysis of the family using the logic of rational action; Coleman (1993) for a treatment of child rearing that employs the rational actor model; Folbre and Hartmann (1988), Mansbridge (1990) and Risman and Feree (1995) for various relevant responses to the use of this model.

3. Although the ideological separation of home and world was powerful throughout this period, the practical separation of these two spheres has always been difficult (if not impossible) to achieve for poor and working-class women who have long participated simultaneously in the public world of paid work and the private sphere of domesticity (see chap. 2 and Weiner [1985]).

4. More specifically, in the United States in 1950, 11.9 percent of women with children under six years of age were employed; in 1960, 18.6 percent; in 1970, 30.3 percent;

in 1979, 43.2 percent; in 1988, 56.1 percent; and in 1993, 58.3 percent (U.S. Bureau of the Census 1994; U.S. Department of Labor 1980). Among married mothers with children under three, for instance, 66.6 percent held paying jobs for all or part of the year in 1992 (Hayghe and Bianchi 1994). Over half of mothers with children less than one year old, and nearly three-quarters of women with children aged six to sixteen, are now working for pay (U.S. Bureau of the Census 1992; U.S. Department of Labor 1991).

5. I recognize that there are important differences among women and mothers along class, racial, and ethnic lines (not to mention age, marital status, and number of children). I will address those issues in later chapters. Throughout much of this introduction, however, I refer either to professional-class career women (for reasons that will become apparent) or to women and mothers in general, focusing on the socially constructed similarities among them.

6. Although the phrase "paid working woman" may at times seem cumbersome, throughout this book I intentionally avoid using the more common expression "working woman" to refer to women who work outside the home. The common usage implies that women who are not working for pay do not actually work. Yet we know that most women who stay at home are engaged in housework, and that mothers who stay at home are also working to care for their children. I do not want to implicitly deny or devalue the unpaid work of these women and therefore consistently refer to women who work for pay as paid working women or employed women.

7. Rachel's belief that bad children are purely the result of bad parenting coexists, curiously, with her sense that much of a child's personality is in the child's genes. After telling me the story of the swat to the butt and reminding me she "never" does this, she also let me know that Kristin was particularly disturbed by it since "she has gentle genes in her and she doesn't think it's right to hit." Although Kristin's gentleness and her belief that violence is not right could easily be interpreted as a result of Rachel's teachings, Rachel nonetheless attributes it to Kristin's nature. As will become clear, such attributions often imply the nature of females.

8. The idea that these are simply two complementary logics that operate in two different contexts is most fully elaborated by Parsons and Bales (1955). Men, they argue, are appropriately "instrumental" in the workplace, while women are appropriately "affective" in the home. And this, they say, is a "functional" solution to the different requirements of the two different spheres. But, as I have suggested, in a society where "affective" women regularly venture out into the "instrumental" workplace, the tension and opposition between the "functional" requirements of the two spheres is brought into striking relief.

9. The portrait of gesellschaft relations corresponds to the rational actor model mentioned earlier. However, while classical social theorists understand this as a relatively recent historical phenomenon originating in the early period of industrialization, rational-actor theorists believe that their model applies universally, to all people, at all times, in all places.

10. Marx and Engels, in a famous passage from the *Manifesto of the Communist Party,* make this point quite eloquently: "The bourgeoisie, wherever it has got the upper hand, has put an end to all feudal, patriarchal, idyllic relations . . . and has left remaining no other nexus between man and man than naked self-interest, than callous 'cash payment.'

It has drowned the most heavenly ecstacies of religious fervour, of chivalrous enthusiasm, of philistine sentimentalism, in the icy water of egotistical calculation. . . . The bourgeoisie has torn away from the family its sentimental veil, and has reduced the family relation to a mere money relation" (Marx and Engels [1848] 1978: 475–76).

11. We see this, for instance, in spouses who keep separate checking accounts and make prenuptial agreements, and in children who sue their parents on the basis of emotional distress.

12. The history of Western child rearing is discussed in depth in chap. 2.

13. See Moore (1958), Sennett (1970), and Stone (1977) for more sophisticated versions of this argument. Sennett contends that the child-centered family inappropriately shields its children, leaving them ill prepared for the harsh reality of life beyond the front porch. Moore believes that specialized child-rearing institutions are far better equipped to provide proper socialization than are idiosyncratic parents — whose "obligation to give affection as a duty to a particular set of persons on account of the accident of birth . . . is a true relic of barbarism" (1958: 163). Stone argues that authoritarian child rearing would be much more effective for disciplining a reliable labor force.

14. Social constructions are not the work of isolated individuals, nor are they static. Our understanding of the social world is constructed through interaction between persons over time, as part of a historical process through which our culture is adjusted, transformed, and re-created on an ongoing basis (see, e.g., Bellah et al. 1985; Berger and Luckmann 1966; Giddens 1984; Mehan 1989, 1983; Mehan and Wood 1975). But culture is not only the product of human interaction; it also produces certain forms of interaction and actually makes possible human interaction as we know it. Socially constructed ideas enable us to think and act at the same time that they limit the range of what is thinkable and doable (Durkheim 1965).

The social construction of culture regularly involves unequal power relations. Some people have more power to "name" and institutionalize culture than others. This, however, does not mean that "the ruling ideas [are] . . . the ideas of the ruling class" (Marx and Engels [1848] 1978: 489). The ruling class is not always interested and does not have *that* much power. Less powerful people not only have the ability to interpret and resist the ideas of those who rule; they also have the power to create their own subcultures and to transform the larger culture as a whole (e.g., Gordon 1988; Hebdige 1979; Piess 1986; Radway 1984; Sewell 1985; Willis 1977).

For some interesting empirical studies that explicitly use the language of social construction, see Garfinkel (1967) on the social construction of "woman"; Mehan et al. (1985) on the social construction of "handicapped students"; Gusfield (1981) on the social construction of the "drinking-driving problem"; Corse (1996) on the social construction of national literary canons; and DeNora (1995) on the social construction of Beethoven's "genius."

15. Although much of this book is dedicated to uncovering and elaborating the socially constructed ideology to which Rachel subscribes, I want to make it clear that the logic to which Rachel's boss subscribes, the logic of rationalized market societies, is also a socially constructed one. Much of classical and contemporary social theorizing is dedicated to making this point (e.g., Polanyi 1944; Sahlins 1976; Weber 1958). The ideology of intensive mothering, however, has received far less attention.

16. See Rossi (1977) for a feminist version of this argument; and Popenoe (1993) for a more recent "family values" version.

17. Many have argued that contemporary notions of appropriate child rearing are far from recommending what is best for our children or our society (e.g., Ariès 1962; Berger 1981a, 1981b; Berger and Berger 1983; Donzelot 1979; Foucault 1978; Kagan 1986; Laing 1972; Lasch 1977; Moore 1958; Plumb 1982; Sennett 1970; Slater 1976; Stone 1977). Others have pointed out that Americans' culturally prescribed image of "good mothering" also tends to contain both an ethnocentric bias and a white, middle-class bias (e.g., Glenn et al. 1994; Kagan 1986; Scheper-Hughes 1992).

18. Here I understand historical context in terms of social structure. The definition of social structure I use includes both social relations (the generally hierarchical systems of social positions, including class, race, ethnicity, gender, occupation, age, etc.) and culture (systems of meaning, including language, symbolic objects and representations, formal and informal rituals, conscious ideologies, and common sense). See Hays (1994).

19. My use of content, carriers, and context as the defining features of ideologies follows from an interpretation of Geertz's (1973: 193–233) outline of the three central theoretical conceptions of ideology. My analysis is also greatly influenced by Mannheim's (1971, 1985) classic works in the sociology of knowledge.

CHAPTER 2: FROM RODS TO REASONING

1. Infants, however, are cared for primarily by their mothers in 43.5 percent of those societies. This, of course, is likely connected to breast-feeding, which, in many instances, is an economic necessity. In all cases, women do more of the child rearing than men, just as female children do more than male children (Whiting and Edwards 1988). This, of course, is probably related to women's subordinate position in most societies.

2. There are a great number of sources on child rearing cross-culturally, especially if one considers works on individual countries. Some relevant general sources include not only those cited above but also the work of Birns and Hay (1988); Margolis (1984); and Rogoff et al. (1976). Of those cited, the general theory I find most compelling is that of Scheper-Hughes (1987, 1992).

3. As Bourdieu aptly points out, "Historization, which apparently relativizes, is a way of avoiding relativity" (1992: 38). In other words, while a look at the history of child rearing may lead one to the conclusion that there are a great number of methods to choose from, it also helps us to see why, in particular contexts, some methods are chosen over others.

4. This does not mean that people don't regularly draw from more than one model and therefore end up embracing two or more potentially contradictory ideas (often in the very same breath). It simply means that ideas are not randomly connected and that there is a *strain* toward making use of one logically cohesive set at any given time.

5. For example, in the case of child care by older children and retirees, the model would supply a set of legitimations that might include, first, the argument that this arrangement would give seniors a sense of fulfillment and an ongoing stake in society through a direct and personal connection with the younger generation and, second, the claim that young caretakers would develop a similar sense of social obligation as well as gaining important training in patience and nurturing behavior.

6. For the argument that a number of ideologies are simultaneously available from which people can pick and choose, see Swidler (1986) on the "tool kit" of culture and Berger (1991) on the "cultural kindling" that is available for gathering off the forest floor.

7. Thus, the relative lack of retrospective histories written about groups other than the middle classes matches the relative lack of attention the ideas of these groups received at the time. Nonetheless, as will become clear, the child-rearing methods of these groups did receive *some* publicity when the white, native-born middle-class population became concerned about their "inadequacies."

8. Although such fears at other times and in other places may have led to tight swaddling clothes, demands for absolute obedience, or the establishment of strict schedules for feeding and toilet training, today we tend to frame the child's uncivilized, fragile, erotic, and demanding characteristics as measures of its special (and ultimately valuable) nature at the same time that we explain them "scientifically" as inevitable stages of development. Nonetheless, the persistence of such fears and the ambivalence they engender is indicated, for instance, in popular satires by Bill Cosby (1986) and Erma Bombeck (1983) and in films like *Honey I Blew Up the Kids.*

9. Swaddling clothes were extremely tight cloth wrappings that prevented the infant from moving its body. By today's standards such restriction seems not only emotionally cruel but potentially harmful to the child's physical development. While swaddling infants was certainly a means to keep them quiet and to minimize the amount of energy expended on them, during the European Middle Ages the more popularly acknowledged purposes spoke to the devaluation of the child and the fear of its fragile and demonic qualities: swaddling clothes were said to force the child's body into its proper adult shape and to restrain the infant who might otherwise harm itself (Stone 1977).

10. This may have begun at an even earlier age among the poor. In 1697, John Locke wrote that the offspring of the poor had to work for some part of the day when they reached the age of three (Laslett 1984).

11. As Locke put it, "Fear and awe ought to give you the first power over their minds, and love and friendship in your riper years to hold it: for the time must come, when they will be past the rod and correction; and then, if the love of you make them not obedient and dutiful . . . I ask, what hold will you have upon them?" (quoted in Greven 1973: 27).

Locke's suggestion here that parents use what might now be called psychological manipulation to control the the child in later years was perhaps the first move toward modern ideas of appropriate child rearing. The popularity of Locke's work is indicated by the fact that it went through twenty-five editions by 1800 (Stone 1977: 279).

12. As an indication of the uneven and incomplete dispersion of this new model, in 1763, two years after the publication of Rousseau's *Julie* (which emphasized parental love and affection), Louis XV issued an ordinance authorizing the parents of children "who had fallen into conduct that might endanger the honor and tranquility of the family" to deport the children to an island in the French Antilles, where they would be put to work under strict supervision (Badinter 1981: 22). And as noted earlier, in France during this time, the use of paid wet nurses was still extremely common.

Stone (1977) also makes it clear that the emergence of the belief in childhood innocence and purity was slow and uneven and notes, for instance, that among devout Protestants the interest in childhood initially took the form of floggings, strict discipline, and repression.

13. As Susanna Wesley wrote in 1732, "As self-will is the root of all sin and misery, so whatever cherishes this in children insures thereafter wretchedness and irreligion; whatever checks and mortifies it, promotes their future happiness and piety" (quoted in Greven 1973: 48).

14. In that these Puritans believed in predestination, one might think that they would not feel the need to busy themselves rearing the perfect child—since God had already determined who was to be saved and who was not. But, as Weber (1958) demonstrates, the belief in predestination actually led the Puritans to engage in a calculated and systematic attempt to provide public signs of the fact that they had been "chosen." A good (hardworking, obedient, and religious) child provided an indication not only that the child was saved but also that the child's parents had been chosen. Appropriate child rearing was, therefore, extremely important.

15. As Kett points out, Puritan children provided their parents "with a form of social security, unemployment insurance, and yearly support" (1983: 239).

If a family did not own a farm or business in which the children could work, the parents were forced to send their children to work in the shops and farms of others. Boston law, for instance, demanded that the poor "dispose of their severall children. . . abroad for servants, to serve by indentures . . . which if they refuse or neglect to do the Magistrates and Selectmen will take their said children from them, and place them with such masters" (Kessler-Harris 1982: 5).

16. Although there is some (implicit) disagreement on its origins, most scholars would probably agree that the rise of the ideology of innocent childhood and maternal virtue occurred in the United States between 1776 and 1830, the precise dates Degler (1980) cites for the creation of the modern family. Kerber (1986) implies that this process began in the 1770s; Sunley (1955) dates the shift from paternal to maternal discipline from 1820 to 1860; Welter (1966) similarly dates the cult of domesticity from 1820 to 1860; Cott (1977) sees it beginning at the turn of the nineteenth century; Philipson (1981) argues that affection replaces authoritarianism in the period 1750–1820; Ryan (1985) dates the rise of the wholly sentimentalized home at 1850; and Sears (1975) claims the "empathic ethos" of child rearing began to emerge in 1790.

17. The idea that George Washington owed it all to his mother was regularly cited and constantly elaborated upon in the literature of the time (Cott 1977; Ryan 1981). The importance of women's role in creating good citizens was also echoed in women's diaries. One mother wrote in 1813, "Governors & kings have only to enact laws & compel men to observe them—mothers have to implant ideas and cultivate dispositions which can alone make good citizens or subjects" (quoted in Cott 1977: 47).

18. It is during this period, beginning in about 1810, that fertility rates for women declined (Hayden 1981: 24). There is no question that the decline in women's fertility and the rising emphasis on the careful rearing of a small number of children are both connected to the decline in child mortality that took place in the era of industrialization (e.g., Collins and Coltrane 1995; Matthaei 1982). The fact that parents could expect most of their children to live to adulthood thus helped to make possible the growth of an ideology of childhood innocence and valorized motherhood. But one should not assume a direct cause-and-effect relation here. First, the ideology of childhood innocence and valorized motherhood took shape *before* child mortality rates began their historical decline.

Further, one should also recognize that women's lower rates of fertility were also connected to women's increasing control over childbearing, to the growing concern that a mother should have sufficient time to spend with each child she bore and, perhaps most important, to the fact that children were becoming less economically useful at the same time that new child-rearing standards were making them more economically expensive to raise. In any case, it is clear that the increasingly intensive nature of child rearing was not just the result of such changes but also a cause.

19. See Cott (1978) on the connection between the claim that women were "passionless" and the rise of their status as keepers of morality.

20. This compares to 43.5 percent of all native-born children of like ages, and 28.4 percent of the foreign-born (Ryan 1981: 168).

21. For the Maternal Association of Utica, the focus on conscience and self-control was symbolized in the maxim "Always act as if your parents are invisibly present" (Ryan 1981: 161).

22. Foreign travelers during this period regularly commented on the "permissiveness" of American child rearing (Cable 1975; Degler 1980). This might be explained, in part, as Catherine Sedgwick did at the time: children "may not appear so orderly," she wrote, "but, deprived of external aid or restraint, the self-regulating machine shows its superiority" (Degler 1980: 98). In this sense, the maternal indulgence that accompanied the stress on children's self-control was at that time understood as permissive, just as it would be later, in the era of Dr. Spock.

23. Rousseauian ideology, which stresses the primitive, natural innocence of children, became increasingly popular during this period (Ehrenreich and English 1978). This popularity could well be interpreted as a nostalgic glorification of "primitive peoples" who lived in worlds not dominated by extensive capitalist markets.

24. At the same time, rural areas continued to use hired girls and women to help out on the farm, as did, for instance, 48 percent of Michigan farmers in 1855 (Dudden 1983).

25. According to the census of 1890, for example, 27.5 percent of servants were black, 26 percent native-born white, and 45 percent foreign or of mixed heritage (Sutherland 1981).

26. From 1880 to 1920, the number of household servants fell by more than half in representative major cities (Hayden 1981: 15).

27. To understand the vast number of immigrants we are talking about, note that in 1855 an estimated three-quarters of the workforce in New York City were immigrants (Stansell 1987: 44).

28. This class demarcation was extended to the belief that middle-class women should stay out of the labor force to maintain their purity while working-class women should participate in paid labor to build their character (Kessler-Harris 1982; Lerner 1969; Stansell 1987). This distinction emerged as early as 1790, when male moralists began to urge poor women to take up factory work lest they be "doomed to idleness and its inseparable attendants, vice and guilt" (Wilson 1982: 123).

29. While this may seem trivial at first glance, the efforts at middle-class reform conducted by the individual employers of domestics should not be underestimated, considering the high percentage of women who worked as domestic servants.

30. To get a sense of the prevalence, intractability, and continued importance of chil-

dren's wage labor during this period, one might note that whereas the campaign against children's labor began in 1870, an enforceable federal law was not created until nearly seventy years later, in 1938. In 1887, for instance, Alabama attempted to set the legal limit of an eight-hour workday for children under fourteen, yet the law proved unmanageable and was repealed in 1894. As late as 1916, the first federal child labor law was declared unconstitutional (Takanishi 1978; Zelizer 1985).

31. Holt's work remained popular for over twenty years; by 1915 his book had gone through seven editions (Cravens 1985; Margolis 1984). Hall was a proponent of "recapitulation theory," believing that each stage of childhood development mimicked the stages of human evolution. His work included surveys designed to "inventory" the minds of children at various stages of development (Ehrenreich and English 1978: 198). Watson's *Psychological Care* sold over 100,000 copies. *Parents' Magazine* told mothers that a copy belonged "on every intelligent mother's shelf" and the *Atlantic Monthly* called it a "godsend to parents" (Hardyment 1983: 173).

32. A Children's Bureau pamphlet of 1930, *Are You Training Your Child to Be Happy?* contained the following advice: "Begin when he is born. Feed him at exactly the same hours every day. Do not feed him just because he cries. Let him wait until the right time. If you make him wait, his stomach will learn to wait. His mind will learn that he can not get things by crying. You do two things for your baby at the same time. You teach his body good habits and you teach his mind good habits" (Lomax et al. 1978: 135).

33. This pamphlet was widely used by poor, working-class, and rural mothers as well as middle-class mothers. The letters such mothers wrote to the Children's Bureau during this era, collected by Ladd-Taylor (1986), testify to their deep concern with the well-being of their children.

34. The settlement-house movement was founded in 1889 by Jane Addams; the first juvenile court was established in 1899, in Chicago; the Playground Association of America in 1906; and the National Kindergarten Association in 1909 (Takanishi 1978; Cavallo 1976; Zelizer 1985).

35. The connections were often direct. For instance, the Children's Bureau was first proposed by a settlement-house founder, and both the first and the second bureau chiefs were longtime settlement-house residents. The first bureau chief was also a close friend of Jane Addams, and the second was the director of enforcement for the first federal child labor law and the founder of the Immigrant Protection League (see Ladd-Taylor 1986).

36. Between 1870 and 1930 the number of immigrants coming to the United States reached a peak (U.S. Bureau of the Census 1982). Like Americans in general, these new groups were crowding into the cities: in 1870 the urban population was 10 million; by 1920, it was 54 million (Hayden 1981: 10). At the turn of the century, this combination meant that one-third to one-half of the populations of major cities were poor immigrants (Kessler-Harris 1982). These were major changes indeed.

37. A further indication of the connection among all these mother and child-centered movements and the growing poor and immigrant populations is the rising public anxiety regarding the high fertility rates of immigrants and the poor, and the low fertility rates of the native-born middle class (Margolis 1984). In other words, there was a concern that the number of "good" people was declining and the number of "bad" people rising.

38. The connection between Frederick Taylor's scientific management and the concern

to structure domestic life efficiently was explicit. In 1912, a *Ladies' Home Journal* series promoting scientific management techniques in the home began each article with a box describing Taylor's techniques for increasing labor efficiency in the laying of bricks. Like the bricklayer, the homemaker was to conduct a detailed analysis of her duties, keeping careful records and making systematic plans with the goal of ever-increasing efficiency. This series generated a record number of requests from readers for further information (Matthaei 1982: 160–61).

39. It is interesting to note that during this period working-class child rearing was defined as permissive, indulgent, and lax — in contrast to the rigid discipline attributed to middle-class parents (Ehrenreich 1989). Twenty years earlier or twenty years later, the definitions would be reversed. Apparently, whatever is defined as good parenting is defined by the middle class as the opposite of working-class parenting.

40. This also explains why women's magazines of this era, unlike any period previously or since, were as much focused on social policy regarding children as on appropriate methods of child rearing (see Stendler 1950).

41. At the same time that children's wage-earning capacity declined, it is interesting to note, the courts increasingly gave mothers, rather than fathers, the custody of children in divorce proceedings (Brown 1981).

42. Indicating the persistence of practices of sibling caretaking, in 1933 public assistance agencies found it necessary to establish a guideline insisting that children had to be at least twelve years of age before being left in charge of their younger siblings (Gordon 1988). Among the poor and working classes at that time, this was considered a ridiculously high standard.

43. Between 1909 and 1917, nineteen states passed labor laws "protecting" women (Kessler-Harris 1982: 187). In addition, struggles for a family wage (which had begun in the mid-nineteenth century among working-class men who were more concerned with protecting their patriarchal rights than with sparing women for gentility) seem to have been particularly successful during this period (Stansell 1987).

44. Weiner (1985) notes that as early as 1914, working-class mothers who were engaged in paid work "approved of values opposed to the employment of women and aspired to leave the labor force," according to a survey taken at the time in New York (103). Komarovsky (1962) argues that working-class women had fully accepted domesticity by the middle of the twentieth century.

Although the ideology of domesticity was, in many respects, imposed on working-class women, this ideology also held out a form of liberation for working-class women — promising freedom from low-paid labor as well as from the double shift of paid work and domestic chores. It could be that this offer of liberation, as much as the enforced imposition, is what ultimately led many working-class women to embrace it.

45. Furthermore, some of these ideas actually may have been, as *Infant Care* suggested, intended to reduce the mother's work load (Ladd-Taylor 1986), though the constant attention to the child demanded by this "professionalization" probably ultimately prolonged the woman's workday. Also, as Cowan (1983) demonstrates, other changes increased a woman's work load during this period, including the fact that men, children, and servants were doing fewer and fewer of the domestic chores.

46. This shift from "moral" to (allegedly) "scientific" categories is in some respects

superficial. It could well be argued that the child's emotional and cognitive development is as much a moral task for twentieth-century moms as it was for mothers of the nineteenth century. Nonetheless, the ideology of nineteenth-century mothering did make it easier to discuss explicitly and self-consciously the social and moral goals involved, whereas the language of the twentieth century makes it easier to treat those same goals as matters of science or of personal choice. Many contemporary mothers are therefore left without a popular linguistic basis to discuss the larger social commitment that is involved in raising a "good" child. (The diminishing prominence of the language of morality, specifically the language of social commitment and the common good, is one of the central themes of *Habits of the Heart* [Bellah et al. 1985].)

47. This continuing trend has been highlighted in recent decades by attempts to oversee the behavior of pregnant women, to control the reproductive process more generally, and to intervene in cases of suspected child abuse and neglect (e.g., Gordon 1988; Kaplan 1994; Martin 1992; Rothman 1989; Tsing 1990).

48. Watson (1928) put it this way, "It is a serious question in my mind whether there should be individual homes for children — or even whether children should know their own parents. There are undoubtedly more scientific ways of bringing up children which probably mean finer and happier children" (5–6).

49. Freud's views of childhood sexuality, it would seem, could potentially threaten the image of childhood innocence and "inherent goodness." Yet, for the most part, the child's explicitly sexual character seems to have been ignored or translated into the child's "affection" for its parents. Spock's (1985) *Baby and Child Care* is the only popular child-rearing manual (to my knowledge) that incorporates a Freudian version of the child's "romantic" and gendered attachment to its parents. Although that attachment might elsewhere be considered perverse or dangerous, Spock has no trouble referring to the same child as one whose "motives are basically good."

50. One might speculate on the significance of the historical coincidence of enforced school attendance removing five-year-old children from the home and the widespread popularity of theories that emphasized the period *before* age five as central to the child's development.

Concern with the psychological development of the child, though not new, became increasingly pronounced during this era and was treated as an issue of national import, as evidenced in the Midcentury White House Conference on Children and Youth dedicated to answering the question "How can we rear an emotionally healthy generation?" (Lomax et al. 1978: 73).

51. Bowlby wrote this despite the fact that he had been raised as a member of the British upper class, among whom the use of nannies was extremely common (Dally 1982). One wonders if he considered such nannies "permanent mother-substitutes."

52. Although most of this literature was concerned with the psychological damage overpowering mothers caused for their children of both sexes, much of the focus actually had to do (explicitly or implicitly) with the problems such mothers caused for their sons.

53. Spock himself actually considered psychoanalytic theory his "most significant contribution to advice on child-rearing" (Bloom 1972: 126). Spock's intimate connection to the Aldriches is evidenced by the fact that Dr. Aldrich (the male member of the husband-and-wife team) read the galleys for *Baby and Child Care,* that Spock shortly thereafter

joined Aldrich in research on child development under the financial support of the Mayo Foundation, and that Spock actually moved into the same neighborhood with the Aldriches when he came to work with them in Minnesota (Bloom 1972). This connection helps to demonstrate the earlier blooming of permissive child-rearing ideas: Spock was, in part, a follower; he did not single-handedly invent this ideology.

54. The first edition of Dr. Spock's manual was published simultaneously in hard cover, as *The Common Sense Book of Baby and Child Care*, and in paperback, as *The Pocket Book of Baby and Child Care* (Zuckerman 1975). Between 1946 and 1973, Spock's manual sold 22 million copies, one for almost every firstborn child in America (Bane 1973).

55. As Zuckerman points out, Spock found the need to remind the mother to remove her wristwatch when bathing the baby and to "hold tight" when she rinsed diapers in the toilet (1975: 188).

56. Vice President Spiro Agnew claimed that student activists of the 1960s "were raised on a book by Dr. Spock and [that] a paralyzing permissive philosophy pervades every policy they espouse" (Bloom 1972: 132).

57. There are many problems with this charge: Spock himself was quite concerned with avoiding the creation of narcissistic children, his advice did in fact contain a healthy dose of morality, and, perhaps most important, he did recommend discipline. But the discipline he recommended was of a certain type. He advised parents to use techniques meant to ensure that children *internalize* discipline — the very techniques that would, theoretically, produce many of the personality traits Spock's critics found most desirable. Whether Spockean-type methods actually do create hedonistic consumers lacking respect for authority is another question, and certainly not one I will try to answer here.

58. Although some have argued that Spock became less permissive over the years (Bloom 1972; Zuckerman 1975), they tend to focus on Spock's advice on scheduling infants and guiding them through toilet training and the like. In his more recent editions, Spock has begun to allow parents a bit more latitude in setting their own schedules, but the central focus is still on the child's wishes, the child's needs, and the child's readiness. More important, it is striking just how much of the text that is dedicated to handling children's behavior is precisely the same in the 1946 and 1985 editions. Overall, the only significant changes in this regard are sections countering the "misinterpretation" of critics who, he argues, inappropriately labeled him as permissive and sections meant to reassure readers that he never believed that love was *all* that was required for appropriate child rearing (e.g., 1985: 8–14, 398–99).

59. In fact, from the statistics currently available, it appears that World War II was not as much of a watershed in women's employment as was once thought. Single and nonwhite women have worked in the wage-labor force fairly continuously since its inception. The participation of white women and married women has shown a steady rise since the 1890s, when (fairly) reliable statistics began to be gathered. However, the number of *mothers* who go out to work for pay does begin to rise in the 1940s and, like women's labor-force participation more generally, their numbers have grown steadily.

CHAPTER 3: "WHAT EVERY BABY KNOWS"

1. Since the time of my interviews, some new authors have begun to rival Brazelton and Leach in popularity. Arlene Eisenberg, Heidi Murkoff, and Sandee Hathaway's *What*

to Expect the First Year (1989) has sold 1,634,554 copies, and Adele Faber and Elaine Mazlish's *How to Talk So Kids Will Listen, and Listen So Kids Will Talk* (1982) has sold 1,335,000 (Lodge 1993). However, given the number of books that Brazelton and Leach have written, the national media attention they have both received, and their proven staying power, many still consider these two, along with Spock, the gurus of contemporary parenting (e.g., Allison 1990; Chira 1994). Further, *What to Expect* and *How to Talk* contain similar advice to that found in the books by Spock, Brazelton, and Leach. Perhaps most important, these latter three were the most popular authors among the mothers I talked to.

A revised and expanded edition of Leach's *Your Baby and Child* was published in 1994, and a revised edition of Spock was published in 1992. In the following analysis, I use the 1986 and 1985 editions, respectively, which at the time of my interviews were the current ones. Although some changes have been made in the later editions, none of the additions or deletions alter the basic logic of child rearing to which these authors subscribe.

I should also point out that although Spock's famous manual is currently entitled *Dr. Spock's Baby and Child Care,* it is actually written with Dr. Michael B. Rothenberg, who is a pediatrician, child psychologist, and an advocate for children's rights.

2. Although Marshall (1991) has done such a study of British child-rearing manuals, Zuckerman (1975) studied earlier editions of Spock in the 1970s, and Ehrenreich and English (1978) examined, in general terms, the child-rearing advice books of the twentieth century, no scholarly analysis has yet been done that focuses specifically on the top-selling contemporary manuals in the United States.

3. Mothers' interpretation of child-rearing advice is discussed at length in chap. 4.

4. Because of Leach's assumption that her readers are educated and competent adults, it is my (unsubstantiated) guess that professional-class mothers (looking for "just the facts," without condescension or a framework that might be interpreted as "old-fashioned") tend to prefer Leach. At the same time, I believe that Leach proposes the most child-centered methods as well as those least compatible with the practical considerations of paid working mothers.

5. As noted, Spock was first published in 1946; Brazelton's earliest book, *Infants and Mothers,* was published in 1969; Leach's *Your Baby and Child* was first published in Great Britain in 1977 (as *Baby and Child*) and in the United States in 1978.

6. In fact, fathers are also outnumbered by children and grandparents as customers for children's books (Roback and Maughan 1995).

7. Despite his tendency toward gender stereotyping, it seems to me that the editors of Spock's later editions have been more careful than those of either Brazelton or Leach in their attempts to remove from the text the assumption that mothers have the primary role in raising children.

8. Leach does not even mention *parents* working for pay until the child begins to attend preschool (between the ages of three and five, depending upon when "he" is "ready"). At this point, Leach realizes that the mother may begin to wonder what to do with her "free time" but argues that "a demanding part-time job is risky," since the child is likely to become ill while attending preschool and the mother will need to be available to stay at home with the sick child (1986: 396). Given the fact that even eight-, ten-, and

fifteen-year-olds can get sick and need to stay at home, one wonders whether the mother might ever be able to take a (demanding and risky) part-time job.

9. In Spock's first (1946) edition, his only discussion of paid working mothers was in a section entitled "Special Problems." He concluded with the following: "The important thing for a mother to realize is that the younger the child the more necessary it is for him to have a steady, loving person taking care of him. . . . If a mother realizes clearly how vital this kind of care is to a small child, it may make it easier for her to decide that the extra money she might earn, or the satisfaction she might receive from an outside job, is not so important after all" (1946: 460). A mother's paid work, however, is no longer a special problem for Spock; the above advice has been deleted.

Brazelton (1983b) dedicates a whole book, *Working and Caring*, to the situation of paid working women. In this book he consistently urges fathers to become more involved in child care. However, it is also in this book that Brazelton writes of *women's* "instinct" to take primary responsibility for the happiness of their families, speaks of how *women* must consistently "switch gears" and become more "flexible, warm, and concerned" when they come home from work, and offers tips on choosing the appropriate day-care situation addressed explicitly to *mothers*.

10. Of the three, Spock (1985) is the one who most favors the language of what is "natural." In *Baby and Child Care* the term is attached to a whole range of phenomena, including not only parental "instincts," "common sense," and "basic human nature" but also "simple societies," psychological drives, personality traits, and social customs, as well as the development of the species and the making of civilization. For Spock, the word *natural* clearly implies a positive quality. And this, it seems to me, is true of Brazelton and Leach as well.

11. Leach's books are more child-centered than Brazelton's as well. Unlike the other two, Leach does not include a single chapter, section, or subsection on the parents' needs. She explains, "'Baby and Child' is written from your baby or child's point of view because, however fashion in child rearing may shift and alter, that viewpoint is both the most important and the most neglected" (1986: 16).

12. Similarly, Brazelton writes, "At home [the baby] becomes surrounded by a protecting and nurturing atmosphere. His desires are anticipated, even encouraged" (1983a: 46).

For Leach, the mother must also anticipate wishes the *toddler* can neither recognize nor formulate. She provides an example of this in terms of encouraging the child's play: "He cannot play well if he has to hunt for what he wants. . . . His things need organizing just as efficiently as a kitchen or a real laboratory. . . . A special drawer in the kitchen for his 'cooking' things . . . a basket of bath-toys could live by the bath, while outdoor toys could have their own place on the balcony or in the shed . . . while things he likes to use in bed can live in his room" (1986: 352–53). This is certainly a picture of a busy and conscientious mother.

13. Even listening to the radio, Leach believes, is a situation that needs to be handled properly: "Don't have talk as background noise. If you like to have the radio on all day, try to keep it to music unless you are actually listening. If you are listening, let him see that you are receiving meaningful communication from the voice he cannot see" (1986: 355).

14. With this in mind, Leach argues that "slower than average speech development"

may result from group-care arrangements with "too low a ratio of adults to children" (1986: 419).

15. Another example of the kind of fragile balance mothers must attend to is provided by Leach. She argues that it is essential for good mothers to provide the toddler simultaneously with just enough protection and just enough autonomy: "If you surround your toddler with too much close care and protection, the need for independence will break out in anger and frustration. If you give too much personal autonomy, too much responsibility for self-care, the need to be close and protected will break out in separation anxiety. Keeping the balance between the two is the essence of your job as parent" (1986: 318). As before, the only way to find this balance is to conscientiously attend to the child's responses at every moment.

16. Leach's idealized image of the completely harmonious mother-child relationship comes out strikingly in her treatment of discipline. For Leach, the issue of discipline does not deserve *any* attention until the child reaches two and a half. Even yelling at the young child is completely out of the question (1986: 273). When she finally does attend to the discipline of the two-year-old, Leach also denies its importance, stating, "A process which ought to be agreeable and interesting both for you and the child is often bedeviled by the heavy word 'discipline.' . . . If you like your child, you may be able to get right through his childhood without ever thinking about 'discipline,' as a topic, at all" (1986: 434). In other words, if you and your child are in harmony, as you should be, you will never have to consider this distasteful topic at all.

Like Leach, Spock and Brazelton think that children under the age of two do not need to be disciplined; mothers must simply meet their babies' needs. For Spock and Brazelton this position translates into the belief that only extreme forms of parental behavior can lead to spoiling the small child, whereas for Leach, the spoiling of a baby is an impossibility. Leach argues that you should not even "allow the idea that he may be getting spoiled to edge its way into your mind" and recommends that you meet all the baby's needs and wants at all times (1986: 193).

17. The emotionally absorbing and labor-intensive aspects of these authors' recommendations regarding discipline are connected to a larger historical trend in Western societies toward the increasing importance of training the child to internalize social (and parental) limits and thus to achieve *self*-discipline. As I have noted, this concern began to be articulated explicitly in American child-rearing advice of the nineteenth century, with the focus on the development of the child's conscience. But the logic of training in self-discipline was fully elaborated only in the permissive era and since then, I would argue, has been put into practice by an increasing number of mothers.

The larger social trend toward self-discipline is highly significant and has been linked, for instance, to the increasing division of labor and the rise of individualism, to the process of rationalization culminating in the development of a centralized state and a market society, to the spread of the ideology of civilization, and to particularly harsh forms of cruelty to the individual psyche (e.g., Collins 1974; Donzelot 1979; Durkheim 1978b; Elias 1978; Freud 1961; Foucault 1979, 1978; Weber, 1958; Weinstein and Platt 1969).

Riesman (1961) and Lasch (1977), among others, argue that the focus on internalized self-discipline has been diminished or eliminated with the twentieth-century rise of a bureaucratized, consumption-oriented society. But the story is actually more complex. The best-selling child-rearing manuals, which emphasize discipline based on love and example rather than on external demands and physical punishment, demonstrate that internalized self-discipline is still understood as the appropriate form. It might be argued that what Riesman and Lasch actually highlight is the tension inherent in child-rearing methods meant to instill self-discipline: that is, the very same constant loving attention that is meant to serve as the foundation for the development of conscience might also breed narcissistic or other-directed personality types. This tension was also highlighted by the charges leveled against Spockean methods in the 1960s.

18. All these authors, of course, imply that it is the mother who will stay at home with the child. Brazelton, for instance, reminds the reader that "there are critical stages of development in *mothering* [that] . . . need to be addressed before a mother returns to work." In a demonstration of his (somewhat feeble) interest in the possibilities for egalitarian parenting, he continues by noting that these critical stages "may be the same for a father, as well, but so far we have not identified them" (1983b: 55, emphasis mine).

19. Leach underscores her distaste for day care when she writes, "Amid millions of words about the importance of finding good day care, there are only a few scattered phrases questioning the desirability of using it at all. . . . The development of infants is predicated on one-on-one relationships. Suppose I'm a day care worker in a center where there is one adult for three babies, the best ratio you will find in any center. . . . How can I fulfill all those needs? I would have to keep two waiting while I say 'Come on, Jonathan, hurry up and suck'" (quoted in Lawson 1991). Leach's concern with the damage caused by day care and "part-time parenting" is the focus of her latest book, *Children First* (1994b).

20. Mothers must also deal with potentially *contradictory* advice on how to make the appropriate day-care choice. For example, whereas Spock argues that "cleanliness and carefulness are a little more important than experience [and] education" (1985: 51), Brazelton tells the reader that the caregiver's education and training are crucial, because an "untrained worker is less likely to have the knowledge necessary to handle his or her own frustrations as well as the babies' demands" (1983b: 120).

21. Brazelton, for instance, suggests that if your child is "listless," you should have her "checked over by an expert" (1987: 38).

22. Actually, Spock sensibly notes that a "milk carton" or "pots and pans" can serve as adequate children's toys (1985: 376), but in the context of all his other advice, this suggestion rings a bit hollow. Leach, on the other hand, clearly implies the expense involved in acquiring the "right" toys: "While nothing you can do will make an urban apartment the ideal environment for a new human being, a wide range of playthings can do a great deal to ensure that your toddler understands the natural world. . . . Making good choices [of playthings] depends on taking a thoughtful look at what the child already has, but it also depends on how your child's thinking is developing and the stage he or she is reaching (1986: 334).

23. One might also note that this arrangement requires the parent to find a workplace that will allow her to cut back her hours or rearrange her work schedule. Such a choice and the search it entails can also be financially draining (if possible at all).

24. Spock's concern with the common good and his prescriptions for building a better

society, one free of selfishness, competition, materialism, and injustice, are laid out in his recent book, *A Better World for Our Children: Rebuilding America's Family Values* (1994).

25. In a later book, *Hide or Seek*, Dobson encourages the reader to teach the child according to "God's value system," which includes not only "devotion to God" but also "respect for authority" and "humbleness of spirit" (1979: 171). The children portrayed in Spock, Brazelton, and Leach are certainly not humble, and the only authority they are to respect is their own. But Dobson's rejection of permissiveness is most explicit in his discussion of discipline; he states, "No other form of discipline is as effective as a spanking when willful defiance is involved" (1979: 93). The problem of willful defiance harkens back to the Puritans, and this connection is further elaborated when Dobson informs the reader that the child's will "is made of steel" and is "at full strength at the moment of birth" (1979: 95).

26. The books listed, as I have noted, are those whose sales now rival the sales of Brazelton and Leach. The magazines listed are the most popular ones among young parents: *Parents* has a circulation of 1.75 million; *Parenting*, 925,000; and *Child*, 600,000 (Brown 1993; Lodge 1993).

CHAPTER 4: SORTING THE MAIL

1. In my sample, the other two child-rearing manuals that mothers listed more than once were *How to Talk So Kids Will Listen and Listen So Kids Will Talk* (1982), by Adele Faber and Elaine Mazlish, and *Dare to Discipline* (1970), by Dr. James Dobson. The most popular child-rearing magazines among mothers in my sample, as is true of the population in general, are *Parents* and *Parenting*. Also mentioned more than once was the magazine *Baby Talk*.

2. One mother elaborated on this latter point: "I've had more incidents where I sit down on a park bench, start talking with another mother, [and] find just what I need to know. Because the books are too idealistic, they just make it sound too easy, and it just doesn't work as easy as it does in the books. . . . Penelope Leach, she's really good to read, but it just isn't practical. . . . Like potty training, she says [mimicking an imagined Penelope in a high, sweet voice], 'Your child will let you know at about two or three [years of age], and just gradually they'll start using the potty.' It just doesn't work that way. And Penelope has them all potty trained by three [again mimicking a sweet and maternal Penelope] 'in just a couple of days.' " The notion that child-rearing manuals contain advice that is impractical and impossible to follow is shared by a number of mothers.

3. One mother expressed this point with some humor: "My mom will tell me [my son] shouldn't have a bottle and I should be potty training him. I tell her, 'Well, I'm lazy, and that's easier for me.' And that's the truth. And I think, he's not *driving* yet, it's no big deal [if] he still has a bottle. He's still a baby. I just don't think that stuff matters." Because she had regular contact with her mother, however, their continuing disagreements over weaning and potty training were something of a problem. In fact, many mothers consider books preferable to face-to-face advice, specifically because "they don't talk back to you" and therefore, "you don't hurt anyone's feelings" when you ignore what they have to say.

4. It is perhaps worth repeating that magazine editors, talk-show hosts, pediatricians,

and the authors of child-rearing manuals did not create the contemporary ideology of appropriate mothering; they simply reproduce it, elaborate it, and tinker with it. Child-rearing advice is therefore not only interpreted and transformed by its audience; it is also collectively produced by the interaction between audiences and authors (in the broadest sense of those terms).

5. Mirroring this calculation is the fact that although Jacqueline has cut back to what she considers a part-time job since she had children, she continues to work fifty hours a week outside the home just to bring in what she considers "enough" money.

6. See the concluding pages of chap. 3 for a brief discussion of Dobson's child-rearing recommendations.

7. "Time-out" is a form of discipline that involves removing a child who has mis-behaved from the company of others. The child is thereby punished through the deprivation of social interaction, and is also provided an opportunity to calm down. Practically speaking, time-out generally means making the child sit quietly in a chair alone or putting the child in an empty room. The rule is that a child should face one minute of time-out for each year of his or her age (thus, a three-year-old would get a three-minute time-out). All of this I learned from mothers, but, as far as I can tell, this method was first used, and named, by educators in the public school system. Time-out, as the reader will recognize, is a practice meant to instill self-discipline. And, as will become clear, it is also one of the most popular forms of discipline among today's mothers.

8. Margaret also finds life as a woman preferable to life as a man: "Women just see life differently, they're more involved with relationships and people's feelings, and love, and warmth, and caring. Whereas men miss a lot. They're so busy trying to make a living and thinking man thoughts. It's tough out there, the competition and the stress. I did that for a while; it was exhausting." As it turns out, this sense that a woman's life of nurturing and warmth is preferable to a man's life of competition and stress is quite common, especially among professional-class women (see chap. 7).

9. Spock, of course, did not recant to the extent that Margaret imagines. But Spock is a powerful figure in child rearing; his ideas are regularly discussed and also regularly misinterpreted. Another mother explained to me that she could not use Spock because his work was far too focused on strict scheduling. Yet another implied much the same thing when she told me a story meant to discredit Spock that she had heard on a Catholic radio station: should your child vomit, Spock supposedly recommended that you leave him lying in the mess, as if to teach him a lesson.

These misinterpretations not only demonstrate the significance of Spock but also indi-cate the disproportionate emphasis given to the ideology of strict scheduling and be-havior modification in the (generationally transmitted) historical memories of many mothers (see chap. 2). Other indications of the persistent power of this ideology are that most of the mothers I talked to felt a strong need to deal with the issue of strict scheduling in one way or another (as if it were a central debate in contemporary child rearing), and some mothers also made explicit their strong opinions against letting the child "cry it out" (which is not suggested by any of the most popular current advisers).

10. Further recognizing the code of intensive mothering, not only does Cindy treat her paid work as something she does for her child, but she also provides legitimations for leaving her child with a day-care provider during the day, explaining that since day care is

now so common and so much better than it once was, "I really don't think it affects the kids that much."

But Cindy, like Jacqueline, also expresses ambivalence regarding what the culture treats as a choice between the intensive mother's appropriate selflessness and the career woman's empowerment. Although she does want to be "the main one" who takes care of her children, she also tells me that women just "don't want to be stereotyped as being in the home having to take care of the kids." (For a more extensive treatment of this issue, see chap. 6.)

11. I do not mean to suggest that Mecca is typical of black, Latina, or welfare mothers, just as I am not suggesting that Jacqueline, Cindy, or Margaret are typical of mothers of their class or race. As is true for the others, it is the unique map of Mecca's personal history and present social circumstances that explains her ideas about child rearing.

12. Class, of course, is a very tricky concept. I use it here as shorthand for differences in income, occupation, and education of self and of spouse (if a spouse is present in the household) and, to a lesser extent, of family of origin. These factors feed into something we might call "class culture." But measuring class culture is even more difficult than attempting to arrive at a standardized rendition of class position. Furthermore, in this study, I ran into the additional problem of measuring the class of women who stay at home. Is husband's income, occupation, and education a good measure of the wife's class? This is certainly debatable. But I will simply bypass such important issues and define class according to the factors outlined above. With this, I establish the two categories I use throughout my analysis: (1) middle class to upper-middle class and (2) working class to working poor and nonworking poor.

I recognize that these categories are not precise and are also not a measure of some absolute truth regarding the social position of these mothers. This is simply my informed guess regarding where they fit. Furthermore, I am fully aware that class is not the only significant category of systematic distinctions among mothers. Notably absent from this analysis is any discussion of race and ethnic differences (not to mention rural/urban and native-born/recent-immigrant differences, which I suspect would also be relevant). Unfortunately, my study was not set up to examine anything beyond distinctions in class and labor-force status.

For suggestive research on racial and ethnic differences in child rearing and family life, see Collins (1991); Collins and Coltrane (1995); Glenn, Chang and Forcey, (1994); Rubin (1994); Stack (1974); and Staples and Mirande (1980).

13. Most of these tendencies have been documented by other scholars of working-class life. See, for instance, Collins (1975); Collins and Coltrane (1995); Kohn (1969); Komarovsky (1962); Lynd and Lynd (1956); Rainwater et al. (1959); Rainwater and Handel (1964); Rubin (1976); and Schneider and Smith (1973). Other analyses that do not treat child rearing specifically but that nonetheless provide relevant portraits of the lives of poor and working-class families include Halle (1984); Polakow (1993); Rubin (1994); and Sidel (1986). A relevant treatment of the maintenance of class boundaries more generally is provided by Lamont (1992).

14. When pressed, most professional-class and wealthy mothers would recognize the existence of poverty in the United States. The point, however, is that they almost never brought it up spontaneously in the course of our interviews. By contrast, the recognition

that there were others with different, more affluent lives came up in nearly every interview I had with working-class and poor mothers.

Mirroring the tendency of social subordinates to recognize social inequalities while their social superiors are less likely to do so, *all* the Latinas and African-Americans I interviewed brought up the importance of teaching kids not to be racist, whereas none of the whites mentioned this. One Latina, for instance, said that her greatest hope was to teach her children "to respect everybody, no matter what color they are, [or their] origin. Just don't be racist, and be humanitarian."

15. Just as professional-class moms rarely mention the existence of working-class and poor moms, they rarely mention finances as a problem. Working-class and poor mothers, on the other hand, regularly bring up this issue, especially with reference to the cost of child care. For instance: "[Money] is the down side of day care. It's because it is a business. And when you're a working mother and you're trying to bring an income into the household, but day care is taking half of it [then there's a problem]. . . . They're expensive. And you've gotta have [medical] insurance for the kids [since my day-care center requires it]. It just adds up."

This same mother spent some time proclaiming her resentment of the rich. When I asked how she imagined life in a "perfect world," she replied: "Everybody would have enough money to take care of their children. And then there wouldn't be any homeless, there wouldn't be any starving people. . . . This is why it ticks me off so much. I get so sick and tired of hearing about how there's no money in the world and then we have a deficit in the government and there's nothing, and then they get on there [pointing to the TV] and they say, 'Well, how much is Oprah Winfrey making this year?' Oh, I don't know, a couple five billion dollars. Well, where's this money coming from if there's no money? There's money. And they're living in these giant mansions in Beverly Hills. . . . It makes me sick. Those people make me ill." Although no other poor or working-class mothers expressed this resentment explicitly, one would guess (and observers such as Phillips [1990] and Ehrenreich [1989] suggest) that at least a few of them felt it. Thus, just as many of these women envy the ability of middle-class mothers to provide their children with all that they want and need, some also resent it.

16. This welfare mother was not unique. First, all four of the welfare mothers I talked to wished that they had paid jobs. One of these mothers told me: "I feel this need to make something of myself. I'm a single parent; I don't want to be a welfare mom 'til my kids are fourteen, fifteen years old. I feel this urgency to make something of my life, to set an example for the children. As far as my morals [go], that's never gonna change. My ideals for raising children, that's never gonna change. . . . [But] I want them to see that I'm a success, in order for them to have an initiative to want to do it. An example. They don't have a father that comes home from the office every day, you know." Mounira had been working, making minimum wage. But when her car broke down, she just couldn't handle it anymore, especially since the paychecks she'd been bringing home, after child care, were little more than what she could make on welfare. Plus, there was health insurance to worry about.

But returning to welfare, though it did relieve the immediate problem for women like Lupe and Mounira, was no panacea. Life at the poverty line creates a whole new set of stresses (see Polakow 1993; Rubin 1994; Sidel 1986). When I asked another welfare mother about her sources of stress, she replied: "It's everything combined: the children, the housecleaning, the having to get them off to school, make sure their homework's done, the bills. The main thing is the bills. You can get rid of twenty bills and next month, they're right back. You can't even die nowadays, because it costs too much. The main stress in the house, I would think, is bills. There's times where I sit there and I pray and I pray. . . . I got to the point where I was having so much stomach problems that I have to take pills. And getting headaches . . . and it was just bills. It was the bills that was driving me insane. We've gotten this far, and we've eaten something. Whether it was a piece of bread and water, we've eaten something every day. So the Lord does provide. So just keep praying, that's all I can do." But it's hard to retain this hope, she admits. The power company had recently turned off her gas and electricity after a particularly cold winter month had left her unable to pay the bill. Although she managed to work out a deal to pay them back on the installment plan, her troubles did not end there. The welfare office contacted her to ask where she'd gotten the money to pay the bill (apparently concerned that she had some outside source of income). They required her to visit their office in person to document the source of the payment before they would send her her monthly check. But getting to the welfare office was difficult — it took three separate buses — and she had to take the kids with her. On this particular occasion, I gave her a ride.

17. The only middle-class mother who focused on the importance of formal education for her children was Ramona, a black woman who had been raised in a working-class family in Jamaica. She had come to the United States as a teenager, acquired a college degree, and married an educated middle-class man. She told me: "I want [my children] to finish college. I want education to be important to them. . . . I think about that a lot. I think our example, my husband and myself, goes a long way. I think our going so far educationally is going to make a big impression on them, because some kids just don't go that far because they don't know anybody who has. It just seems beyond their reach." Ironically, then, this particular middle-class woman actually underscored the reason most middle-class mothers do not feel the need to focus on education when discussing appropriate mothering. Ramona felt certain that a mother's attention to education was key to raising children appropriately precisely because it was her own mother's pressure on her to get an education that had helped Ramona to rise to the middle class. For middle-class mothers whose membership in that class seemed less precarious, this was not an issue.

18. This interest does not mean that working-class and poor moms actually read child-rearing manuals more than professional-class and affluent moms do (although they do seem more interested in radio and television programs on child rearing). The point here is that less financially fortunate mothers seem more likely to admire and look up to the so-called experts. The idea of class differences in the valuation of expert advice is supported by Blau (1964).

19. This squares with Lareau's (1987) argument that working-class parents are less likely than their middle-class counterparts to participate in their children's schooling, in part because they tend to believe that teachers are more competent than they are.

20. These findings are confirmed by Erlanger (1974). Using national studies of the 1960s and 1970s, he argues that although there is a statistically significant relationship between social class and the use of corporal punishment, that relationship is relatively weak. In other words, the received wisdom that working-class parents hit their kids far

more often than do middle-class parents is overdrawn. Both Erlanger and I agree, however, with Kohn's (1969) argument that working-class parents tend to focus on teaching their children to conform to external rules, whereas middle-class parents tend to stress the development of internal standards of behavior.

21. The labor-intensive aspects of providing choices and negotiating with the child are considered in greater detail in chap. 5.

22. Again, I want to emphasize that although these differences are real, it is not as if all working-class mothers spank their children and all professional-class mothers negotiate with theirs. A number of less financially fortunate mothers are just as adamant as Rachel is about the "no spanking" rule, and many also use time-out. At the same time, there are professional-class mothers like Margaret who think that spanking is absolutely necessary and that giving the child choices is a ridiculous idea. Overall, the majority of mothers share the same basic ideas about discipline and good child rearing. Nonetheless, as my attention to class differences demonstrates, I believe such differences are significant.

CHAPTER 5: INTENSIVE MOTHERING

1. Given my argument regarding class differences in mothering, throughout this chapter I have been careful to represent equally the stories of working-class, poor, middle-class, and upper-middle-class mothers, unless otherwise noted. And given the frequent argument (which is further elaborated in chaps. 6 and 7) that paid working mothers are likely to be less committed to intensive mothering than stay-at-home mothers, I have also been careful to represent those two groups equally.

2. I wish to make it clear that my emphasis in this chapter, as throughout the book, is on *ideas* about mothering rather than on practices. What mothers actually do may be quite different from what they say. But their ideas are significant, not only because ideas incline one toward certain practices but also because ideas are themselves a form of cultural practice and because it is ideas that produce the ideological tensions that account for the cultural contradictions of motherhood.

3. In many cases, the primary male adult in the household is not the husband of the mother or the biological father of the children. He may be a father, brother, or other relative or a friend or lover of the mother. But in almost all the households in my sample, the male adult present was the husband of the mother and took the role of father to the children. Given this, I try to alternate their titles and hope the reader will bear with me.

4. One international study by the High/Scope Educational Research Foundation found an even more dramatic difference, with American mothers, on average, taking charge of watching over children for 10.7 hours each day, compared to fathers at .7 hours, both parents at .9 hours, and care by others at 3.7 hours. These American mothers spent more hours as primary caregivers than mothers in any of the other countries in the study, which included Belgium, China, Finland, Germany, Hong Kong, Nigeria, Portugal, Spain, and Thailand (Owen 1995).

Another indirect indicator of gender differences in responsibility for child care is the fact that of the one in five United States households managed by a single-parent, 85 to 90 percent are headed by women (Sorrentino 1990).

5. Although the increasing number of teenagers who work for pay seems to be an indication that older children are taking on more responsibility and that parents may be

requiring more of such children, the fact is that the majority of these teenagers do not contribute the money they earn to the family economy. Instead, they use it to buy clothes and cars and to pay for leisure activities (Waldman and Springen 1992). The higher incidence of teenage employment, in this sense, may simply be an indication that teenagers are becoming increasingly feverish consumers.

6. For the uninitiated, mothers distinguish between commercial day-care centers, which employ a staff of caregivers and occupy a physical space used exclusively for child care, and family day-care arrangements, in which the caregiver (usually a mother herself) attends to other people's children in her own home. Nelson (1994) provides an interesting analysis of the tensions faced by family day-care providers who are simultaneously mothers and paid workers in a setting that is simultaneously home and the site of work.

7. Two-thirds of the mothers in my small sample said that they wanted their husbands to do more; the rest said they did not. The paid working mothers were actually much less likely than the stay-at-home moms to say that their husbands should do more. Although this might be partially explained by the fact that the husbands of employed working moms generally spend more time caring for their children than the husbands of mothers who stay at home, none of these husbands actually do half the work. If we calculate the work hours of a mother who has paid employment against a mother who stays at home with the kids, the former is the one who still suffers the larger "leisure gap" (see Hochschild 1989).

8. The notion that fathers can be dangerous is related to the belief that men in general tend to be more dangerous than women. When asked about their gender preference in making the choice of alternative caregivers, four-fifths of the mothers said they would prefer a woman and the rest said they had "no preference"; *none* said they would prefer a man. Although some seemed to base this answer on their belief that men are incompetent, more often than not it was connected to the notion that men can be dangerous. One mother explained her preference for a woman caregiver in this way: "Because there's so much in the news about men doing stuff to little girls. . . . It's not that I don't think that a man wouldn't be good with kids. It's just that I don't need to have that extra worry of 'Is he a weirdo?' " In other words, men are perceived as possible child molesters. It was never suggested that a woman might be a pedophile.

9. The fact that mothers often consider men incompetent as caregivers is also underscored by the fact that the mothers in my sample almost never went to male friends or relatives for advice on how to raise children.

10. For similar treatments of how women seem to collude with men in making gender inequalities in parenting appear fair, see, for instance, Hochschild (1989) and LaRossa and LaRossa (1981).

11. Such ambivalent feelings regarding male help in child rearing were not unusual. This mother oscillates between praising her husband's interest in the kids and doubting his competence: "[My husband's] real good at [child rearing]. [The children] really love being with him. . . . But there's some times when I'm dissatisfied about how he does it 'cause he does things differently and claims there's more than one way to do something. But then I claim that there are ways and then there are better ways. But it's just that I spend so much time with them that I have learned to anticipate a lot of things. He's getting better. He didn't used to want me to tell him too much. But he's learned that I'm a useful

source of information when it comes to dealing with the kids. Still, he tends to be more lenient with them. Since he doesn't have to spend as much time with them, he doesn't realize the consequences of breaking a few rules that mommy's worked so hard all week to instill."

12. Men's tendency to be playful in their interactions with children at the same time they tend to ignore the necessities of physical care has been documented by others (e.g., Hood 1986; Parke 1981).

13. See, for instance, Hochschild (1989) on the "economy of gratitude"; Hartmann (1981b) on the "mechanism of redistribution"; and Collins (1992) on women's "status cultures."

14. Owing largely to my lack of foresight in devising the interview schedule and questionnaire, I did not ask these mothers a direct question such as: "Do you think your commitment to mothering is the result of male domination, your childhood training, or genetics?" I would be very interested in their responses. But even if I had such data, the either/or answers required might mask the very real sense of ambiguity that mothers express regarding this matter.

15. I should note that the national media also contributed to and affirmed the sense that Dahmer's mother was a central player in this drama, by covering her story on television and in print. The point is, however, that mothers and reporters *share* the underlying belief that the killer's mother was, at least in part, responsible for his actions as an adult.

16. This emotional response becomes even more striking when one realizes that this question was asked just five minutes into the interview. Although I had talked to these mothers by phone several times before our meeting, I was still a stranger to them, and we had had little chance to talk about kids and child rearing. Yet their feelings about life without children were so strong that, as I say, a number of them cried spontaneously in front of me, a stranger. As many of them told me, no childless person can fully understand how deeply they feel this.

17. Over half of the mothers I interviewed used precisely those words — lonely, empty, or missing something. Answers that would also fit into this category included "miserable," "sad," "depressed," "a great sense of loss," "desperate," and "unfulfilled." When these expressions of loneliness and emptiness are added to the others, nearly all of the mothers I spoke to expressed similar reasons for the sadness they experienced at the thought of not having a child.

The only answers that fell outside this group included "richer" (with a laugh), "curious," and, in an expression of ambivalence that was telling: "They're a lot of work. . . . [But] when I grow old I want to have someone there for me, and, you know, be able to say, 'these are my kids.' "

18. As the reader may have noticed by now, the condemnation of selfishness is a recurring theme among mothers. You will hear it over and over throughout this chapter, and I will discuss it at greater length in chap. 7.

19. As I noted earlier, one could argue that including affection as a minimal requirement is debatable. There is evidence that our present-day understanding of the necessity of a particular level and form of affection is as much a social construction as the ideology of intensive mothering in general. Nonetheless, I include it here since it is so widely and deeply understood as an absolute requirement.

For a particularly interesting treatment of the historical connection between the social construction of maternal affection and our affection toward pets, see Tuan (1984)

20. Thus, the quotes and stories in the following discussion of labor-intensive techniques (up to, but not including, the treatment of paid caregivers) are all taken from such mothers. However, a number of working-class and poor mothers also mentioned the use of reasoning, negotiation, explanation, distraction, and time-out. The difference is the extent to which these two groups of women expounded upon such methods; it is therefore primarily a difference in degree rather than in kind.

21. The reader may note that Karen uses the pronoun "we" to emphasize that both she and her husband practice these methods. By Karen's account, her husband is very much involved in the raising of their children. But it is Karen who cut back her paid work hours to stay home when her first daughter was born; her husband, on the other hand, works two jobs and is away from the house most of the time. The story of the "bombshell" that hit the house whenever the father was left alone to care for the children was Karen's story.

22. This method of positive reinforcement, as many will recognize, is widely used with younger children in public schools and probably, like "time-out," originated there.

23. Not surprisingly, fathers are generally perceived as less willing to use the negotiation, reasoning, and explanation required to avoid spankings and saying no. For instance: "[My husband] thinks that with little boys, 'Okay, he's talking back, give him a spanking.' Whereas I'll tell [my son] why. If he gets a spanking, is it going to make him want to stop talking back? I don't think so."

24. Cooperative day-care centers (where parents rotate caring for one another's children), on-the-job day-care facilities, and state-subsidized child-care centers are rare, though a number of mothers say that they wish there were more, especially on-the-job facilities, which would be convenient and allow them to visit the kids during lunch hours and breaks.

While the best-selling child-rearing advisers recommend that mothers find a center that pays its child-care workers well, most paid working mothers simply can't afford them. This is true despite the fact that, as we know, the people (mainly women) who care for children are paid extremely low wages. In 1984, over half of market-based child-care workers and 90 percent of caregivers working in private homes earned poverty-level wages (Collins and Coltraine 1995). Noble (1993) notes that "people who take care of zoo animals make on average nearly $2,500 a year more than most workers at childcare centers." The highest-paid teacher at a child-care center makes, on average, nearly $4,000 a year less than the average female worker with a high school diploma — even though most such teachers have had college-level training in child development (Noble 1993).

25. From my survey questionnaire, other indicators of the labor-intensive nature of socially appropriate child rearing include: four-fifths of these mothers breast-fed for an average of twenty months per child; over three-quarters of the mothers read to their children daily; the same proportion talk to someone about their children on a daily basis; all read books and magazines on child rearing; and all take their children on special outings at least once a week, and some as frequently as several times a day. But, as the reader will note, these indicators are not nearly as powerful as the descriptions that mothers provide.

26. The average couple whose oldest child is under six years old spends 10 percent more overall than the average couple with no children (Exter 1992). By one estimate, which excludes the cost of childbirth and college tuition, raising a child from birth through high school graduation will cost from $151,170 to $293,400, depending on one's income level. Thirty years ago, economists estimated that parents would spend between $13,408 and $69,333 (Wright 1991). Even after adjusting for inflation, this is a dramatic increase.

For discussions of the booming industry in providing children with designer toys, clothes, and accessories, see Groves (1990), Lawson (1990), and Strom (1991). Experts in the child-products industry estimate that sales rose by at least 10 percent per year from 1988 to 1991, while the nation's birthrate (after years of decline) was rising only 3 to 4 percent (Strom 1991). Working-class and poor women are less able to afford such fashions and accessories, but this does not mean that they are always able to ignore their children's demands for them.

27. Even though, as I have noted, hired caregivers are very poorly paid, child care eats up a good percentage of family income, especially, of course, in poor and working-class families. On average, those whose family income is under $15,000 a year spend 23 percent of it on child care; those making $15,000 to $49,999 spend between 12 percent and 7 percent, with the percentage falling as the income rises; and those earning over $50,000 spend 6 percent of their income on child care ("Who's Minding the Children?" 1993).

In fact, more than one mother noted that the cost of child care eats up most of her income from paid work. It is also significant that these mothers tend to speak as if such costs appropriately come out of their salaries rather than their husbands' (e.g., "after child care costs, I hardly make anything").

28. Conjugal relationships can fall apart, but that special relationship between mother and child persists. One woman comments on this in her answer to the question "Does having a child make you feel closer to other women?": "Definitely close to other mothers. But it makes me feel more distant from women who don't have kids. They seem selfish. No, that's too strong. But they're missing something. When they get old, they'll be without that special relationship. It's just that they miss out on loving, on that. When they're older, maybe they get divorced, maybe their husband dies, and then what do they have?"

CHAPTER 6: THE MOMMY WARS

1. It seems to me that the popular-culture images of both the traditional mother and the supermom tend to be portraits of professional-class women; the life-styles of working-class and poor women are virtually ignored. Hochschild (1989) does a particularly nice job of describing the image of a professional-class supermom, an image that our society pastes on billboards and covers in full-page ads in popular magazines: "She has that working-mother look as she strides forward, briefcase in one hand, smiling child in the other. Literally and figuratively, she is moving ahead. Her hair, if long, tosses behind her; if it is short, it sweeps back at the sides, suggesting mobility and progress. There is nothing shy or passive about her. She is confident, active, 'liberated.' She wears a dark tailored suit, but with a silk bow or colorful frill that says, 'I'm really feminine underneath.' She has made it in a man's world without sacrificing her femininity. And she has

done this on her own. By some personal miracle, this image suggests, she has managed to combine what 150 years of industrialization have split wide apart — child and job, frill and suit, female culture and male" (1).

2. Women's decisions to remain childless or to become stay-at-home mothers or paid working mothers are based in social-structural circumstances. Kathleen Gerson's *Hard Choices: How Women Decide about Work, Career, and Motherhood* (1985) focuses precisely on this issue.

3. For discussions of this war in its various forms, see, for instance, Berger and Berger (1983); Gerson (1985); Ginsburg (1989); Hunter (1991, 1994); Klatch (1987); and Luker (1984).

4. The fact that people use ideological work to come to terms with their social circumstances does not mean that people's ideas are purely the result of their social position. An individual's ideas may well be the reason he or she came to that position in the first place. There is, as Berger points out, a dialectical relationship between ideas and circumstances. And neither one's ideas nor one's position is a matter of completely "free" or individual choice. Both are socially shaped.

5. A full half of the paid working women in my sample were employed only part-time. Nationally, approximately 33 percent of the married mothers employed in 1992 worked part-time; the remaining 67 percent worked full-time, that is, 35 hours or more per week (Hayghe and Bianche 1994). When one adds to this reality the facts that a number of stay-at-home mothers engage in forms of temporary or hidden paid work (such as child care for others) and that all mothers tend to move in and out of the labor force over time, it becomes clear that there is actually a *continuum* rather than a sharp divide between the statuses of paid working mothers and stay-at-home mothers. Nonetheless, the mothers in my sample systematically defined themselves as either paid working mothers or stay-at-home mothers and focused on the divide rather than on the continuum, as their arguments in this chapter make clear.

6. Over one-third of the stay-at-home mothers I talked to planned to enter the paid labor force within the next five years, one-third were not sure if they would or not, and just under one-third felt sure that they would stay at home for at least another five years. These figures compare with the eighteen of twenty paid working mothers who planned to continue working outside the home; only two hoped they would at some point be able to stay at home with the kids.

Two of the eighteen stay-at-home mothers in my sample wanted to stay home *indefinitely*. Here's how one of them explained her position: "I don't want to go to work. I enjoy being [at home]. I enjoy it. I don't mind if somebody would call me a housewife or a homemaker. It doesn't bother me. I'm not a feminist. There's no need for me to be out there. For the amount of money I made, it's not worth it." Her concluding remark is, of course, telling. But poorly paid jobs are not the only reason that mothers want to stay home, as Margaret's story (from chap. 4) demonstrates. It should also be recognized that many women want to work outside the home even if their jobs pay poorly.

7. This can be hard on a mother too. For instance: "[My friend] was working full-time, and she came to the baby-sitter's, and her daughter was just kind of clinging to the baby-sitter and wouldn't come to her. And that was it for her. She quit her job."

8. This same argument is also found in popular-press pieces such as "The Managerial

Mother" (Schneider 1987). Since the time of these interviews a number of the middle-class employed mothers I know (nearly all of whom are academics) have made this same argument: that they are more "organized, efficient, and effective" as moms because their paid work trains them to develop those skills, just as their double shift forces them to be organized, efficient, and effective *all* the time. In fact, many of these mothers argue that the professionalism they learn as working women explains their intensive mothering. The problem with this explanation is that the ideology of intensive motherhood, as I have shown, is not confined to middle-class, paid-working mothers. Many other women argue that it is mothering itself that teaches them to be more organized, efficient, and effective as mothers and as workers.

But there is some truth in what my paid professional women friends say. Although intensive mothering has a much broader social basis, there are reasons why middle-class mothers on the one side, and paid working women on the other, are, in some respects, more intensive in their mothering. It makes sense that women who are both middle-class and paid professionals add to this an overlay of training in organization and focused commitment to their assigned tasks. But this only explains differences in degree; it does not explain the larger social grounding for the ideology of intensive mothering.

9. My sample is too small to make any definitive comment on this, but the numbers are as follows: half of the paid working mothers in my study say that children and home are more important for a woman than work, whereas only one-quarter of the stay-at-home mothers respond in this way (with the remainder providing the "it depends" response). And, it is interesting to note, professional-class and affluent paid-working mothers are the group most likely to say that home and children are more important and rewarding than careers; nearly three-quarters of them respond this way.

10. While the historical increase in the use of day-care facilities and alternative care-givers might be seen as an attempt to lessen the cultural contradictions of motherhood, it should be recognized that, historically speaking, mothers rarely did the job of raising children alone: rural families often had live-in help and relied on older siblings to take care of the younger ones; working-class women in urban areas also relied on older children as well as on friends and neighbors; and many upper-class women depended upon servants, nannies, and nursemaids (see chap. 2). Although there does seem to have been a period during the 1950s and 1960s when families were less able to obtain and less likely to use help in raising children, today's alternatives to exclusively maternal care are probably in large measure a simple *substitute* for the help that was previously available. Furthermore, it is important to note that the expectations for the task are much higher today than they once were, that mothers must therefore expend much time and energy seeking out and assuring the maintenance of the proper day-care situation, and that the use of day care coexists with increased expectations for mothers to make up for the hours their children spend under the care of others.

CHAPTER 7: LOVE, SELF-INTEREST, POWER, AND OPPOSITION

1. I was actually quite surprised when a majority of mothers spontaneously brought up their tendency to reflect on their own childhoods. Regarding their attempts to re-create what was good, this mother was typical: "There were things that my mother did that I strongly approved of. So I carry those forward. . . . I think the gut-level stuff comes

right from there, that I was treated in a certain way that felt good to me." Regarding their struggle to avoid the mistakes of their parents, another mother provides an example: "What I'm doing with [my daughter] is I'm repairing the stuff that I didn't get when I was a child, you see. . . . I'm having a childhood with her that I didn't have." On this point, DeMause's argument clearly resonates with the beliefs of contemporary mothers. The universality of this phenomenon, however, remains to be demonstrated empirically.

2. Although many would attempt to correct such theorists by explaining that women are not naturally mothers but are instead *trained* to be mothers through explicit gender socialization or more deeply hidden psychoanalytic processes (e.g., Bernard 1975; Chodorow 1978; Gilligan 1982; Weitzman 1975), it should be recognized that the logic of the love analysis, in and of itself, does not account for such differential gender socialization. The reality and power of gender socialization, however, is indisputable. In my study this is evident not only in how mothers consider themselves primarily responsible for mothering and how deep that sense of responsibility runs, but also in the awareness of many mothers that, no matter how hard they may try to avoid it, they tend to treat their male and female children differently. Over half of the mothers in my sample were sure they did so (or would do so) regularly. Boys are "rough," you buy them trains and Ninja Turtles, and take them to see dinosaurs. Girls are "cute," you buy them dolls, "dress them up," and "pamper" them. While the other half of the mothers I spoke with explicitly stated that they *try* to respond to their children as "individuals," many of them also went on to wonder whether they might unintentionally or on occasion treat their sons and daughters differently. Most mothers in both groups insisted that their differential gender treatment was not a matter of imposing gender roles on their children: "It's just their personality," they would tell me, or "they seem to be born that way" and "I follow *their* interests, not my own." No matter how unintentionally differentiation may occur, it seems quite possible that the majority of mothers do participate in the perpetuation of gender-role socialization. To understand the roots of this socialization, however, one must look beyond arguments about the natural propensity to love one's children.

3. As Becker puts it, a mother seeking to "maximize family income . . . is led by the invisible hand of self-interest to act as if she is altruistic toward her benefactor" (1981: 179). According to this logic, however altruistic a mother may appear, she is, in fact, simply maximizing efficiency in a calculated pursuit of self-interested gain.

4. See Held (1990) and Risman and Feree (1995) for explicit critiques of the use of rational-choice theory to understand mothering. See Folbre and Hartmann (1988) for an explicit treatment of the reasons why women should be understood as rational actors.

5. Taking this logic to its extreme, Becker (1981) argues that, whether mothers work or not, they always weigh the costs of caring for children against the potential benefits of the child's future status or economic success. If the rate of return on their investment in children is expected to be high, parents will invest more in the "quality" of their children. Thus, for Becker, Jewish families invest more in their children's education than do African-Americans, since the Jewish family can expect a long-term payoff on this investment. For African-Americans, however, the future is less certain (1981: 110). Using the same logic, Becker writes, "Parents would be more likely to put their inferior rather than their superior children up for sale or adoption" (1981: 98–99).

6. As I have suggested, the most extreme version of this argument is found in the work

of Gary Becker (1981). Bits and pieces of this analysis can be found in Coleman (1993); Folbre and Hartmann (1988); Hofferth and Moore (1979); Huber and Spitze (1988); Margolis (1984); Moore and Hofferth (1979); and Pleck (1985), among others. The most sophisticated and subtle version of this analysis is found in Gerson (1985). Although her argument implies the scenario outlined above, her central claims are that women are knowledgeable agents rather than passive victims, that they make reasoned choices about housework and child care based on their adult experiences (rather than on their early childhood socialization), and that their experiences and choices are constituted by structural opportunities and constraints. Her structural argument provides an opening for elaborating on the wider circumstances that are the backdrop for the social construction of women's experiences and choices — and this is a crucial opening, as will become clear.

7. See Collins (1992) for a relevant treatment of the ways women's housework and household consumption are used by women as a means to gain and retain social status.

8. For various pieces of these historical analyses, see Collins (1971a, 1985); Degler (1980); Ehrenreich and English (1978); Hayden (1981); Ryan (1981); and Watt (1957).

9. Although some may attempt to argue that the emotional rewards that mothers experience as a result of nurturing the child, caring for the child, playing with the child, and loving the child are the self-interested gains that mothers seek, this is an altogether different concept of self-interest than is implied by the "rational choice" model. To treat the joy that is derived from caring for another as a form of personal profit stretches the logic of self-interest so far as to make it completely meaningless.

10. I borrow the notion of "social assets" from Karl Polanyi. Using the word *man* to refer to both men and women, he writes: "Man is a social being. . . . Man's economy, as a rule, is submerged in his social relationships. He does not act so as to safeguard his individual interests in the possession of material goods: he acts so as to safeguard his social standing, his social claims, his social assets. He values material goods only in so far as they serve this end" (1944: 46).

11. As Donzelot puts it, "Parents no longer have the right, as they had in the Dark Ages, to turn their children into failures" (1979: 225). Donzelot also points out that middle-class women have been particularly useful to the state, not only in their work of internally monitoring their own families but also in that they have regularly been enlisted in attempts to establish agencies meant to monitor the behavior of poor and working-class families.

12. In historical terms, this argument is implied by McGlone (1971), Ryan (1985), and Stansell (1987), among others. With reference to today's mothering, this argument is implied by many, including Anzaldua (1987); Bourdieu (1977); Bourdieu and Passeron (1977); Bowles and Gintis (1973, 1976); Chow (1989); Cliff (1983); Collins (1991); Glenn, Chang, and Forcey (1994); Joseph (1981); Lareau (1987); MacLeod (1987); Matute-Bianchi (1986); and Wilcox (1982). One could also add to this analysis the forms of power that undergird the systematic privileging of those with the "right" sexual orientation (e.g., Rich 1983; Rubin 1984).

13. More precisely, half state that women have it better, about one-third that men have it better, and the rest argue that neither men nor women have it better. Although I expected that they would respond to this question in terms of men's greater access to wealth and power, they instead answered in terms of whose life-style they would choose.

It is also interesting to note that working-class and poor women were far more likely than middle-class women to say that men have it better, at the same time that middle-class mothers were far more likely to identify themselves as "feminists." These apparent contradictions clearly deserve further exploration.

14. See Chafetz (1990) and Jackman (1994) for versions of this argument.

15. This argument can also explain how forms of gender socialization and psychological processes that serve to reproduce certain types of mothering were first set in motion: both follow from male domination and the separation of spheres that attended the development of capitalism and the centralized state. Chodorow's (1978, 1974) and Benjamin's (1988) arguments about the reproduction of mothering fit into this framework and are also connected to arguments focusing on love. That is, both would argue that maternal love is very deep and emotionally powerful at the same time that they argue that the reason this love is maternal rather than parental is to be found in historically specific systems of domination. Rothman's (1989) view of mothering also fits with analyses of both love and unequal power. Unfortunately, I cannot do justice to the complexity and sophistication of their arguments here.

Since readers familiar with Chodorow's argument in particular will recognize the extent to which it could be used to explain intensive mothering, a further point of clarification may be in order. Her analysis of the complex psychoanalytic processes involved in parent-child relations and childhood-identity formation is the most powerful argument available for making sense of the way that the gendered nature of parenting is reproduced over generations and the fact that mothering seems such a deep and integral part of women's identities. This argument, however, cannot fully explain the development and persistence of intensive mothering. First, the ideology of intensive mothering is a far more elaborate set of beliefs than the emotional attachment that Chodorow describes. Second, the logic of Chodorow's argument would lead us to believe that the more women shared parenting with others (e.g., day care) and the more women had a chance to gain power and status in the world outside the home (e.g., paid work), the less attached to mothering they would become. As I have shown, this does not seem to hold true.

16. For a further analysis of why such practices would make perfect sense in modern market societies, see Bowles and Gintis (1976); Moore (1958); and Sennett (1970). Many Marxist feminists and socialist feminists have also implied that child rearing might be most equitably and effectively accomplished in a rationalized, institutional setting under the control of the state (e.g., Bentson 1984; Firestone 1984; Hartmann 1981a; Kollantai 1980). All these arguments challenge the widely accepted belief that children are best prepared for life in this society by currently prescribed child-rearing methods. Although the alternatives they propose may seem unacceptable, they do demonstrate that the value of today's child-rearing methods is not self-evident.

17. Compared to the other three analyses outlined in this chapter, this argument gets less press and is rarely made relevant to contemporary mothering. There are, however, a number of researchers that provide hints of this analysis. One of the more direct treatments of contemporary womanhood in these terms is Hunt and Hunt (1987). Countless scholars have recognized and analyzed the cultural logic that understands the home as a privatized, nurturing "haven" that stands in opposition to the public world outside it (esp. Ariès 1962; Coontz 1992; Elshtain 1981, 1974; Hareven 1989, 1976; Laslett 1978,

1973; Weintraub 1996; Zaretsky 1976). The works of Cott (1977); Kerber (1986); Matthaei (1982); and Smith-Rosenberg (1975) are particularly useful in offering historical clues. Broader arguments about trends countering the logic of self-interest or power seeking can be found, for instance, in the work of Bellah et al. (1985); Berger et al. (1974); Polanyi (1944); Sahlins (1976); Watt (1957); and Wolfe (1989). Arguments about the resistance of social subordinates are many, though I found those of Gordon (1988), Hebdige (1979), and Piess (1986) particularly illuminating in this context. Although it is Lasch (1977) who lent contemporary popularity to the notion that the family is "a haven in a heartless world," his argument is that the family no longer serves this purpose.

I owe a special debt to Jeff Weintraub, who first introduced me to this line of analysis and convinced me of its significance.

18. See Silver (1996) for a particularly nice rendition of friendship in these terms. Friendships are valued, he argues, precisely to the extent that they *invert* the norms of the larger society.

19. The question of making child rearing a public issue is a highly complex one, littered with land mines. To maintain child rearing as a private enterprise conducted by men and women in the (hypothetically) secluded haven of the home continues to absolve the public sphere from the values implied in the ideology of intensive mothering. On the other hand, many are appropriately concerned that the state and the marketplace, as they are presently constituted, would not provide appropriate leadership in a reconfiguration of family life. Attempts to find a compromise between these two extremes have not yet met with great success. Today, for instance, we find politicians simultaneously calling for a return to "family values" and for the substitution of welfare with "work-fare." The tensions are apparent.

Bibliography

Acker, Joan. 1988. "Class, Gender, and the Relations of Distribution." *Signs* 1 (3):473–97.

Ahlburg, Dennis A., and Carol J. DeVita. 1992. "New Realities of the American Family." *Population Bulletin* 47 (2):2–43.

Aldrich, C. Anderson, and Mary M. Aldrich. 1938. *Babies Are Human Beings*. New York: Macmillan.

Allen, Jeffner. 1983. "Motherhood: The Annihilation of Women." Pp. 315–30 in *Mothering: Essays in Feminist Theory*, edited by Joyce Trebilcot. Savage, Md.: Rowman and Littlefield.

Allison, John. 1990. "Parenting Books for a New Generation." *American Bookseller* 13 (12):129.

Anderson, Michael. 1971. *Family Structure in Nineteenth-Century Lancashire*. Cambridge: Cambridge University Press.

Anzaldua, Gloria. 1987. *Borderlands/La Frontera: The New Mestiza*. San Francisco: Spinsters/Aunt Lute.

Ariès, Phillipe. 1962. *Centuries of Childhood: A Social History of Family Life*. Translated by Robert Baldick. New York: Vintage.

"At S & S, Spate of Bestsellers onto Audio Tape." 1992. *Publishers Weekly*, November 2, 28.

Badinter, Elisabeth. 1981. *Mother Love: Myth and Reality*. New York: Macmillan.

Bane, Mary Jo. 1973. "Book Reviews." *Harvard Educational Review* 43 (4):669–81.

———. 1976. *Here to Stay: American Families in the Twentieth Century*. New York: Basic.

Banks, Joseph A. 1954. *Prosperity and Parenthood*. London: Routledge and Kegan Paul.

Becker, Gary S. 1981. *A Treatise on the Family*. Cambridge: Harvard University Press.

Beecher, Catherine. 1846. *A Treatise on Domestic Economy: For the Use of Young Ladies at Home and at School*. New York: Harper and Bros.

Beekman, Daniel. 1977. *The Mechanical Baby: A Popular History of the Theory and Practice of Child Raising*. Westport, Conn.: Lawrence Hill.

Bellah, Robert, Richard Madsen, William M. Sullivan, Ann Swidler, and Steven M. Tipton. 1985. *Habits of the Heart: Individualism and Commitment in American Life*. Berkeley: University of California Press.

———. 1991. *The Good Society*. New York: Knopf.

Benjamin, Jessica. 1988. *The Bonds of Love: Psychoanalysis, Feminism, and the Problem of Domination*. New York: Pantheon Books.

Bentson, Margaret. 1984. "The Political Economy of Women's Liberation." Pp. 239–47 in *Feminist Frameworks: Alternative Theoretical Accounts of the Relations between Women and Men*, edited by Alison M. Jaggar and Paula S. Rothenberg. New York: McGraw-Hill.

Berger, Bennett. 1981a. *Survival of a Counterculture*. Berkeley: University of California Press.

———. 1981b. "Liberating Child Sexuality: Commune Experiences." Pp. 247–54 in *Children and Sex*, edited by Larry L. Constantine and Floyd M. Martinson. Boston: Little, Brown.

———. 1991. "Structure and Choice in the Sociology of Culture." *Theory and Society* 20 (1):1–19.

Berger, Brigitte, and Peter Berger. 1983. *The War over the Family: Capturing the Middle Ground*. Garden City, N.Y.: Anchor.

Berger, Peter, Brigitte Berger, and Hansfried Kellner. 1974. *The Homeless Mind: Modernization and Consciousness*. New York: Vintage.

Berger, Peter, and Thomas Luckmann. 1966. *The Social Construction of Reality*. New York: Doubleday.

Bernard, Jessie. 1975. *Women, Wives, Mothers: Values and Options*. Chicago: Aldine.

Bielby, William T., and Denise D. Bielby. 1989. "Family Ties: Balancing Commitments to Work and Family in Dual Earner Households." *American Sociological Review* 54: 776–89.

Birns, Beverly, and Dale F. Hay. 1988. *The Different Faces of Motherhood*. New York: Plenum.

Blau, Zena Smith. 1964. "Exposure to Child-Rearing Experts: A Structural Interpretation of Class-Color Differences." *American Journal of Sociology* 6:596–608.

Bloch, Ruth. 1978. "American Feminine Ideals in Transition: The Rise of the Moral Mother, 1785–1815." *Feminist Studies* 4 (2):101–26.

———. 1987. "Gendered Meanings of Virtue in Revolutionary America." *Signs* 13 (1): 37–58.

Bloom, Lynn Z. 1972. *Doctor Spock: Biography of a Conservative Radical*. New York: Bobbs-Merrill.

Blumberg, Rae Lesser, ed. 1991. *Gender, Family, and Economy: The Triple Overlap*. Newbury Park, Calif.: Sage.

Bombeck, Erma. 1983. *Motherhood: The Second Oldest Profession.* New York: Mc-Graw-Hill.

Boswell, John. 1988. *The Kindness of Strangers.* New York: Pantheon.

Bourdieu, Pierre. 1977. "Cultural Reproduction and Social Reproduction." Pp. 487–511 in *Power and Ideology in Education,* edited by Jerome Karabel and A. H. Halsey. Oxford: Oxford University Press.

——. 1984. *Distinction: A Social Critique of the Judgement of Taste.* Translated by Richard Nice. Cambridge: Harvard University Press.

——. 1992. "Thinking About Limits." *Theory, Culture, and Society* 9 (1):37–49.

Bourdieu, Pierre, and Jean-Claude Passeron. 1977. *Reproduction in Education, Society and Culture.* London: Sage.

Bowlby, John. 1952. *Maternal Care and Mental Health.* 2d ed., series 2. Geneva: World Health Organization.

Bowles, Samuel, and Herbert Gintis. 1973. "IQ in the U.S. Class Structure." *Social Policy* 3:65–96.

——. 1976. *Schooling in Capitalist America.* New York: Basic.

Bradshaw, John. 1990. *Homecoming: Reclaiming and Championing Your Inner Child.* New York: Bantam.

Brazelton, T. Berry. 1983a. *Infants and Mothers.* New York: Delacorte.

——. 1983b. *Working and Caring.* Reading, Mass.: Addison-Wesley.

——. 1987. *What Every Baby Knows.* New York: Ballantine.

——. 1989. *Families: Crisis and Caring.* New York: Ballantine.

Brown, Carol. 1981. "Mothers, Fathers, and Children: From Private to Public Patriarchy." Pp. 240–67 in *Women and Revolution,* edited by Lydia Sargent. Boston: South End Press.

Brown, Patricia Leigh. 1993. "Magazines Remake Family, or Vice Versa." *New York Times,* August 19.

Cable, Mary. 1975. *The Little Darlings: A History of Child-Rearing in America.* New York: Scribner.

Calhoun, Daniel. 1973. *The Intelligence of a People.* Princeton: Princeton University Press.

Campbell, D'Ann. 1984. *Women at War with America: Private Lives in a Patriotic Era.* Cambridge: Harvard University Press.

Carnoy, Martin, and Henry M. Levin. 1985. *Schooling and Work in the Democratic State.* Stanford: Stanford University Press.

Cavallo, Dom. 1976. "Social Reform and the Movement to Organize Children's Play during the Progressive Era." *History of Childhood Quarterly* 3:509–22.

Chafetz, Janet Saltzman. 1990. *Gender Equity: An Integrated Theory of Stability and Change.* Newbury Park: Sage.

Cherlin, Andrew. 1981. *Marriage, Divorce, Remarriage.* Cambridge: Harvard University Press.

"Childcare Bestsellers." 1991. *Publishers Weekly,* June 14, 64.

Chira, Susan. 1994. "Still Guilty after All These Years: A Bouquet of Advice Books for the Working Mom." *New York Times Book Review,* May 8, 11.

Chodorow, Nancy. 1974. "Family Structure and Feminine Personality." Pp. 43–66 in

Woman, Culture, and Society, edited by Michelle Z. Rosaldo and Louise Lamphere. Stanford: Stanford University Press.

———. 1978. *The Reproduction of Mothering.* Berkeley: University of California Press.

Chodorow, Nancy, and Susan Contratto. 1982. "The Fantasy of the Perfect Mother." Pp. 54–75 in *Rethinking the Family: Some Feminist Questions,* edited by Barrie Thorne. New York: Longman.

Chow, Esther Ngan-Ling. 1989. "The Feminist Movement: Where Are All the Asian American Women?" Pp. 362–77 in *Making Waves,* edited by Asian Women United of California. Boston: Beacon.

Cleverly, John, and D. C. Phillips. 1986. *Visions of Childhood: Influential Models from Locke to Spock.* New York: Teachers College Press.

Cliff, Michelle. 1983. "If I Could Write This in Fire I Would Write This in Fire." Pp. 16–30 in *Home Girls: A Black Feminist Anthology,* edited by Barbara Smith. New York: Kitchen Table: Women of Color Press.

Coleman, James S. 1993. "The Rational Reconstruction of Society." *American Sociological Review* 58:1–15.

Collins, Patricia Hill. 1991. *Black Feminist Thought.* New York: Routledge.

Collins, Randall. 1971a. "A Conflict Theory of Sexual Stratification." *Social Problems* 19:3–21.

———. 1971b. "Functional and Conflict Theories of Educational Stratification." *American Sociological Review* 36: 1002–19.

———. 1974. "Three Faces of Cruelty: Towards a Comparative Sociology of Violence." *Theory and Society* 1 (4):415–40.

———. 1975. *Conflict Sociology.* New York: Academic.

———. 1985. *Sociology of Marriage and the Family: Gender, Love, and Property.* Chicago: Nelson Hall.

———. 1992. "Women and the Production of Status Cultures." Pp. 213–31 in *Cultivating Differences: Symbolic Boundaries and the Making of Inequality,* edited by Michèle Lamont and Marcel Fournier. Chicago: University of Chicago Press.

Collins, Randall, and Scott Coltrane. 1995. *Sociology of Marriage and the Family: Gender, Love, and Property.* 4th ed. Chicago: Nelson-Hall.

Coontz, Stephanie. 1992. *The Way We Never Were: American Families and the Nostalgia Trap.* New York: Basic.

Corse, Sarah M. 1996. *Nationalism and Literature: The Politics of Culture in Canada and the United States.* Cambridge: Cambridge University Press.

Cosby, Bill. 1986. *Fatherhood.* Garden City, N.Y.: Doubleday.

Cott, Nancy F. 1977. *The Bonds of Womanhood: 'Woman's Sphere' in New England, 1780–1835.* New Haven: Yale University Press.

———. 1978. "Passionlessness: An Interpretation of Victorian Sexual Ideology, 1790–1850." *Signs* 4:219–36.

Cowan, Ruth Schwartz. 1976. "Two Washes in the Morning and a Bridge Party at Night: The American Housewife between the Wars." *Women's Studies* 3 (2):147–72.

———. 1983. *More Work for Mother: The Ironies of Household Technology from the Open Hearth to the Microwave.* New York: Basic.

Cravens, Hamilton. 1985. "Child-Saving in the Age of Professionalism, 1915–1930." Pp.

415–88 in *American Childhood: A Research Guide and Historical Handbook,* edited by Joseph M. Hawes and N. Ray Hiner. Westport, Conn.: Greenwood.

Dally, Ann. 1982. *Inventing Motherhood: The Consequences of an Ideal.* London: Burnett.

Darnton, Nina. 1990. "Mommy vs. Mommy." *Newsweek,* June 4.

Davidson, Cathy N. 1986. *Revolution and the Word: The Rise of the Novel in America.* New York: Oxford University Press.

Degler, Carl N. 1980. *At Odds: Women and the Family in America from the Revolution to the Present.* Oxford: Oxford University Press.

Delphy, Christine. 1984. *Close to Home: A Materialist Analysis of Women's Oppression.* Translated and edited by Diana Leonard. Amherst: University of Massachusetts Press.

DeMause, Lloyd. 1974. "The Evolution of Childhood." *History of Childhood Quarterly* 1 (4):503–75.

Demos, John. 1970. *A Little Commonwealth: Family Life in Plymouth Colony.* New York: Oxford University Press.

———. 1986. *Past, Present, and Personal.* New York: Oxford University Press.

DeNora, Tia. 1995. *Beethoven and the Construction of Genius: Musical Politics in Vienna, 1792–1803.* Berkeley: University of California Press.

Dobson, Dr. James. 1970. *Dare to Discipline.* Wheaton, Ill.: Tyndale House.

———. 1979. *Hide or Seek.* Old Tappan, N.J.: Fleming H. Revell.

Donzelot, Jacques. 1979. *The Policing of Families.* New York: Pantheon.

Douglas, Ann. 1988. *The Feminization of American Culture.* New York: Anchor.

Dudden, Faye E. 1983. *Serving Women: Household Service in Nineteenth-Century America.* Middletown: Wesleyan University Press.

Durkheim, Emile. 1965. *The Elementary Forms of the Religious Life.* New York: Free Press.

———. 1978a. "Review of Ferdinand Tönnies: Gemeinschaft and Gesellschaft." Pp. 115–22 in *Emile Durkheim on Institutional Analysis,* edited by Mark Traugott. Chicago: University of Chicago Press.

———. 1978b. "Two Laws of Penal Evolution." Pp. 153–80 in *Emile Durkheim on Institutional Analysis,* edited by Mark Traugott. Chicago: University of Chicago Press.

Ehrenreich, Barbara. 1989. *Fear of Falling: The Inner Life of the Middle-Class.* New York: HarperCollins.

Ehrenreich, Barbara, and Deirdre English. 1978. *For Her Own Good: Fifty Years of Experts' Advice to Women.* New York: Doubleday.

Eisenberg, Arlene, Heidi Murkoff, and Sandee Hathaway. 1989. *What to Expect the First Year.* New York: Workman.

Elias, Norbert. 1978. *The History of Manners.* New York: Pantheon.

Elshtain, Jean Bethke. 1974. "Moral Woman and Immoral Man: A Consideration of the Public-Private Split and Its Political Ramifications." *Politics and Society* 4:453–73.

———. 1981. *Public Man, Private Woman.* Princeton: Princeton University Press.

Elster, Jon. 1989. *Nuts and Bolts for the Social Sciences.* Cambridge: Cambridge University Press.

Epstein, Cynthia Fuchs. 1988. *Deceptive Distinctions: Sex, Gender, and the Social Order.* New Haven: Yale University Press.

Erlanger, Howard S. 1974. "Social Class and Corporal Punishment in Childrearing: A Reassessment." *American Sociological Review* 39 (1):68–85.

Exter, Thomas G. 1992. "Big Spending on Little Ones." *American Demographics* 14 (2):6.

Eyer, Diane E. 1992. *Mother-Infant Bonding.* New Haven: Yale University Press.

Faber, Adele, and Elaine Mazlish. 1982. *How to Talk So Kids Will Listen and Listen So Kids Will Talk.* New York: Avon.

Finkelstein, Barbara. 1985. "Casting Networks of Good Influence: The Reconstruction of Childhood in the United States, 1790–1870." Pp. 111–52 in *American Childhood: A Research Guide and Historical Handbook,* edited by Joseph M. Hawes and N. Ray Hiner. Westport, Conn.: Greenwood.

Firestone, Shulamith. 1984. "The Dialectic of Sex." Pp. 136–43 in *Feminist Frameworks: Alternative Theoretical Accounts of the Relations between Women and Men,* edited by Alison M. Jaggar and Paula S. Rothenberg. New York: McGraw-Hill.

Folbre, Nancy, and Heidi Hartmann. 1988. "The Rhetoric of Self-Interest: Ideology and Gender in Economic Theory." Pp. 184–203 in *The Consequences of Economic Rhetoric,* edited by Arjo Klamer, Donald N. McCloskey, and Robert M. Solow. Cambridge: Cambridge University Press.

Forward, Susan, with Craig Buck. 1989. *Toxic Parents: Overcoming Their Hurtful Legacy and Reclaiming Your Life.* New York: Bantam.

Foucault, Michel. 1978. *The History of Sexuality.* Vol. 1, *An Introduction.* New York: Vintage.

——. 1979. *Discipline and Punish.* New York: Vintage.

Fraiberg, Selma. 1977. *Every Child's Birthright: In Defense of Mothering.* New York: Basic.

Freud, Sigmund. 1961. *Civilization and Its Discontents.* New York: Norton.

Friedan, Betty. 1963. *The Feminine Mystique.* New York: Dell.

Fuqua, Robert W., and Dorothy Labensohn. 1986. "Parents as Consumers of Child Care." *Family Relations* 35:295–303.

Garfinkel, Harold. 1967. *Studies in Ethnomethodology.* Englewood Cliffs, N.J.: Prentice-Hall.

Geboy, Michael J. 1981. "Who Is Listening to the 'Experts'? The Use of Child Care Materials By Parents." *Family Relations* 30:205–10.

Geertz, Clifford. 1973. *The Interpretation of Cultures.* New York: Basic.

Gerson, Kathleen. 1985. *Hard Choices: How Women Decide about Work, Career, and Motherhood.* Berkeley: University of California Press.

Giddens, Anthony. 1984. *The Constitution of Society: Outline for the Theory of Structuration.* Berkeley: University of California Press.

Gilligan, Carol. 1982. *In a Different Voice: Psychological Theory and Women's Development.* Cambridge: Harvard University Press.

Ginsburg, Faye D. 1989. *Contested Lives: The Abortion Debate in an American Community.* Berkeley: University of California Press.

Glaser, Barney G., and Anselm L. Strauss. 1980. *The Discovery of Grounded Theory: Strategies for Qualitative Research.* New York: Aldine.

Glenn, Evelyn Nakano, Grace Chang, and Linda Rennie Forcey. 1994. *Mothering: Ideology, Experience, and Agency.* New York: Routledge.

Goffman, Erving. 1977. "The Arrangement between the Sexes." *Theory and Society* 4:301–331.

Goldin, Claudia. 1990. *Understanding the Gender Gap: An Economic History of American Women.* New York: Oxford University Press.

Goldthorpe, J. E. 1987. *Family Life in Western Societies: A Historical Sociology of Family Relationships in Britain and North America.* Cambridge: Cambridge University Press.

Goode, William J. 1970. *World Revolution and Family Patterns.* New York: Free Press.

Goodman, Ellen. 1990. "Bridging the Guilt Gap." *Los Angeles Times,* May 12.

Goody, Jack. 1983. *The Development of the Family and Marriage in Europe.* Cambridge: Cambridge University Press.

Gordon, Linda. 1988. *Heroes of Their Own Lives: The Politics and History of Family Violence.* New York: Penguin.

Gordon, Michael. 1968. "Infant Care Revisited." *Journal of Marriage and the Family* 30: 578–83.

Gottlieb, Beatrice. 1993. *The Family in the Western World.* New York: Oxford University Press.

Greenberger, Ellen, and Robin O'Neil. 1990. "Parents' Concerns about Their Child's Development: Implications for Fathers' and Mothers' Well-Being and Attitudes toward Work." *Journal of Marriage and the Family* 52:621–35.

Greven, Philip J. 1970. *Four Generations: Population, Land and Family in Colonial Andover, Massachusetts.* Ithaca: Cornell University Press.

———. 1973. *Child-Rearing Concepts, 1628–1861: Historical Sources.* Itasca, Ill.: Peacock.

Groves, Martha. 1990. "Mothers of Invention." *Los Angeles Times,* September 5.

Gusfield, Joseph. 1981. *The Culture of Public Problems: Drinking-Driving and the Symbolic Order.* Chicago: University of Chicago Press.

Habermas, Jürgen. 1987. *The Theory of Communicative Action.* Vol. 2, *Lifeworld and System: A Critique of Functionalist Reason.* Translated by Thomas McCarthy. Boston: Beacon.

———. 1989. *The Structural Transformation of the Public Sphere: An Inquiry into a Category of Bourgeois Society.* Translated by Thomas Burger with the assistance of Frederick Lawrence. Cambridge: MIT Press.

Hackett, Alice Payne. 1967. *Seventy Years of Best Sellers, 1895–1965.* New York: Bowker.

Halle, David. 1984. *America's Working Man.* Chicago: University of Chicago Press.

Harding, Sandra. 1986. *The Science Question in Feminism.* Ithaca: Cornell University Press.

Hardyment, Christina. 1983. *Dream Babies: Three Centuries of Good Advice on Child Care.* New York: Harper and Row.

Hareven, Tamara K. 1976. "Modernization and Family History, Perspectives on Social Change." *Signs* 2:190–207.

———. 1989. "American Families in Transition: Historical Perspectives on Change." Pp. 39–56 in *Family in Transition,* edited by Arlene S. Skolnick and Jerome H. Skolnick. 6th ed. Glenview, Ill.: Scott, Foresman.

Hartmann, Heidi. 1981a. "The Unhappy Marriage of Marxism and Feminism: Towards a More Progressive Union." Pp. 1–41 in *Women and Revolution: A Discussion of the Unhappy Marriage of Marxism and Feminism,* edited by Lydia Sargent. Boston: South End Press.

———. 1981b. "The Family as the Locus of Gender, Class, and Political Struggle: The Example of Housework." *Signs* 6 (3):366–94.

Hayden, Dolores. 1981. *The Grand Domestic Revolution: A History of Feminist Designs for American Homes, Neighborhoods, and Cities.* Cambridge: MIT Press.

Hayghe, Howard V., and Suzanne M. Bianchi. 1994. "Married Mothers' Work Patterns: The Job-Family Compromise." *Monthly Labor Review* 117 (6):24–30.

Hays, Sharon. 1994. "Structure and Agency and the Sticky Problem of Culture." *Sociological Theory* 12 (1):57–72.

Hebdige, Dick. 1979. *Subculture: The Meaning of Style.* London: Methuen.

Held, Virginia. 1983. "The Obligations of Mothers and Fathers." Pp. 7–20 in *Mothering: Essays in Feminist Theory,* edited by Joyce Trebilcot. Savage, Md.: Rowman and Littlefield.

———. 1987. "Feminism and Moral Theory." Pp. 111–28 in *Women and Moral Theory,* edited by Eva Feder Kittay and Diana T. Meyers. Totowa, N.J.: Rowman and Littlefield.

———. 1990. "Mothering Versus Contract." Pp. 287–304 in *Beyond Self-Interest,* edited by Jane J. Mansbridge. Chicago: University of Chicago Press.

Heilbroner, Robert. 1988. "The Coming Meltdown of Traditional Capitalism." *Ethics and International Affairs* 2:63–77.

Hewlett, Sylvia Ann. 1987. *A Lesser Life: The Myth of Women's Liberation in America.* New York: Warner.

———. 1991. *When the Bough Breaks: The Cost of Neglecting our Children.* New York: Basic.

Hochschild, Arlie, with Anne Machung. 1989. *The Second Shift: Working Parents and the Revolution at Home.* New York: Viking.

Hofferth, Sandra L., and Kristin A. Moore. 1979. "Women's Employment and Marriage." Pp. 99–124 in *The Subtle Revolution: Women at Work,* edited by Ralph Smith. Washington, D.C.: Urban Institute.

Hood, Jane. 1986. "The Provider Role: Its Meaning and Measurement." *Journal of Marriage and the Family* 48:349–59.

Huber, Joan, and Glenna Spitze. 1988. "Trends in Family Sociology." Pp. 425–48 in *Handbook of Sociology,* edited by Neil J. Smelser. London: Sage.

Hunt, David. 1970. *Parents and Children in History: The Psychology of Family Life in Early Modern France.* New York: Basic.

Hunt, Janet G., and Larry L. Hunt. 1987. "Male Resistance to Role Symmetry in Dual-Earner Households: Three Alternative Explanations." Pp. 192–203 in *Families and Work,* edited by Naomi Gerstel and Harriet Engel Gross. Philadelphia: Temple University Press.

Hunter, James Davison. 1991. *Culture Wars: The Struggle to Define America.* New York: Basic.

———. 1994. *Before the Shooting Begins: Searching for Democracy in America's Culture War.* New York: Free Press.

Ishii-Kuntz, Masako, and Scott Coltraine. 1992. "Predicting the Sharing of Household Labor: Are Parenting and Housework Distinct?" *Sociological Perspectives* 35 (4):629–47.

Jackman, Mary. 1994. *The Velvet Glove: Paternalism and Conflict in Gender, Class, and Race Relations.* Berkeley: University of California Press.

Johnson, Miriam. 1988. *Strong Mothers, Weak Wives: The Search for Gender Equality.* Berkeley: University of California Press.

Jones, Jacqueline. 1985. *Labor of Love, Labor of Sorrow: Black Women, Work, and the Family from Slavery to the Present.* New York: Basic.

Joseph, Gloria. 1981. "The Incompatible Menage à Trois: Marxism, Feminism, and Racism." Pp. 91–107 in *Women and Revolution: A Discussion of the Unhappy Marriage of Marxism and Feminism,* edited by Lydia Sargent. Boston: South End Press.

Kagan, Jerome. 1986. "The Psychological Requirements of Human Development." Pp. 373–83 in *Family in Transition,* edited by Arlene S. Skolnick and Jerome H. Skolnick. 5th ed. Boston: Little, Brown.

Kamerman, Shelia B. 1995. "Starting Right: What We Owe to Children under Three." Pp. 457–65 in *Diversity and Change in Families: Patterns, Prospects, and Policies,* edited by Mark Robert Rank and Edward L. Kain. Englewood Cliffs, N.J.: Prentice-Hall.

Kanter, Rosabeth Moss. 1978. "Jobs and Families: Impact of Working Roles on Family Life." *Children Today* 7:11–15, 45.

Kaplan, E. Ann. 1994. "Look Who's Talking, Indeed: Fetal Images in Recent North American Visual Culture." Pp. 121–37 in *Mothering: Ideology, Experience, and Agency,* edited by Evelyn Nakano Glenn, Grace Chang, and Linda Rennie Forcey. New York: Routledge.

Keniston, Kenneth, and the Carnegie Council on Children. 1977. *All Our Children: The American Family under Pressure.* New York: Harcourt Brace Jovanovich.

Kerber, Linda K. 1986. *Women of the Republic: Intellect and Ideology in Revolutionary America.* London: Norton.

Kessler-Harris, Alice. 1982. *Out to Work: A History of Wage-Earning Women in the United States.* Oxford: Oxford University Press.

Kett, Joseph F. 1983. "The Stages of Life, 1790–1840." Pp. 229–54 in *The American Family in Social Historical Perspective,* edited by Michael Gordon. New York: St. Martin's.

Klatch, Rebecca E. 1987. *Women of the New Right.* Philadelphia: Temple University Press.

Kohn, Melvin L. 1969. *Class and Conformity: A Study in Values.* Homewood, Ill.: Dorsey Press.

Kollantai, Alexandra. 1980. "The Social Basis of the Woman Question." Pp. 58–73 in *Selected Writings of Alexandra Kollantai,* edited by A. Holt. New York: Norton.

Komarovsky, Mirra. 1962. *Blue-Collar Marriage.* New Haven: Yale University Press.

Ladd-Taylor, Molly. 1986. *Raising a Baby the Government Way: Mothers' Letters to the Children's Bureau, 1915–1932.* New Brunswick: Rutgers University Press.

Laing, R. D. 1972. *The Politics of the Family, and Other Essays.* New York: Vintage.

Lamont, Michèle. 1992. *Money, Morals, and Manners.* Chicago: University of Chicago Press.

Lareau, Annette. 1987. "Social Class Differences in Family-School Relationships." *Sociology of Education* 60:73–85.

LaRossa, Ralph, and Maureen LaRossa. 1981. *Transition to Parenthood: How Infants Change Families.* Beverly Hills: Sage.

Lasch, Christopher. 1977. *Haven in a Heartless World.* New York: Basic.

Laslett, Barbara. 1973. "The Family as a Public and Private Institution." *Journal of Marriage and the Family* 35:480–92.

———. 1978. "Family Membership, Past and Present." *Social Problems* 25:476–90.

Laslett, Peter. 1984. *The World We Have Lost.* New York: Scribner.

Lawson, Carol. 1990. "For Stylish Babies: Zebra-Skin Diapers and Neon Strollers." *New York Times,* October 11.

———. 1991. "Advice on Child Care From, of All People, a Mother and a Doctor." *New York Times,* June 13.

Leach, Penelope. 1986. *Baby and Child: From Birth to Age Five.* New ed. London: Penguin.

———. 1989. *Babyhood.* New York: Knopf.

———. 1994a. *Your Baby and Child: From Birth to Age Five.* Rev. and exp. New York: Knopf.

———. 1994b. *Children First: What Our Society Must Do — and Is Not Doing — for Our Children Today.* New York: Knopf.

Lerner, Gerda. 1969. "The Lady and the Mill Girl: Changes in the Status of Women in the Age of Jackson." *Midcontinent American Studies Journal* 10 (1):5–15.

Lévi-Strauss, Claude. 1971. "The Family." Pp. 261–86 in *Man, Culture, and Society,* edited by Harry L. Shapiro. New York: Oxford University Press.

———. 1974. "Reciprocity, The Essence of Social Life." Pp. 36–47 in *The Family: Its Structures and Functions,* edited by Rose Laub Coser. New York: St. Martin's.

Levine, David. 1977. *Family Formations in an Age of Nascent Capitalism.* New York: Academic.

Litwak, Eugene. 1960a. "Geographic Mobility and Extended Family Cohesion." *American Sociological Review* 25:385–94.

———. 1960b. "Occupational Mobility and Extended Family Cohesion." *American Sociological Review* 25:9–21.

Lodge, Sally. 1993. "Raising Today's Kids by the Book." *Publishers Weekly,* October 18, 36–41.

Lomax, Elizabeth M. R., Jerome Kagan, and Barbara Gutmann Rosenkrantz. 1978. *Science and Patterns of Child Care.* San Francisco: Freeman.

Luker, Kristin. 1984. *Abortion and the Politics of Motherhood.* Berkeley: University of California Press.

Lynd, Robert S., and Helen Merrell Lynd. 1956. *Middletown: A Study in Modern American Culture.* New York: Harcourt, Brace.

MacCleod, Jay. 1987. *Ain't No Makin' It.* Boulder: Westview.

MacDonald, Cameron. "Selling Ourselves Short: Advice to Women in the 80s and the Mystique of Independence." University of California, Berkeley, typescript.

McGlone, Robert Elno. 1971. "Suffer the Children: The Emergence of Modern Middle-Class Family Life in America, 1820–1870." Ph.D. diss., University of California, Los Angeles.

MacKinnon, Catharine A. 1982. "Feminism, Marxism, Method, and the State: An Agenda for Theory." *Signs* 7:515–44.

———. 1987. *Feminism Unmodified*. Cambridge: Harvard University Press.

Mainardi, Pat. 1970. "The Politics of Housework." Pp. 447–54 in *Sisterhood Is Powerful*, edited by Robin Morgan. New York: Vintage.

Mannheim, Karl. 1971. "Conservative Thought." Pp. 132–222 in *From Karl Mannheim*, edited by Kurt H. Wolff. New York: Oxford University Press.

———. 1985. *Ideology and Utopia*. San Diego: Harcourt Brace Jovanovich.

Mansbridge, Jane J., ed. 1990. *Beyond Self-Interest*. Chicago: University of Chicago Press.

Margolis, Maxine. 1984. *Mothers and Such: Views of American Women and Why They Changed*. Berkeley: University of California Press.

Marshall, Harriet. 1991. "The Social Construction of Motherhood: An Analysis of Childcare and Parenting Manuals." In *Motherhood: Meanings, Practices, and Ideologies*, edited by Ann Phoenix, Anne Woollett, and Eva Lloyd. London: Sage.

Martens, Peter L. 1990. "The Desired Image of the Child." *Sociology and Social Research* 74 (3):146–49.

Martin, Emily. 1992. *The Woman in the Body: A Cultural Analysis of Reproduction*. Boston: Beacon.

Marx, Karl, and Friedrich Engels. [1848] 1978. *The Marx-Engels Reader*. Edited by Robert C. Tucker. 2d ed. New York: Norton.

Matthaei, Julie A. 1982. *An Economic History of Women in America*. New York: Schocken.

Matute-Bianchi, Maria Eugenia. 1986. "Ethnic Identities and Patterns of School Success and Failure among Mexican-Descent and Japanese American Students in a California High School: An Ethnographic Analysis." *American Journal of Education* 95:233–55.

May, Elaine Tyler. 1988. *Homeward Bound: American Families in the Cold War Era*. New York: Basic.

Mead, Margaret. 1962. "A Cultural Anthropologist's Approach to Maternal Deprivation." Pp. 45–62 in *Deprivation of Maternal Care: A Reassessment of Its Effects*, edited by Mary D. Ainsworth, R. B. Andry, Robert G. Harlow, S. Lebovici, Margaret Mead, Dane G. Prugh, and Barbara Wootton. Geneva: World Health Organization.

Mead, Margaret, and Martha Wolfenstein. 1955. *Childhood in Contemporary Cultures*. Chicago: University of Chicago Press.

Mechling, Jay E. 1975. "Advice to Historians on Advice to Mothers." *Journal of Social History* 9:44–63.

Mehan, Hugh. 1983. "The Role of Language and the Language of Role." *Language and Society* 12 (3):1–39.

———. 1989. "Oracular Reasoning in a Psychiatric Setting." Pp. 160–77 in *Conflict Talk*, edited by A. D. Grimshaw. Cambridge: Cambridge University Press.

Mehan, Hugh, Alma Hetweck, and J. Lee Meihls. 1985. *Handicapping the Handicapped: Decision Making in Students' Careers*. Stanford: Stanford University Press.

Mehan, Hugh, and H. Wood. 1975. *The Reality of Ethnomethodology*. New York: Wiley-Interscience.

Milkman, Ruth. 1987. *Gender at Work: The Dynamics of Job Segregation by Sex during World War II*. Chicago: University of Illinois Press.

Mills, C. Wright. 1959. *The Sociological Imagination*. New York: Oxford University Press.

Moore, Barrington, Jr. 1958. *Political Power and Social Theory: Six Studies*. Cambridge: Harvard University Press.

Moore, Kristin A., and Sandra L. Hofferth. 1979. "Women and Their Children." Pp. 125–58 in *The Subtle Revolution: Women at Work*, edited by Ralph Smith. Washington, D.C.: Urban Institute.

Moraga, Cherrie, and Gloria Anzaldua, eds. 1981. *This Bridge Called My Back: Writings by Radical Women of Color*. New York: Kitchen Table: Women of Color Press.

Nelson, Margaret K. 1994. "Family Day Care Providers: Dilemmas of Daily Practice." Pp. 181–210 in *Mothering: Ideology, Experience, Agency*, edited by Evelyn Nakano Glenn, Grace Chang, and Linda Rennie Forcey. New York: Routledge.

Noble, Barbara Presley. 1993. "Worthy Child-Care Pay Scales." *New York Times*. April 18.

Oakley, Ann. 1981. "Interviewing Women: A Contradiction in Terms." Pp. 30–61 in *Doing Feminist Research*, edited by Helen Roberts. London: Routledge and Kegan Paul.

Ogburn, William F. 1962. "The Changing Functions of the Family." Pp. 157–63 in *Selected Studies in Marriage and the Family*, edited by Robert F. Winch, Robert McGinnis, and Herbert R. Barringer. Rev. ed. New York: Holt, Rinehart, and Winston.

Owen, Kelly. 1995. "U.S. Dads Lag in Child-Care Duties, Global Study Finds." *Los Angeles Times*, February 19.

Parke, Ross. 1981. *Fathers*. Cambridge: Harvard University Press.

Parsons, Talcott. 1954. "The Kinship System of the Contemporary United States." Pp. 233–50 in *Essays in Sociological Theory*. Glencoe, Ill.: Free Press.

———. 1962. "Age and Sex in the Social Structure of the United States." Pp. 68–81 in *Selected Studies in Marriage and the Family*, edited by Robert F. Winch, Robert McGinnis, and Herbert R. Barringer. Rev. ed. New York: Holt, Rinehart, and Winston.

Parsons, Talcott, and Robert F. Bales. 1955. *Family, Socialization and Interaction Process*. New York: Free Press.

Pateman, Carole. 1983. "Feminist Critiques of the Public/Private Dichotomy." Pp. 281–303 in *Public and Private in Social Life*, edited by S. I. Benn and G. F. Gaus. New York: St. Martin's.

———. 1988. *The Sexual Contract*. Stanford: Stanford University Press.

Peterson, Susan Rae. 1983. "Against 'Parenting.'" Pp. 62–69 in *Mothering: Essays in Feminist Theory*, edited by Joyce Trebilcot. Savage, Md.: Rowman and Littlefield.

Philipson, Ilene. 1981. "Child Rearing Literature and Capitalist Industrialization." *Berkeley Journal of Sociology* 26:57–73.

Phillips, Kevin. 1990. *The Politics of Rich and Poor: Wealth and the American Electorate in the Reagan Aftermath*. New York: Random House.

Piess, Kathy. 1986. *Cheap Amusements*. Philadelphia: Temple University Press.

Platt, Anthony M. 1977. *The Child Savers: The Invention of Delinquency*. 2d ed. Chicago: University of Chicago Press.

Pleck, Joseph H. 1985. *Working Wives, Working Husbands*. Beverly Hills: Sage.

Plumb, J. H. 1982. "The New World of Children." Pp. 285–315 in *The Birth of a*

Consumer Society: The Commercialization of Eighteenth-Century England, edited by Neil McKendrick, John Brewer, and J. H. Plumb. Bloomington: Indiana University Press.

Polakow, Valerie. 1993. *Lives on the Edge: Single Mothers and Their Children in the Other America.* Chicago: University of Chicago Press.

Polanyi, Karl. 1944. *The Great Transformation.* Boston: Beacon.

Polatnick, M. 1983. "Why Men Don't Rear Children: A Power Analysis." Pp. 21–40 in *Mothering: Essays in Feminist Theory,* edited by Joyce Trebilcot. Savage, Md.: Rowman and Littlefield.

Pollitt, Katha. 1992. "Are Women Morally Superior to Men?" *The Nation,* December 28, 799–807.

Popenoe, David. 1993. "Parental Androgyny." *Society* 30 (6):6–11.

Poster, Mark. 1978. *Critical Theory of the Family.* New York: Seabury.

Radway, Janice. 1984. *Reading the Romance: Women, Patriarchy, and Popular Literature.* Chapel Hill: University of North Carolina Press.

Rainwater, Lee, Richard P. Coleman, and Gerald Handel. 1959. *Workingman's Wife: Her Personality, World, and Life Style.* New York: Oceana.

Rainwater, Lee, and Gerald Handel. 1964. "Changing Family Roles in the Working Class." Pp. 70–77 in *Blue-Collar World: Studies of the American Worker,* edited by Arthur B. Shostak and William Gomberg. Englewood Cliffs, N.J.: Prentice-Hall.

Rapp, Gail S., and Sally A. Lloyd. 1989. "The Role of 'Home as Haven' Ideology in Child Care Use." *Family Relations* 38:426–30.

Rapp, Rayna, Ellen Ross, and Renate Bridenthal. 1979. "Examining Family History." *Feminist Studies* 5 (1):174–200.

Rich, Adrienne. 1983. "Compulsory Heterosexuality and Lesbian Existence." Pp. 177–205 in *Powers of Desire: The Politics of Sexuality,* edited by Ann Snitow, Christine Stansell, and Sharon Thompson. New York: Monthly Review Press.

Riesman, David. 1961. *The Lonely Crowd: A Study of the Changing American Character.* New Haven: Yale University Press.

Risman, Barbara, and Myra Marx Feree. 1995. "Making Gender Visible." *American Sociological Review* 60 (5):775–82.

Roback, Diane, and Shannon Maughan. 1995. "Children's Bookselling Survey: On the Road to Recovery." *Publishers Weekly,* May 1.

Rodgers, Daniel T. 1980. "Socializing Middle-Class Children: Institutions, Fables, and Work Values in Nineteenth-Century America." *Journal of Social History* 1 (3):354–67.

Rogoff, Barbara, Martha Julia Sellers, Sergio Pirrotta, Nathan Fox, and Sheldon H. White. 1976. "Age of Assignment of Roles and Responsibilities to Children: A Cross-Cultural Survey." Pp. 249–68 in *Rethinking Childhood: Perspectives on Development and Society,* edited by Arlene Skolnick. Boston: Little, Brown.

Rossi, Alice. 1977. "A Biosocial Perspective on Parenting." *Daedalus* 106 (2):1–31.

———. 1984. "Gender and Parenthood." *American Sociological Review* 49:1–19.

Rothman, Barbara Katz. 1989. *Recreating Motherhood: Ideology and Technology in a Patriarchal Society.* New York: Norton.

Rothman, Shelia M. 1978. *Woman's Proper Place: A History of Changing Ideals and Practices, 1870 to the Present.* New York: Basic.

Rousseau, Jean-Jacques. 1964. *Emile, Julie and Other Writings*. Edited by R. L. Archer. New York: Barron's Educational Series. *(Julie* originally published in 1761; *Emile* in 1762.)

Rubin, Gayle. 1984. "Thinking Sex: Notes for a Radical Theory of the Politics of Sexuality." Pp. 267–317 in *Pleasure and Danger,* edited by Carole S. Vance. New York: Routledge, Chapman, and Hall.

Rubin, Lillian B. 1976. *Worlds of Pain: Life in the Working-Class Family*. New York: Basic.

———. 1983. *Intimate Strangers: Men and Women Together*. New York: Harper and Row.

———. 1994. *Families on the Fault Line*. New York: HarperCollins.

Ruddick, Sara. 1982. "Maternal Thinking." Pp. 76–94 in *Rethinking the Family: Some Feminist Questions,* edited by Barrie Thorne and Marilyn Yalom. New York: Longman.

Ryan, Mary P. 1981. *Cradle of the Middle Class: The Family in Oneida County*. Cambridge: Cambridge University Press.

———. 1985. *The Empire of the Mother: American Writing about Domesticity, 1830–1860*. New York: Harrington Park.

Sacks, Karen. 1984. "Generations of Working Class Families." Pp. 15–38 in *My Troubles Are Going to Have Trouble with Me: Everyday Trials and Triumphs of Women Workers,* edited by Karen Brodkin Sacks and Dorothy Remy. New Brunswick: Rutgers University Press.

Sahlins, Marshall. 1976. *Culture and Practical Reason*. Chicago: University of Chicago Press.

Scheper-Hughes, Nancy, ed. 1987. *Child Survival: Anthropological Perspectives on the Treatment and Maltreatment of Children*. Boston: D. Reidel.

———. 1992. *Death without Weeping: The Violence of Everyday Life in Brazil*. Berkeley: University of California Press.

Schneider, David M., and Raymond T. Smith. 1973. *Class Differences and Sex Roles in American Kinship and Family Structure*. Englewood Cliffs, N.J.: Prentice-Hall.

Schneider, Phyllis. 1987. "The Managerial Mother." *Working Woman,* December, 117–26.

Schwartz, Felice. 1989. "Management Women and the New Facts of Life." *Harvard Business Review* 67 (1):65–77.

Sebald, Hans. 1976. *Momism: The Silent Disease of America*. Chicago: Nelson-Hall.

Sears, Robert R. 1975. *Your Ancients Revisited: A History of Child Development*. Chicago: University of Chicago Press.

Sennett, Richard. 1970. *Families against the City: Middle Class Homes of Industrial Chicago, 1872–1890*. Cambridge: Harvard University Press.

Sewell, William, Jr. 1985. "Ideologies and Social Revolutions: Reflections on the French Case." *Journal of Modern History* 57 (1):57–85.

Shorter, Edward. 1974. "Comment." Response to "The Evolution of Childhood," by Lloyd DeMause. *History of Childhood Quarterly* 1 (4):593–97.

———. 1977. *The Making of the Modern Family*. New York: Basic.

Sidel, Ruth. 1986. *Women and Children Last: The Plight of Poor Women in Affluent America*. New York: Viking.

Silver, Allan. 1996. " 'Two Different Sorts of Commerce' — Friendship and Strangership in Civil Society." In *Public and Private in Thought and Practice: Perspectives on a Grand Dichotomy,* edited by Jeff Weintraub and Krishan Kumar. Chicago: University of Chicago Press.

Slater, Philip. 1968. *The Glory of Hera: Greek Mythology and the Greek Family.* Boston: Beacon.

———. 1976. *The Pursuit of Loneliness: American Culture at the Breaking Point.* Boston: Beacon.

Smith, Daniel Blake. 1983. "Autonomy and Affection: Parents and Children in Chesapeake Families." Pp. 209–28 in *The American Family in Social Historical Perspective,* edited by Michael Gordon. New York: St. Martin's.

Smith, Ralph, ed. 1979. *The Subtle Revolution: Women at Work.* Washington, D.C.: Urban Institute.

Smith-Rosenberg, Carroll. 1975. "The Female World of Love and Ritual: Relations between Women in Nineteenth-Century America." *Signs* 1:1–29.

Sorrentino, Constance. 1990. "The Changing Family in International Perspective." *Monthly Labor Review* 113 (3):41–56.

Spock, Benjamin M. 1946. *The Pocket Book of Baby and Child Care.* New York: Pocket Books.

———. 1994. *A Better World for Our Children: Rebuilding American Family Values.* Bethesda, Md.: National Press.

Spock, Benjamin M., and Michael B. Rothenberg. 1985. *Dr. Spock's Baby and Child Care.* New York: Pocket Books.

———. 1992. *Dr. Spock's Baby and Child Care.* 6th ed., rev. and updated. New York: Pocket Books.

Stacey, Judith. 1983. *Patriarchy and Socialist Revolution in China.* Berkeley: University of California Press.

———. 1986. "Are Feminists Afraid to Leave Home? The Challenge of Conservative Pro-Family Feminism." Pp. 208–37 in *What Is Feminism?* edited by Juliet Mitchell and Ann Oakley. New York: Pantheon.

———. 1991. "Backward toward the Postmodern Family: Reflections on Kinship and Class in the Silicon Valley." Pp. 17–34 in *America at Century's End,* edited by Alan Wolfe. Berkeley: University of California Press.

Stack, Carol B. 1974. *All Our Kin: Strategies for Survival in a Black Community.* New York: Harper and Row.

Stansell, Christine. 1987. *City of Women: Sex and Class in New York, 1789–1860.* Chicago: University of Illinois Press.

Staples, Robert, and Alfredo Mirande. 1980. "Racial and Cultural Variations among American Families: A Decennial Review of the Literature on Minority Families." *Journal of Marriage and the Family* 42:157–73.

Stendler, Celia B. 1950. "Sixty Years of Child Training Practices: Revolution in the Nursery." *Journal of Pediatrics* 36:122–34.

Stone, Lawrence. 1977. *The Family, Sex and Marriage in England, 1500–1800.* New York: Harper and Row.

Strom, Stephanie. 1991. "Creating the Well-Groomed Child." *New York Times,* July 6.

Sunley, Robert. 1955. "Early Nineteenth-Century Literature on Child Rearing." Pp. 150–67 in *Childhood in Contemporary Cultures*, edited by Margaret Mead and Martha Wolfenstein. Chicago: University of Chicago Press.

Sutherland, Daniel E. 1981. *Americans and Their Servants: Domestic Service in the United States from 1800 to 1920*. Baton Rouge: Louisiana State University Press.

Swidler, Ann. 1986. "Culture in Action." *American Sociological Review* 51:273–86.

Takanishi, Ruby. 1978. "Childhood as a Social Issue: Historical Roots of Contemporary Child Advocacy Movements." *Journal of Social Issues* 34 (2):8–28.

Tilly, Louise A., and Joan W. Scott. 1987. *Women, Work, and Family*. New York: Routledge.

"The Top 25 of the '80s: Nonfiction Bestsellers." 1990. *Publishers Weekly*, January 5, 5.

Tsing, Anna Lowenhaupt. 1990. "Monster Stories: Women Charged with Perinatal Endangerment." Pp. 282–99 in *Uncertain Terms*, edited by Faye Ginsburg and Anna L. Tsing. Boston: Beacon.

Tuan, Yi-Fu. 1984. *Dominance and Affection: The Making of Pets*. New Haven: Yale University Press.

U.S. Bureau of the Census. 1982. *Statistical Abstract of the United States*. Washington, D.C.: Government Printing Office.

———. 1992. *Statistical Abstract of the United States*. Washington, D.C.: Government Printing Office.

———. 1994. *Statistical Abstract of the United States*. Washington, D.C.: Government Printing Office.

U.S. Bureau of Labor Statistics. 1991. *Consumer Expenditure Survey, 1988–89*. Washington, D.C.: Government Printing Office.

U.S. Department of Commerce. 1991. *Fertility of American Women*. Current Population Reports, series P-20, no. 454. Washington, D.C.: Government Printing Office.

U.S. Department of Labor. 1980. *Perspectives on Working Women: A Databook*. Bulletin 2080. Washington, D.C.: Government Printing Office.

———. 1989. *Facts on Working Women*. No. 89–3. Washington, D.C.: Government Printing Office.

———. 1991. *Working Women: A Chartbook*. Bulletin 2385. Washington, D.C.: Government Printing Office.

Ulrich, Laurel Thatcher. 1982. *Good Wives: Image and Reality in the Lives of Women in Northern New England, 1650–1750*. New York: Oxford University Press.

Varenne, Hervé. 1977. *Americans Together: Structured Diversity in a Midwestern Town*. New York: Teachers College Press.

Vincent, Clark E. 1951. "Trends in Infant Care Ideas." *Child Development* 22:199–210.

Waldman, Steven, and Karen Springen. 1992. "Too Old, Too Fast? Millions of American Teenagers Work, but Many May Be Squandering Their Futures." *Newsweek*, November 16, 80.

Watson, John B. 1928. *Psychological Care of Infant and Child*. New York: Norton.

Watt, Ian. 1957. *The Rise of the Novel*. Berkeley: University of California Press.

Weber, Max. 1958. *The Protestant Ethic and the Spirit of Capitalism*. New York: Scribner.

———. 1978. *Economy and Society.* Berkeley: University of California Press.

Weiner, Lynn Y. 1985. *From Working Girl to Working Mother: The Female Labor Force in the United States, 1820–1980.* Chapel Hill: University of North Carolina Press.

Weinstein, Fred, and Gerald M. Platt. 1969. *The Wish to Be Free: Society, Psyche, and Value Change.* Berkeley: University of California Press.

Weintraub, Jeff. 1996. "The Theory and Politics of the Public/Private Distinction." In *Public and Private in Thought and Practice: Reflections on a Grand Dichotomy,* edited by Jeff Weintraub and Krishan Kumar. Chicago: University of Chicago Press.

———. (forthcoming). *Freedom and Community: The Republican Virtue Tradition and the Sociology of Liberty.* Berkeley: University of California Press.

Weisner, Thomas, and Ronald Gallimore. 1977. "My Brother's Keeper: Child and Sibling Caretaking." *Current Anthropology* 18:169–89.

Weiss, Nancy Pottishman. 1978. "The Mother-Child Dyad Revisited: Perceptions of Mothers and Children in Twentieth Century Child-Rearing Manuals." *Journal of Social Issues* 34 (2):29–45.

Weitzman, Lenore J. 1975. "Sex-Role Socialization." Pp. 105–44 in *Women: A Feminist Perspective,* edited by Jo Freeman. Palo Alto: Mayfield.

Welter, Barbara. 1966. "The Cult of True Womanhood, 1820–1860." *American Quarterly* 18:151–74.

Whiting, Beatrice Blyth, and Carolyn Pope Edwards. 1988. *Children of Different Worlds.* Cambridge: Harvard University Press.

"Who's Minding the Children?" 1993. *New York Times.* January 28.

Wilcox, Kathleen. 1982. "Differential Socialization in the Classroom: Implications for Equal Opportunity." Pp. 270–309 in *Doing the Ethnography of Schooling,* edited by G. D. Spindler. New York: Holt, Rinehart, and Winston.

Willis, Paul E. 1977. *Learning to Labor: How Working Class Kids Get Working Class Jobs.* New York: Columbia University Press.

Wilson, Joan Hoff. 1982. "The Illusion of Change: Women and the American Revolution." Pp. 117–36 in *Our American Sisters: Women in American Life and Thought,* edited by Jean E. Friedman and William Shade. Lexington, Mass.: Heath.

Wishy, Bernard. 1968. *The Child and the Republic: The Dawn of Modern American Child Nurture.* Philadelphia: University of Pennsylvania Press.

Wolfe, Alan. 1989. *Whose Keeper? Social Science and Moral Obligation.* Berkeley: University of California Press.

Wolfenstein, Martha. 1953. "Trends in Infant Care." *American Journal of Orthopsychiatry* 23:120–30.

———. 1955. "Fun Morality: An Analysis of Recent American Child-Training Literature." Pp. 168–78 in *Childhood in Contemporary Cultures,* edited by Margaret Mead and Martha Wolfenstein. Chicago: University of Chicago Press.

Wright, Jeanne. 1991. "The High Cost of Kids." *Los Angeles Times,* November 12.

Wylie, Philip. 1942. *Generation of Vipers.* New York: Rinehart.

Zaretsky, Eli. 1976. *Capitalism, the Family, and Personal Life.* New York: Harper and Row.

———. 1982. "The Place of the Family in the Origins of the Welfare State." Pp. 188–224 in *Rethinking the Family: Some Feminist Questions,* edited by Barrie Thorne. New York: Longman.

Zelizer, Viviana A. 1985. *Pricing the Priceless Child.* New York: Basic.

Zuckerman, Michael. 1975. "Dr. Spock: The Confidence Man." Pp. 179–207 in *The Family in History,* edited by Charles E. Rosenberg. Philadelphia: University of Philadelphia Press.

Index